Disruptive Situations

In the series *Sexuality Studies*,
edited by Janice Irvine and Regina Kunzel

ALSO IN THIS SERIES:

Andrew Israel Ross, *Public City/Public Sex: Homosexuality, Prostitution, and Urban Culture in Nineteenth-Century Paris*

Heike Bauer, *The Hirschfeld Archives: Violence, Death, and Modern Queer Culture*

Ryan Murphy, *Deregulating Desire: Flight Attendant Activism, Family Politics, and Workplace Justice*

Heike Bauer, *Sexology and Translation: Cultural and Scientific Encounters across the Modern World*

Lynette Chua, *Mobilizing Gay Singapore: Rights and Resistance in an Authoritarian State*

Thomas A. Foster, *Sex and the Founding Fathers: The American Quest for a Relatable Past*

Colin R. Johnson, *Just Queer Folks: Gender and Sexuality in Rural America*

Lisa Sigel, *Making Modern Love: Sexual Narratives and Identities in Interwar Britain*

DISRUPTIVE SITUATIONS

*Fractal Orientalism and
Queer Strategies in Beirut*

GHASSAN MOUSSAWI

TEMPLE UNIVERSITY PRESS
Philadelphia • Rome • Tokyo

TEMPLE UNIVERSITY PRESS
Philadelphia, Pennsylvania 19122
tupress.temple.edu

Copyright © 2020 by Temple University—Of The Commonwealth System
    of Higher Education
All rights reserved
Published 2020

Library of Congress Cataloging-in-Publication Data

Names: Moussawi, Ghassan, 1985– author.
Title: Disruptive situations : fractal Orientalism and queer strategies in Beirut /
    Ghassan Moussawi.
Other titles: Sexuality studies.
Description: Philadelphia : Temple University Press, 2020. | Series: Sexuality studies |
    Includes bibliographical references and index. | Summary: "Uses ethnographic research
    from LGBT and queer subjects to challenge how sexuality has been used to provide an
    exceptional narrative about contemporary Beirut and modernity. Offers an alternative
    narrative that highlights the power of everyday life disruptive situations in shaping
    LGBT life and queer strategies of survival"—Provided by publisher.
Identifiers: LCCN 2019039562 (print) | LCCN 2019039563 (ebook) |
    ISBN 9781439918494 (cloth) | ISBN 9781439918500 (paperback) |
    ISBN 9781439918517 (pdf)
Subjects: LCSH: Sexual minorities—Lebanon—Beirut—21st century. | Gender-
    nonconforming people—Lebanon—Beirut—21st century. | Gays—Travel—Lebanon—
    Beirut—21st century. | Social stability—Lebanon—Beirut—21st century. | Beirut
    (Lebanon)—Social conditions—21st century.
Classification: LCC HQ76.2.L42 B4565 2020 (print) | LCC HQ76.2.L42 (ebook) |
    DDC 306.76095692/5—dc23
LC record available at https://lccn.loc.gov/2019039562
LC ebook record available at https://lccn.loc.gov/2019039563

♾ The paper used in this publication meets the requirements of the American National
Standard for Information Sciences—Permanence of Paper for Printed Library Materials,
ANSI Z39.48-1992

Printed in the United States of America

9 8 7 6 5 4 3 2 1

For Beirut

For the victims of all the senseless violence and

those who continue to live amid al-wad'

Contents

Acknowledgments

I write this a few weeks after the tragic passing of my dear friend and graduate school colleague Jason Phillips—two months before his dissertation defense. Jason's kindness, intellect, and generosity have inspired me and so many of his friends in countless ways. He left us too soon, but we will continue to celebrate his life.

This book would not have been possible without the generous and invaluable support of so many individuals who believed in and engaged with this project at various stages and reminded me of the importance of putting this out in the world.

The seeds of this project started during my first term of graduate school in a seminar with Arlene Stein, my dissertation chair and adviser, on the sociology of culture. Many thanks go to Arlene for believing in this project and for providing constant support and encouragement. She has been a wonderful mentor and friend since my first day at Rutgers University. Arlene encouraged me to be methodologically open and flexible and pushed me to be a better and clearer writer, always thinking about how to make my work accessible. Judy Gerson's unwavering support and instrumental advice throughout graduate school shaped how I approach my research and taught me how to embrace vulnerability in the research process. She showed me that a good mentorship relationship is based on mutual respect and honesty. I am truly grateful. I thank Ann Mische for introducing me to fractals. I am very grateful for her belief in my project and for her genuine enthusiasm, guidance, and friendship, even after moving to Notre Dame. I am thankful for Zakia Salime's critical comments, feedback, and advice, which pushed me theoretically and helped me think about my broader contributions to multiple fields of study. Roderick Ferguson's feedback, advice, and support have been vital and pushed me to think outside disciplinary boundaries. His work continues to inspire and inform my own understandings of queer theory in many ways. I cannot thank Ashley Currier enough for all her mentorship, guidance, generosity, and friendship and for reading several drafts of chapters for this book. She has been there for me in countless ways and in every stage of this process.

I was fortunate to learn from supportive faculty at Rutgers University, including Ethel Brooks, Phaedra Daipha, Carlos Decena, Paul McLean, Julie Phillips, Robyn Rodriguez, Louisa Schein, and Richard Williams. At Rutgers, I also had the great privilege of being a Graduate Student Fellow at the Institute for Research on Women seminar "Decolonizing Gender/Gendering Decolonization," where I benefited from the feedback of Thea Abu El-Haj, Simone Alexander, Ashley Falzetti, Nicole Fleetwood, Annie Fukushima, Nadia Guessous, Juno Parreñas, and Sarah Tobias. I thank Nicole Fleetwood for pushing me to realize and highlight the tensions and anxieties of the field. I also thank my graduate school friends: Brittany Battle, Shruti Devgan, Nada El-Kouny, Victoria Gonzalez, Elizabeth Luth, Rosemary Ndubuizu, Jason Phillips, and Theresa Simpson.

At the University of Illinois, I owe many thanks for the support of my awe-inspiring colleagues in gender and women's studies and sociology. In the Department of Sociology, I thank Asef Bayat, Cynthia Buckley, Brian Dill, Behrooz Ghamari-Tabrizi, Zsuzsa Gille, Tim Liao, Anna-Maria Marshall, Ruby Mendenhall, Daniel Steward, and Assata Zerai. I thank the Department of Gender and Women's Studies for the warm welcome. My thanks specifically go to Teresa Barnes, Toby Beauchamp, Ruth Nicole Brown, Jodi Byrd, Karen Flynn, Maryam Kashani, Chantal Nadeau, Fiona Ngô, Mimi Thi Nguyen, and Siobhan Somerville. I am grateful to Karen Flynn for her support and uplifting conversations and for reminding me to "keep it real." Many thanks go to Chantal Nadeau for her friendship and for reading several earlier drafts of this book and pushing me to write catchier and clearer titles. Siobhan Somerville has been a mentor like no other. I am forever grateful for her support. Her engagement with my project at multiple stages has been transformational. She read countless drafts of the book and has always been generous with her time and feedback. She helped me see my contributions when I thought I had none. In addition, I offer heartfelt thanks to the dedicated staff in these departments. I am grateful for Shari Day and Mina Seaton. Shari Day has made everything possible and has been the kindest friend one could ask for. I thank Jacque Kahn and Virginia Swisher for all the amazing work they do.

Colleagues across campus have been very supportive, and I am grateful for conversations and friendships with Tariq Ali, Valeria Bonatti, J. B. Capino, Vincent Cervantes, Jenny Davis, Chris Eng, Hadi Esfahani, Jessica Greenberg, Faye Harrison, Waïl Hassan, Deanna Hence, Linda Herrera, Billy Huff, Brian Jefferson, John Karam, Craig Koslofksy, Isabel Molina, Jennifer Monson, Ellen Moodie, Parthiban Muniandy, Mauro Nobili, Cynthia Oliver, Naomi Paik, Dana Rabin, Junaid Rana, Gilberto Rosas, Sandra Ruiz, Krystal Smalls, Mark Steinberg, and David Wilson. My Chemex and Gali time with Sandra Ruiz has kept me afloat. I am fortunate to be her friend and to work alongside her. Jennifer Monson is a kind and generous soul who has introduced me to other ways of thinking about and feeling the world. I am very grateful. I thank Maria Gillombardo, Craig Koslofksy, and Carol Symes for organizing the First Book Writing Group; Craig and Maria read countless drafts of my prospectus and offered crucial feedback. Cynthia Oliver has been incredibly supportive and gave me feedback on multiple grant applications. I thank her.

Susan Koshy welcomed me to the Unit for Criticism and Interpretive Theory and gave me vital feedback on my project in its earliest phases. I thank her for her support. Antoinette Burton has supported me since I joined the University of Illinois. She has been very generous with her time and has given me extensive and tremendous feedback on earlier chapter drafts. I am forever grateful for her intellectual generosity and for the inspiring spaces and dialogues she creates on campus.

Asef Bayat and Linda Herrera very warmly welcomed me when I moved to Illinois and continue to be truly generous and supportive. I am extremely grateful. My gratitude also goes to Hadi Esfanahi and Niloofar Shambayati, who immediately welcomed me to the community. I am so happy and fortunate to have met Cynthia Degnan and to be her friend. I also thank Alicia Beck, Tim Shea, and Karie Wolfson for their support. Many thanks go to Karen Haboush. The memory of her kindness and wisdom remain with me and helped me throughout this process.

Reading Martin Manalansan's work in my first year of graduate school transformed how I think of queer theory. To be his colleague—even if for only two years at the University of Illinois—was such an honor and joy. I am very grateful for his friendship, brilliant mind, and fabulousness.

Graduate students at the University of Illinois make my job more rewarding and stimulating. Special thanks go to my wonderful research assistant, Shwetha Delanthamajalu, for her careful attention and help with organizing my interview data. It is such a pleasure to work alongside my mentees Miguel Avalos, Shwetha Delanthamajalu, and Jessennya Hernandez and to think with them about their fantastic projects. I thank them for making me strive to be a better mentor. I continue to engage with and learn from the projects of numerous graduate students from both my Gender and Sexuality and Queer Theory seminars, including Alana Ackerman, Miguel Avalos, Shwetha Delanthamajalu, Nehal Elmeligy, Breanna Escamilla, Daniel Gonzalez, Jessennya Hernandez, Cierra Humphrey, Heba Khalil, Bri Lafond, Leslie Morrow, and Po-Chia Tseng. I thank them for creating and valuing collaborative learning spaces, for embracing vulnerability in their research and questions, and for inspiring with their contagious passion.

I am very grateful to those who invited me to present parts of my book in progress. Thanks go to the audiences at the Sexualities Project at Northwestern University, the University of Cincinnati, and the University of Chicago. Various stages of this book were supported by the Woodrow Wilson Dissertation Fellowship for Women's Studies; the Institute for Research on Women at Rutgers University; and at the University of Illinois, the Illinois Program for Research on the Humanities and the College Campus Research Board's Humanities Release Time and Multiracial Democracy Grant. Special thanks go to Siobhan Somerville for organizing my book manuscript workshop and to both her and Salvador Vidal-Ortiz for the most helpful feedback on an earlier version of my manuscript. Many thanks go to Maryam Kashani and Mimi Thi Nguyen for taking the most detailed and helpful notes during my manuscript workshop.

I thank the Sexpots Writing Group, who welcomed me and gave me great feedback on Chapter 4: Sinikka Elliott, Patrick Grzanka, Emily Mann, Vrushali Patil, Jyoti Puri, and Evren Savci. I am thankful for conversations, feedback, and tremendous insights from remarkable colleagues at other institutions: Chris Barcelos, Shantel Buggs, Héctor Carrillo, Moon Charania, Cati Connell, Sara Crawley, Steve Epstein, Theo Greene, Kimberly Kay Hoang, Angela Jones, Kerwin Kaye, Greggor Mattson, Nadine Naber, Bandana Purkayastha, Chandan Reddy, and Atef Said.

Theo Greene, my friend and coconspirator, and I will continue to hold each other up. I am grateful to Vrushali Patil, dear friend and collaborator, for the fantastic work she does and for giving me the opportunity to present my work. Salvador Vidal-Ortiz, mentor, friend, and collaborator, is an incredible source of support, and I am so fortunate to think alongside and with him. His commitment and integrity are truly inspiring. Jyoti Puri taught me to let the project breathe and reminded me countlessly that I have something important to say. I am eternally grateful for her support, engagement with my work, and unmatched kindness. I am beyond fortunate to continually learn from Vrushali, Salvador, and Jyoti as scholars and people.

At the American University of Beirut, special thanks go to Kirsten Scheid and Livia Wick, both of whom taught me to value the beauty and importance of ethnographic methods. I am grateful for my dear friends in Beirut, whom I miss deeply: Romy-Lynn Attieh, Lynn Darwich, Rima Majed, Lamia Moghnieh, Zakaria Nasser, and Zeina Osman. Daily phone calls with Rima Majed during the last year of writing this book sustained me. I thank her for helping me better think of sectarianization and sect. Zeina Osman inspires me in so many ways. I am grateful for her friendship, quirky wisdom, and all the conversations we have had about *al-wad'*. I thank Victor Chedid, who was a supportive friend during early stages of the writing process. Alexander Ammerman taught me to write and appreciate literature. I am so grateful that our paths crossed and saddened by his passing too soon. I also thank all my interlocutors for trusting me and sharing their worlds with me. Without them, this book would not have been possible. I hope I did justice to the stories they shared. Any fault is mine.

Thanks go to Miriam Salah for designing the fractal Orientalism figures. I thank Janice Irvine for providing feedback and for supporting this project and including it as part of the Sexuality Series at Temple University Press. In addition, I thank Aaron Javsicas, Gary Kramer, Ashley Petrucci, and the whole team at Temple University Press. Particular thanks go to Sara Cohen, who believed in this project in its earliest forms and helped me better articulate its contributions. Sara patiently guided me through the process of publishing as a first-time author and answered all the questions I had. Sarah Munroe took on the project during the last year, and I cannot thank her enough for all the amazing work she has done. Sarah's extensive feedback has tremendously shaped this book. Any author would be fortunate to work with her. Many thanks also go to the anonymous reviewers at Temple University Press and Minnesota University Press who provided immensely generative and helpful feedback.

I thank my parents, Haifa Harmalani and Ali Moussawi, for supporting me and teaching me the importance of reading and writing early on in my life. Though not always content with my career choices, they stood by me. I hope my description of *al-wad'* does justice to their experiences. I also thank my dear sister and friend, Sarah Moussawi, for being there and always asking about my project. I love her dearly and hope for a future in which we live closer to each other.

I owe thanks to Erik Wade, who has been there with me during the toughest periods of graduate school. He taught me how to close-read, and

I am still very jealous of his skills. He remains my closest friend. Though we are oceans apart, he was there during the writing and rewriting of this book. I have not met a more selfless person, and I hope I can someday return his kindness. Last, I thank Maddie and Nina, my cat-babies and family in Illinois. Maddie has been my companion for the past five years and has sat patiently next to me every morning while I write. Maddie and Nina are constants in a world of everyday disruptions and change.

An earlier version of Chapter 1 was previously published as Ghassan Moussawi, "Queering Beirut, the Paris of the Middle East: Fractal Orientalism and Essentialized Masculinities in Gay Travelogues," *Gender, Place and Culture: A Journal of Feminist Geography* 20, no. 7 (2013): 858–875. It is reprinted by permission of Informa UK Limited, trading as Taylor and Francis Group, www.tandfonline.com. An earlier version of Chapter 2 was previously published as Ghassan Moussawi, "Queer Exceptionalism and Exclusion: Cosmopolitanism and Inequalities in 'Gay Friendly' Beirut," *Sociological Review* 66, no. 1 (2018): 174–190, https://doi.org/10.1177/0038026117725469. (Copyright © 2018 SAGE Publications.) It is reprinted by permission of SAGE Publications. Sections of an earlier version of Chapter 4 appeared in Ghassan Moussawi, "Not 'Straight' but Still a 'Man': Negotiating Non-heterosexual Masculinities in Beirut," in *Introducing the New Sexuality Studies*, 3rd ed., ed. Steven Seidman and Nancy Fischer (New York: Routledge, 2016), 152–159. (Copyright © 2016 Nancy L. Fischer and Steven Seidman.) These sections are reproduced with permission of the Licensor through PLSclear.

DISRUPTIVE SITUATIONS

Introduction

While "the World Is Beiruting Again"

When the [civil] war ended, it appeared that the things I was
saying were too big. It's like I used to dream more; now I dream
less. . . . I wanted the war to end so I could fulfill my dreams.
It ended, and then everything started appearing smaller and less
significant.

    —HANA, in *Phantom Beirut*

Beirut is Reliving its Golden Age: with an intensity to live that
is strangely contagious and an energy that is nowhere else to be
found.

    —*PARIS MATCH* BILLBOARD IN BEIRUT, 2010

Beirut, whether it's the Paris of the Middle East or not, might once
again become a great city.

    —MICHAEL TOTTEN, "Can Beirut Be Paris Again?"

We really can't afford another war. We are exhausted. We already
live in a state of everyday war. Anxiety and fear of the unknown, it
causes depression, you know?

    —CAB DRIVER IN BEIRUT, May 2019

In July 2009, the *New York Times* published an article celebrating Beirut, the capital of Lebanon, as the "Provincetown of the Middle East," where "gay men and women from other Arab countries and the West are increasingly vacationing." The journalist, Patrick Healy, described the choice of vacationing in Beirut as "all the more sexy and thrilling for some because they feel they are living on the edge and discovering a gay culture that is freshly evolving" (Healy 2009). Such descriptions of Beirut do not circulate in a vacuum. Lebanon, a sectarian, Muslim-majority country, has often been regarded as exceptional in the Arab world for its seeming diversity and cosmopolitanism. Following the assassination of Lebanese prime minister Rafic Hariri in 2005 and the Syrian troops' withdrawal from Lebanon later that year, contemporary Euro-American presses hailed Beirut as a new gay-friendly tourist destination in the Middle East. Euro-American presses describe gay life using linear narratives of progress, gauging improvements in the rise of "tolerant" attitudes and the growth of Western-style gay identities, gay-friendly spaces, and lesbian, gay, bisexual, and transgender (LGBT) organizations. These representations use neoliberal logics to produce a Beirut where both people and places are made intelligible, commodified, and ready for consumption. Thus, they sell Beirut as a city that is welcoming and accommodating to Western gay tourists to the extent that they describe it as "the chameleon city, catering to any desire," where anything one wants can be found in abundance (Masri 2009).

I came across Healy's article in August 2009, a few weeks after arriving in the United States to pursue my Ph.D. I not only did not know what or where Provincetown was—the famous LGBT vacation destination in Cape Cod, Massachusetts—but also could not relate to the experiences that Healy narrates. Reading Healy's account of Beirut's gay friendliness made me question the extent to which I and my friends in Beirut had experienced the city as gay friendly. My research found a growing trend of Euro-American articles and gay travelogues encouraging gay men from Western Europe and North America to visit Beirut. Such descriptions simultaneously liken life in Beirut to and distance it from that in Euro-American cities, while often reminding readers that Beirut is still *in* the Middle East. These articles make similar distinctions between parts of Beirut that are progressive and gay friendly (*like* the West) and those that are not (*similar to* other parts of the Arab world). Once hailed as the "Paris of the Middle East," Beirut has seemingly recovered from Lebanon's fifteen-year civil war (1975–1990) and now presents an exciting, different, and relatively safer yet somewhat dangerous option for travelers in the Middle East. Gay tourism to Beirut, however, is a newly emerging phenomenon. The articles I found were clearly directed to a white Euro-American audience of gay men, and they left me puzzled: Who has these experiences of gay Beirut, and who gets to speak of gay life in Beirut?

This book challenges both popular and academic representations of contemporary Beirut as exceptional, while highlighting everyday-life disruptions in Beirut. I argue that these representations rely on discourses of sexuality (especially LGBT identity) that construct Beirut as "modern" in relation to other sites in the Middle East (and other parts of Lebanon). In addition, they use a market-driven, neoliberal framework that constructs Beirut as the object of both consumer desire (tourism) and foreign investment. The Orientalist logics of these representations occur on multiple levels, which, in contemporary culture, take the form of what I call "fractal Orientalism." As an alternative to these exceptionalist representations of Beirut, the book focuses on Beirut as it is lived by my LGBT interlocutors, who are primarily women and genderqueer persons. Rather than analyze LGBT identity formation per se, the book analyzes practices, particularly what I call queer strategies of everyday life, that my interlocutors use to navigate ongoing daily disruptions in Beirut. In doing so, the book highlights the centrality of everyday-life disruptions as a defining feature of life in contemporary Beirut—a condition that confounds existing Foucauldian models of power that rely on distinctions between normative and nonnormative positionings (or situations). Thus, the book exposes the inherent "stability" that is assumed in these conceptions of queer theory and offers an alternative theoretical lens that instead highlights disruptions and precarity as normative conditions of everyday life. My use of "queer" follows queer theorist Siobhan Somerville's (2014) conceptualization of "queer" as a verb, an action, and a relation. I use the term "queer" both in relation to nonnormative gender and sexuality and in reference to the larger social condition of everyday disruptions. That is, a *queer* situation refers to an anomalous condition in relation to what we perceive as normative (for example, imminent disruptions versus stability).

Tourism and Disruptions in Beirut

Despite decades of violent conflict and political instability, Lebanon has maintained its tourism and service industry on which its economy is highly dependent. The government promotes tourism by highlighting Lebanon and Beirut's exceptionalism and cosmopolitanism (see Lebanon Ministry of Tourism, n.d.). While most of the tourists are Lebanese expatriates who live abroad, there has been a growing informal gay tourism industry, which, even though not endorsed by the state, is run by Lebanese tourism groups such as Lebtour and the International Gay and Lesbian Travel Association (IGLTA) (discussed in more detail in Chapter 1).

Depictions of Beirut's openness and cosmopolitanism cite Lebanon's religious and sectarian diversity and "nascent" gay life as signs of exceptionalism and modernity in the Middle East.[1] Hariri's assassination in 2005 and the resulting Syrian troop withdrawal from Lebanon were regarded as a turning point in recent Lebanese history, especially with regard to possibilities for a new democracy and political reform. However, in the months and years after 2005, the beliefs and promises of a new beginning and the possibilities for the expansion of civil liberties were countered by the stark reality of more state-led oppression targeting already-marginalized groups in Lebanon (Makarem 2011, 106).

As sociologist Rima Majed (2016) illustrates, the Syrian troops' withdrawal from Lebanon in 2005 inaugurated a new phase in Lebanese postwar history. Majed notes that social movements and political alliances shifted away from primarily Pan-Arab and pro-Palestinian mobilizations to a focus on internal politics and heightened calls for civil liberties. Violence and daily disruptions took on various manifestations in the years that followed. The period between 2005 and 2008 witnessed a series of targeted assassinations against prominent journalists and politicians who were critical of the Syrian regime; a number of explosions in various neighborhoods in Beirut; a thirty-three-day Israeli war against Lebanon in 2006; a war between the Lebanese Armed Forces and a radical Islamist Sunni group in the Nahr El Bared Palestinian refugee camp in northern Lebanon in 2007; and an internal violent conflict in May 2008 in Beirut between supporters of Hezbollah and supporters of the government and the Future Movement, a political party led by Hariri's son. Political deadlocks became endemic in the post-2005 phase of Lebanon's history. There were two periods of political standstill when Lebanon had no president, from November 2007 to May 2008 and from May 2014 to October 2016.

As the Arab uprisings began to spread, their effects were felt in most countries in the region, even those—such as Lebanon—that did not witness a revolutionary wave. In the summer of 2012, the Syrian uprising started to shift into a full-blown war. The escalation in Syria spilled over to Lebanon, manifesting itself as armed clashes between Sunni Muslim groups who opposed the Syrian regime and mainly Muslim Alawite groups who supported the regime in the northern city of Tripoli and the southern city of Sidon. By that time, the polarization around the Special Tribunal for Lebanon concerning Hariri's assassination had also intensified. The year 2012 witnessed a number of assassinations targeting general security officers. As the conflict in Syria developed and with Hezbollah's direct involvement in the war in Syria, the internal security situation in Lebanon deteriorated. In 2013, Beirut also became a target of numerous Islamic State of Iraq and the Levant (ISIL) suicide bombings and attacks. From 2013 to 2015, there were fourteen ISIL car bombings and suicide attacks, mostly aimed at civilians and checkpoints in the predominantly working- to middle-class Shia southern suburbs of Beirut. This culminated in November 2015 when an ISIL suicide bombing in the predominantly working-class Shia Burj al-Barajneh neighborhood in the southern suburbs led to the death of eighty-nine people and wounded more than two hundred (see discussion in the Conclusion).

Al-Wad: Defining a Queer Situation

Life in Beirut remained highly precarious. Suicide bombings targeted civilians and army checkpoints, and there were shortages of basic services (such as daily electricity blackouts and the lack of clean drinking water). A citywide garbage crisis began in 2015, which has not officially been resolved, "when a huge landfill site closed and government authorities failed to implement a contingency plan in time to replace it; dumping and burning waste on the streets became widespread. The campaign group Human Rights Watch calls it 'a national health crisis'" (Smith Galer 2018).

For as long as I can remember, people in Beirut have used the term *al-wad* to capture the complexity of everyday violence, disruptions, and lack of basic services. *Al-wad* is the Arabic equivalent of the term "the situation," which can also refer to "circumstance(s); condition(s); position; setting; . . . state (of affairs or things as they are)" or "status."[2] "The situation," then, is a general and nebulous term, commonly used in post–civil war Lebanon to refer to the shifting conditions of instability in the country that constantly shape everyday life. It simply refers to the ways that things are, the normative ordering of things and events. However, it produces feelings of constant unease, anticipation of the unknown or what the future might bring, and daily anxieties. Perhaps this feeling is best captured by my conversation with a cab driver in May 2019, when the driver describes the feelings of anxiety and fear of the unknown that *al-wad* produces as living "in a state of everyday war."

It is not uncommon for people to use unclear terms when speaking about conflicts, which serve as vague containers for histories (and ongoing situations) of trauma, violence, and struggles. For example, people in Lebanon distinguish between "the events" (*al-ahdath*) in reference to the Lebanese civil war (1975–1990) and "the situation" (*al-wad*). In a place where there is no shared narrative or history of the civil war or postwar reconciliation among people, these vague terms help keep a form of peace. Though one might wish to analogize *al-wad* to "the Troubles" in Northern Ireland or "the Conflict" between Israel and Palestine, it does not carry the same connotation or even affective resonance, since the term "situation," unlike "trouble" or "conflict," does not necessarily convey something negative. *Al-ahdath*, which is similar to *al-wad*, is a disaffected and nebulous term, yet it signifies more than just "the everyday situation." However, *al-ahdath*, the Conflict, and the Troubles all refer to conflicts and histories of partition that are racialized.

Having such a seemingly neutral and nebulous term to describe circumstances of a place and people reflects the difficulty of finding words that can capture or express what the situation actually is. "The situation" is a term that in English might refer to a particular situation and might not carry much weight; in the Lebanese context, however, *al-wad'* is a loaded term. In Beirut, people share their anxieties and experiences of *al-wad'* as imminent disruptions and refer to it in conversations with one another without having to explain. The term establishes a shared sense of knowledge and feeling among people in Lebanon. A person who needs to have the term explained is marked as an outsider to *al-wad'*. Because there is no clear beginning or end to *al-wad'*—it is constantly changing—what remains is its disruptive and affective elements. Perhaps the power of *al-wad'* is its generality and untranslatability to those who do not experience it as a daily, precarious, and normative state. What happens when the way that things are or the normative baseline implies constant yet shifting disruptions? My interlocutors use the term *al-wad'* to name a condition but also to reveal the kinds of queer tactics or strategies that become necessary under such disruptive conditions. These queer tactics also gesture toward an expansive understanding of queerness—one that does not necessarily link to LGBT identities but to practices of negotiating everyday life.

This book uses the concept of *al-wad'* in two ways: (1) to describe the historical context and the backdrop of the research and to capture the challenges and precarity that shape everyday life and (2) to serve as a metaphor and analytical tool to help understand queer strategies of everyday life in Beirut. The queer strategies enacted by my interlocutors also disrupt dominant discourses of Beirut's exceptionalism and gay life in Beirut. My use of the term "disruptive situations" might betray the concept of *al-wad'*, since it assumes that there are moments or times when life is not disrupted. *Al-wad'* is the situation that is always disruptive. It serves as a description as well as a metaphor for the challenges and precarity as a result of war and strife that shape quotidian life; it occurs when the out of the ordinary becomes the normal. In other words, *al-wad'* is a way of describing queer times. Though language ultimately fails in articulating or accounting for what *al-wad'* actually is, affect does not.

Exceptionalism as "Fractal Orientalism"

Despite the disruptive effects of *al-wad'*, in 2013, when violence from the Syrian war had already spilled over to Lebanon and Beirut, the U.S.-based urban policy magazine *City Journal* published an article by American journalist Michael Totten titled "Can Beirut Become Paris Again? Freed from Syrian Domination, Lebanon's Capital Could Shine." In the article, Totten (2013) considers how the war and devastation in Syria had the unintended effect of making Beirut "potentially shine" again: "Today, the shoe is on the other foot. Syria, not Lebanon, is suffering the horrors of civil war. With Syria's Bashar al-Assad possibly on his way out—or at least too busy to export mayhem to his neighbors—will Beirut have the chance to regain its lost glory?" Taking into account the everyday violence and disruptions of *al-wad'*, how might we make sense of the numerous representations of Beirut being circulated in Euro-American publications, including Healy's (2009) celebration of gay tourism in Beirut and Totten's (2013) hopeful vision for Beirut to return to its "former glory"? While Beirut of the 1970s and 1980s (and sometimes 1990s) continues to be represented as dangerous and war-torn in the U.S. imagination, as depicted, for example, in the 2018 Hollywood movie *Beirut* (filmed in Morocco), contemporary Beirut is also hailed as the "Provincetown of the Middle East." These Orientalist depictions, though seeming to be at odds, complement each other. Current fighting, tensions, and violence in Beirut become described as a natural state of the Middle East and are not easily understood or explained as war. At first glance, these representations appear to be "traditional" Orientalism, or what Edward Said (1978) describes as historical discursive misrepresentations of the Middle East that tend to paint it as homogeneous and backward, in opposition to the progressive and diverse West. Orientalism relies on irreconcilable binaries and differences between the West and the Middle East to explain the region, cities, and peoples of the Middle East. However, on closer examination, I suggest that these contemporary neoliberal representations of Beirut use and rely on fractal Orientalism, or Orientalisms within the Middle East.

Fractals, or "nested dichotomies" (Abbott 2001, 9), are geometric patterns that repeat themselves infinitely across multiple scales and contexts. These geometric patterns are found in nature, such as in plants, leaves, and snowflakes, where exactly the same shape is simultaneously reproduced on multiple levels that keep repeating themselves (Peitgen and Richter 1986). Fractals usually hide in plain sight, such as in nature, and therefore are often hard to identify.[3] Unlike Orientalism, which does not account for the multiple scales by which binaries are produced and circulated, fractal Orientalism shows how the same binaries simultaneously operate on global, regional, and local scales. While I draw on the effects of fractal Orientalism in the example of Beirut, it is useful for other sites that are shaped by similar histories and relations of power. As a theoretical lens, it is an imperial structure or imposition that functions concurrently at the transnational, regional, national, and city levels; hence, it provides us with a multiscalar spatial model that uncovers how distinctions are made, circulated, and remade.

Since fractal Orientalism simultaneously operates on multiple scales and a fractal takes the same shape as the whole, we can choose to focus on one level or scale of the fractal and still get a narrative that seems complete. Fractal Orientalism uses relational distinctions to produce Lebanon as exceptional and gay friendly—that is, "modern," but only within the context of the Arab Middle East. In addition, the supposed gay friendliness attributed to Beirut obscures ongoing conditions of instability in Beirut and Lebanon. Rather than take for granted that Orientalism produces a single binary of East-West, this book zooms in and out to capture the multiple layers by which fractal Orientalism works.

Disruptive Situations seeks to uncover the underlying processes of fractal Orientalism that make it possible to think of Beirut as exceptional and to unpack how queerness gets produced: what is considered "queer" and who are considered as "legitimate" LGBT subjects. The process and act of situating Beirut and Beirutis as exceptional in relation to various "others" make it possible to recount multiple stories and experiences of Beirut. Naming Beirut the Paris (or Provincetown) of the Middle East is an act of situating Beirut in relation to both Middle Eastern and Euro-American cities. Beirut is likened to Paris yet distanced from it, because Beirut is in the Middle East. These narratives suggest that Beirut has some qualities of the presumably progressive Paris, yet it is not entirely Paris since it also shares qualities with other (not-so-progressive) cities in the Middle East.

Fractal Orientalism illustrates how transnational discourses of national and sexual exceptionalism operate on multiple scales. They are multifaceted and circulate at global (not just in the West), regional, and local levels; they are informed by and in touch with one another. Thus, the binaries of traditional versus modern and backward versus progressive are used to distinguish the Middle East from Europe, Lebanon from other countries in the Arab Middle East, and Beirut from other cities in Lebanon. Fractal Orientalism makes it possible to distinguish Lebanese gays from others in the Arab World and the West.

This book challenges how sexuality has been used to provide an exceptional narrative about contemporary Beirut and modernity. It offers an alternative to the fractal Orientalist narratives of Beiruti and Lebanese exceptionalism and instead uses the queer materialities of *al-wad'* to understand LGBT people's queer strategies of everyday life in Beirut. While fractals are useful for thinking about the multiscalar production of binaries and discursive misrepresentations of Beirut and Lebanon, they have their limitations in fully accounting for how differences are negotiated, felt, and experienced. *Al-wad'*, however, is not about representations; rather, it is used to invoke a felt experience of what the situation actually *does*: its material consequences and effects. Rather than an empirical description of *al-wad'*, I offer LGBT people's experiences of *al-wad'* as an alternative framework to fractal Orientalism. I investigate LGBT people's "queer strategies" in navigating anxieties, violence, and disruptions of everyday life, with a focus on queer subjectivities and access to space.

My goal is to intervene in Orientalist representations of gender and sexuality in the Arab world. Current representations (including scholarly work) on gender and sexuality in the Middle East rely on binaries and a flattened understanding of culture as a site of difference. This book builds on theoretical work that analyzes and critiques linear narratives of progress and modernity that are grounded in gay neoliberal ideals of coming out and visibility (Massad 2007; Puar 2007; Reddy 2011).[4] However, it departs from such works by privileging the affective dimensions of such discourses and the ways that LGBT individuals articulate and negotiate them in their everyday lives. What does it mean to think of Beirut as exceptional? Where does *al-wad'* fare in such representations? How do various groups of individuals experience *al-wad'*? How can learning about LGBT people's everyday-life strategies help us better understand both *al-wad'* and the shifting precarious conditions of daily life? Such questions animate this book.

(Un)Exceptional Disruptions and the Study of LGBT Lives

Disruptive Situations offers a methodological intervention in the study of queer lives by mobilizing the voices of LGBT people in understanding larger questions about war, violence, and precarity. It draws our attention to how disruptions and violence become familiar and calls into question what constitutes "ordinary" and "mundane" aspects of queer lives. Moving away from perspectives that view disruptions as a reflection of exceptionalism or triumphalism, the book highlights queer tactics or strategies of everyday life. Queer tactics or strategies are not just a theorization. They are enactments of political strategies that are not always calculated but essential in navigating the difficulties of daily life: for example, how LGBT individuals access space, move throughout the city, cross checkpoints, and connect with others. Though the book focuses on practices that LGBT people enact, queer strategies of navigating *al-wad'* are not necessarily enacted only by LGBT people. They are also quotidian political practices enacted against oppressive regimes that name and control certain individuals as nonnormative.

Focusing on local manifestations of everyday-life precarity and disruptions in Beirut, I ask: How do queer strategies of everyday life better help us understand "the situation" and the precarious? Unlike an event (such as a natural disaster, a state of emergency, or war), al-wad' does not have a clear beginning or process of unfolding.[5] Rather than try to make sense of its different manifestations or my interlocutors' understanding of "the situation," my focus on queer strategies helps me get at *how* "the situation" gets lived and negotiated.[6] Based on ethnographic research, "deep hanging out" (Geertz 1998), and life interviews with LGBT individuals in Beirut in the periods 2008–2009 and 2013–2014, *Disruptive Situations* intervenes in, and disrupts, portrayals of Arab LGBT persons as homogeneous minorities. Unlike current ethnographic and interview-based research, it does not study gay Beirut or seek to document gay life in the city.[7] It is less concerned with questions of whether gay life exists in Beirut, what forms it takes or how it looks, or what gay subjects do; rather, my objects of study are the *queer tactics* enacted by my interlocutors rather than the people themselves. I move away from analyses that conceptualize LGBT people as a discernible category or minority and assume that queer subjects in the Arab world are always in the process of resisting or adopting Western conceptions of LGBT identities. My interlocutors do not situate their lives along the lines of this rejection-adoption dichotomy. They do not simply adopt LGBT identities; nor do they really attempt to fit their lives within the dominant Euro-American LGBT framework. The majority understand their sexual subjectivities to be intertwined with their class, gender, and religious sect. Rather than document or look for the possibilities of LGBT life, I ask what everyday-life queer tactics can tell us about local and regional politics. By asking what everyday queer tactics have to say about queer life in contexts where precarity and disruptions are the conditions of everyday social and culture life, I raise questions that apply to spaces beyond Beirut.

One of the unintended consequences of working in and on a place such as contemporary Beirut is the necessity of grappling with the question of how we understand a social phenomenon like gender or sexual nonnormativity in a place that is so shaped by political turmoil and multiple disruptions. Traditionally, literature on nonnormative gender and sexualities in the Arab Middle East focuses on marginality of LGBT and queer communities (Whitaker 2006; El-Feki 2013). However, another growing body of research looks at the multiple positions that LGBT individuals occupy, beyond their nonnormative gender and sexualities (Ritchie 2010; Makarem 2011; Naber and Zaatari 2014; Merabet 2014). For example, anthropologist Nadine Naber and feminist researcher Zeina Zaatari (2014) examine the antiwar activism of

LGBT and feminist organizations in Beirut, focusing on their humanitarian and relief work during the Israeli war against Lebanon in 2006 rather than only on their LGBT activism. Naber and Zaatari document the effects of the transnational war on terror by shifting the lens "away from the center of power (the empire) to the everyday lives of feminist and queer activists living the war on terror from the ground up" (2014, 92). I build on Naber and Zaatari's work by emphasizing what queer strategies of everyday life can tell us about larger everyday-life disruptions and violence, which are emblematic of what's happening at the geopolitical level. While Naber and Zaatari focus on a state of emergency during the Israeli war against Lebanon in 2006 as an example and extension of the war on terror, I look at disruptions that are not easily captured by a particular moment or incident. These everyday-life disruptions are not seen as states of emergency but as normative aspects of daily life in Beirut. I consider how gender, class, and normativity simultaneously shape LGBT individuals' queer tactics of everyday life and their engagements with discourses of cosmopolitanism and national exceptionalism in Beirut.

Anthropologist Sofian Merabet's (2014) *Queer Beirut* also pays careful attention to the constitutive role of sect and class in understanding sexual subjectivities in Beirut. In his ethnography of "queer Beirut," Merabet does an excellent job of capturing the experiences of inhabiting and moving through the streets of Beirut (and beyond), taking us on a journey through a number of neighborhoods and the ways that spaces have become coded as "gay friendly" by gay men. His focus on sexual difference, rights, and normalized homophobia sheds light on space making and identity acquisition. *Disruptive Situations*, however, explores a different kind of ethnography. While Merabet raises questions about sexual subjectivities, he does so by attending to the everyday performative and bodily practices of men and the construction of urban gay or what he refers to as "queer spaces"—and the changing landscapes of gay spaces in Beirut. Using queer methods, this book focuses on queer strategies of everyday life rather than an approach that minoritizes LGBT people, and it sheds light on larger questions of disruption, coloniality, and power. It destabilizes the seemingly coherent narrative of queer exceptionalism in Beirut by attending to everyday-life disruptions and the transnational flow of discourses of modernity, progress, and cosmopolitanism. Unlike *Queer Beirut*'s focus on Lebanese men and gay Beirut, this book does not privilege Lebanese gay cisgender men; rather, it centers women and genderqueer persons.

Disruptive Situations extends emerging scholarship on transnational queer studies, urban studies, and social-scientific and interdisciplinary research that employs queer methods and political economies of sexuality in understanding social life, including but not limited to sexuality (Allen 2011; Benedicto 2014; Cantú 2009; El-Tayeb 2011; Haritaworn 2015; Perez 2015; Puri 2016). In addition, it complicates transnational queer and sexuality studies and queer theory.[8] I am indebted to queer of color critique (Cohen 1997; Ferguson 2004; Muñoz 1999; Reddy 2011) for decentering whiteness in our understanding of queer theory and for illustrating the ways that queer theory is "an explicitly racialized project" (Vidal-Ortiz 2019, 75).[9] Queer of color critique also decenters sexual-identity categories and instead focuses on people's relation to state power. However, by doing so, it unwittingly takes the nation-state as a category of analysis for granted. Because of the theory's near-exclusive focus on U.S. racial formations and its overreliance on the state, it falls short in accounting for the transnational. Transnational and geopolitical structures and lenses are necessary for understanding local formations. Thus, building on queer of color critique, I focus on what queer strategies of everyday life tell us about geopolitical and transnational formations in Beirut.

While the field of queer studies destabilizes identities and interrogates modes of knowing about the social world, its reliance on categories of normativity has been understated. That is, queer theory presumes a normative standard that needs to be "shaken" or "upset." The notion of *al-wad'*, however, illustrates the impossibility of establishing that distinction (normative-nonnormative) in any consistent or continuous way over time and space. Therefore, I ask what becomes of queer life when conditions of everyday life upset the tethering of a normative baseline that queer theory presumes exists. In other words, what analyses can queer studies offer when everyday-life disruptions and precarity are the *conditions* of social and cultural life? By regarding normativity as a contested category, I shed light on the tensions between queer modes of life and an already-disruptive or *queer situation*.

Queering Lebanese Exceptionalism

Discourses on Lebanon's exceptional status in the Middle East have their roots in the colonial French Mandate that founded Lebanon as a country primarily for the protection of Christians and other religious minorities in the Arab Middle East.[10] Prior to the 1975–1990 civil war, Beirut was often described as the Middle Eastern equivalent of Paris and also as the "Switzerland of the Middle East," particularly for its banking industry, nightlife, and flourishing art scene. Contemporary discourses on Beiruti exceptionalism emerge from the neoliberal policies of the Rafic Hariri governments of the 1990s, which employed discourses on openness and progress to attract foreign investments—particularly from the Arab Gulf—to rebuild the country after the fifteen-year civil war. However, narratives concerning progress are narratives about capital, neoliberalism, and consumption. Prior to the civil war, downtown Beirut had been a major hub for all Lebanese, but during reconstruction, Hariri's governments and the company Solidere transformed it into a high-end shopping district, an exclusive space primarily for the consumption of high-end goods and food catering mostly to tourists from the Gulf (Masri 2010).[11]

Since 2005, with the increase in assassinations of anti-Syrian politicians, journalists, and activists, and later ISIL suicide bombings in Lebanon, tourism advertisements focused mostly on rebranding the safety of Lebanon. The Lebanese Ministry of Tourism's advertisements cater predominantly to Lebanese diaspora and tourists from the Arab Gulf. While not being able to deny *al-wad'*, these advertisements redefine safety, suggesting that to be safe is to be in a familiar (and familial) setting and to be reunited with family and friends. For example, a 2007 advertisement titled "Lebanon the Safest Country on Earth" explicitly stated that "there is no safer place than in the arms of your loved ones." In 2013, in another ad, titled "Don't Go to Lebanon," the Lebanese Ministry of Tourism cast as narrator the famous Lebanese singer Assi Helani, who recited a number of practices that people in general are cautioned not to do:

> They say don't stay in the sun too long, but is there anything more beautiful than the sun? They say too much food is bad for you, but is there something better than food? They say don't stay out too long, but is there something more fun than partying? They say stay away from arguments, but is there anything more beautiful than democracy? They say stay away from Lebanon, but is there something more beautiful than Lebanon?

This advertisement acknowledges the risks of visiting Lebanon, especially those issued by Euro-American governments and Arab Gulf states; however, at the same time, it reshapes the discourse by inviting Lebanese expatriates to visit, using the notion that breaking the rules is an exciting adventure.[12]

In addition to the state and local tourism organizations, fractal Orientalist discourses on Lebanese and Beiruti exceptionalism have and continue to globally circulate in Euro-American media and press. For example, journalist Michael Totten simultaneously employs fractal Orientalist distinctions at the global, regional, and local scales to account for life in Beirut and Lebanon. At the global and regional levels Totten (2013) makes the following distinction:

Beirut is nevertheless by far the most cosmopolitan, liberal, and even Western of Arab cities. To an extent, you can chalk that up to the cultural influence of Lebanese Christians and imperial France. But the Sunni half of town is no less culturally developed than the Christian. Art galleries, fantastic bookstores, film and music festivals, and even gay bars—unthinkable in Baghdad or Cairo—proliferate in both parts of the city.

Totten (2013) claims that Beirut, although not Paris, is the "most cosmopolitan, liberal, and even *Western* of Arab cities." This fractal Orientalist positioning makes it possible for Totten to situate Beirut as more Western in relation to its Arab counterparts yet not Western *enough* in relation to its Euro-American counterparts. He cites French and Lebanese Christians' influences as a distinguishing factor in Beirut. However, he is surprised that Sunnis are "no less culturally developed" than their Christian counterparts, pointing out that they too have galleries, bookstores, festivals, and even gay bars. In doing so, Totten gauges culture and progressiveness of a place and people by looking for the presence of Western conceptions of art and culture. However, for Totten to establish Beirutis' exceptionalism in the Arab world, his use of fractal Orientalism makes it necessary to contrast it to Cairo and Baghdad, where such cultural events remain "unthinkable."

Totten not only makes distinctions between Beirut and other cities in the Arab world but also distinguishes locally between the Lebanese themselves. He celebrates imperialism and French colonialism, citing it as the cause for Lebanon's and Lebanese Christians' exceptionalism:[13]

The Christian half of the city sustained less damage during the [civil] war than the Sunni half did, and it is consequently the more French-looking of the two today. Its culture is also more French, since many Lebanese Christians feel a political, cultural, and religious kinship with France and the French language that Lebanese Muslims do not. The western side of the city is more culturally Arab and also, since so many of its buildings were flattened during the war, architecturally bland. Though the Sunnis there are more liberal and cosmopolitan than most Sunni Arabs elsewhere, their culture, religion, language, and loyalties are, for the most part, in sync with those of their more conservative Middle Eastern neighbors. (Totten 2013)

To highlight Beirut's exceptionalism and cosmopolitanism, Totten looks for signs of "Frenchness" in the city, which he finds in the Christian rather than the Muslim areas. Lebanese Christians become hailed as the bearers of Beirut's cosmopolitanism, whereas Muslims—Sunnis in particular—are depicted as more traditional since they have affinities with their counterparts, their "conservative Middle Eastern neighbors." Totten continues by contrasting the majority Shia southern suburbs of Beirut, or al-Dahiyeh,[14] to Christian areas in Beirut:

> The *dahiyeh* looks and feels like a ramshackle Iranian satellite, even though you can walk there from central Beirut in an hour. Once known as the "belt of misery," the area is still a slum. Most of the buildings are 12-story apartment towers built without permits or attention to aesthetics of any kind—especially the French kind. There are places in East Beirut where, if you try hard enough and squint, you could fool yourself into believing that you're in France. You could never get away with that in the *dahiyeh*. (Totten 2013)

Totten continues to use the adoption of French aesthetics as a barometer or a sign of the progressiveness of Beirut. Any resemblance to France becomes the example of whether a place can be considered cosmopolitan. Presumably Totten is not talking about the Parisian suburbs (*banlieues*), where North African French and Muslims live, but other parts of France that he considers cosmopolitan. At the same time, resemblance to an imagined Iran, which he links to the Shia southern suburbs, suggests a space that is backward and lacks culture. His use of fractal Orientalism is even more pronounced when distinguishing between the Lebanese themselves: Christians (being more progressive and "cultured") versus Muslims (and Shias in particular, who have "no bearing to culture"; Totten 2013). Totten's article demonstrates how Western representations create the fractal Orientalist comparisons, but these discourses are also taken up and circulated in Beirut by the Lebanese themselves.

Lebanese development, reconstruction, and urban-planning companies such as Solidere heavily rely on such discourses to advertise (and sell) Beirut. For example, they cite Euro-American newswires and journalistic accounts of Lebanon to promote Beirut. On a research trip to Beirut in the summer of 2010, I came across advertisements for a high-end shopping and restaurant promenade that reproduced selections from Euro-American magazine articles that highlighted the fact that Beirut is regaining its place as a top tourism destination (see Figures I.1, I.2, and I.3). The circulation of statements such as "Beirut is back on the map" and "the revival of a landmark," by Western news outlets such as the British Broadcasting Corporation, Agence

FIGURE I.1. "The World Is Beiruting Again," 2010. (Photograph by the author.)

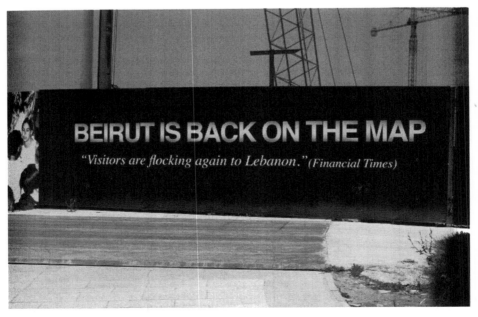

FIGURE I.2. "Beirut Is Back on the Map," 2010. (Photograph by the author.)

FIGURE I.3. "The Revival of a Landmark," 2010. (Photograph by the author.)

France-Presse, the *Financial Times*, and the *New York Times*, illustrates that Beirut is lucrative for foreign investors and as a new tourist destination. Most notable is the advertisement taken from Agence France-Presse, which states: "The World is Beiruting Again: Brimming with Style, Beirut Is Regaining Its Reputation as a Shopper's Paradise." What does it mean for the world to be "Beiruting" again? Given these advertisements, "Beiruting" as a verb signifies an act of consumption and commodification. More specifically, Beiruting becomes equated to style and luxury shopping. Here, the political economy of progress becomes directly related to particular neoliberal patterns of consumption and the selling of places.

One of the main questions this book asks is: Who has access to and gets to engage in the consumptive practices of Beiruting? While the world is seemingly Beiruting again, there is no consensus about whether Beirut has become or has "regained its title as Paris of the Middle East" (Sherwood and Williams 2009) or whether Beirut can be Paris again (Totten 2013). To queer the term "Beiruting," I use it as a verb and ask: How do my interlocutors and I "Beirut"? The idea of Beiruting, and what it means to Beirut, pairs with another major question: Who experiences Beirut as gay friendly?

Modern "Gays"

Transnational discourses about modernity and progress, currently animated by the specter of a unitary Islam, often use sex and sexuality to determine a society's progressiveness (Bracke 2012). Sexual politics, as queer theorist Judith Butler argues, often link modernity "to sexual freedom, and the sexual freedom of gay people in particular is understood to exemplify a culturally advanced position, as opposed to one that would be deemed pre-modern" (2010, 105). In other words, the realm of "sexual freedom" determines how people and places are positioned and assessed in relation to one another in transnational narratives of modernity and progress (Cruz-Malavé and Manalansan 2002; Reddy 2011). These transnational discourses of progress employ mainstream gay visibility as markers of freedom of expression and signs of national/cultural progress (Manalansan 1995). Similar to sociologist Lionel Cantú (2009), I am less interested in tracing where these discourses come from and whether LGBT identifications are imported or not (Vidal-Ortiz 2019). Rather, the focus here is on how discourses of sexual progress and modernity are circulated and articulated in Beirut. More specifically, I pay attention to the political economy of these discourses by centralizing the role of power in how they travel and how they make certain designations of people and places possible. For example, while discourses of progress designate certain neighborhoods in Beirut to be more "modern," people, too, take up these discourses in various ways, whether to discount, reproduce, or redefine themselves and others. Ultimately, as Chapter 2 describes, narratives of progress are not unidirectional but take on multiple manifestations. I acknowledge the slippages between categories of cosmopolitan, secular, exceptionalism, and modernity. Instead of trying to parse out and use these concepts neatly, they are used as brought up in the field, particularly to show their grit, messiness, and entanglements.[15] For example, while I used terms such as "openness" and "inclusive," my interlocutors used designations such as "gay friendly" and "cosmopolitan."

Among the challenges faced while conducting fieldwork in Beirut was explaining to my friends and acquaintances the topic of my research. Many assumed that working on queer subjectivities in Beirut meant working on identity acquisition and LGBT communities, or "gay life" in Beirut. I did not initially frame queer experiences only in terms of LGBT individuals' lives and had intended to include individuals whose sexual lives and experiences are not considered normative in Lebanon and do not benefit from heterosexual privilege, such as asexual individuals and single mothers. However, even by focusing on LGBT people's narratives and strategies, I am able to touch on multiple experiences that are beyond sexuality. In explaining my research, the term "queer" is used as a shorthand for and interchangeably with LGBT people. In a May 2013 fieldwork trip to Beirut, an acquaintance, Sura, asked me about my research. I explained that it is about queer subjectivities. She directly responded by saying, "Oh, there aren't a lot of people identifying as queer anymore here. They used to, but now, since there is more openness, people don't need to identify as queer. They can just say, 'I am gay.'" Queer as identification, according to her, gave people the possibility to live in and inhabit multiple worlds. In addition, it could also be used as a "cover" for lesbian or gay. What is striking about her claim is the assumption that with time and more acceptance, nonheterosexual individuals are more likely to identify as gay instead of queer. Hence, she conceives of queerness and gayness teleologically: One precedes the other, and each identification is based on and derived from the political situation and the safety of the actors. Two points are worth noting: First, for Sura, queer is used to blur "gayness" and hence acts as a safer identification that people would abandon over time when they feel safer. Second, Sura does not make distinctions regarding what forms of gay visibilities might be safer and for whom and how the form might differ based on gender, class, and context. To think about who is accepted is to always have to think about gender, class, race, and religious sect and how they inform one's position and one's possibility of being accepted for *being* queer. Framing societal acceptance of LGBT people as an undifferentiated group, as Sura does, glosses over the multiple exclusions and inequalities that constitute and are constitutive of nonnormative and LGBT formations and spaces in Beirut.

Others who asked about my research often followed up by bringing up the issue of gay marriage in Europe and the United States, pointing out that "we" in Lebanon are still stuck in the past, despite it being 2013–2014. Such explanations employ linear narratives of progress that perceive gay marriage as the pinnacle of gay and lesbian acceptance. In addition, they locate neoliberal concepts and understandings of rights, acceptance, and diversity, often coded as "modern," in Western Europe and North America and point out that "we" have yet to catch up. Such examples suggest that tolerance and a celebration of gender diversity, sexual diversity, and visibility signify the cultural advancement of Lebanese society.[16] While Lebanon is imagined as more modern than other Arab countries in this fractal Orientalist comparison, it still lags behind its Euro-American counterparts.

Beyond the International Gay

On July 28, 2012, the Lebanese Internal Security forces raided a pornographic cinema in the district of Bourj Hammoud in Beirut and arrested thirty-six men accused of engaging in what was termed "indecent and immoral acts" ("Lebanese Authorities" 2012). This raid, as has been discussed on various internet social-media outlets, was directly linked to an episode of the Lebanese talk show *Enta Horr* (You are free) on the Lebanese TV station MurrTelevision (MTV) a few days before the arrests, when the host had outed such cinemas and exposed what he referred to as the "deviance" and homosexuality that takes place in "such places." Following the arrests, gay men and transgender women were taken to the infamous Hobeich police station in the neighborhood of Hamra in West Beirut and subjected to anal examinations and probes to "prove" whether they had engaged in homosexual activities.[17] These "tests of shame," as local activists have called them, were performed by forensic doctors and sparked an outrage within Lebanese LGBT circles and a number of mainstream media outlets. However, days after the tests, a decree was issued by the Lebanese Order of Physicians, Lebanon's main medical association, "making these anal examinations unlawful and warning doctors they would face disciplinary measures if they carried out the act" ("Lebanese Authorities" 2012).

Although same-sex behavior is technically illegal in Lebanon and can be punished by up to one year in prison, Beirut has been recently represented as a more open city for LGBT individuals than other cities in the Arab world, primarily because of the somewhat open gay and lesbian events, bars, clubs, and an LGBT travel agency (Moussawi 2013). I use "Technically illegal" because Article 534 of the French Penal Code explicitly outlaws "sexual acts that are contrary to nature" without defining such acts. However, the law has been and can be used as proxy for same-sex sexual acts (Makarem 2011). Despite the depiction of Beirut as a "safe haven for homosexuals" in the Arab world and a "beacon of hope" for many gay Arabs (Zoepf 2007), stories of arrests and crackdowns are not unheard of, and they especially target individuals or groups of people who already occupy marginalized positions in society (Makarem 2011). In addition, the antisodomy law, like other laws in Lebanon, does not apply to those who have "connections" (*wasta*), which afford people protections because of their association with famous political figures, factions, or political groups (Naber and Zaatari 2014).

LGBT rights in Lebanon continue to be vexed. In May 2018, Lebanese General Security forced the cancellation of Beirut Pride, a nine-day event for International Day against Homophobia and Transphobia (IDAHOT), because it claimed that these events did not get its approval (Human Rights Watch 2018). One of the organizers, Hadi Damien, was arrested by police officers who showed up at an IDAHOT public reading event. Damien was held overnight at the Hobeich police station and asked to sign a pledge to cancel the activities (Barrington 2018). In July 2018, the Lebanese Court of Appeals in Mount Lebanon reexamined Article 534 of the Lebanese Penal

Code and "issued a new judgment holding that homosexuality is not a crime" (Hajj 2018). This was a historical and unprecedented act. While individual judges have considered the article to be problematic, especially since "natural sex acts" are undefined and ambiguous, and hence have refused to use it to prosecute same-sex sexual relations, this decision was made not by individual judges but by a court majority (Hajj 2018).

Although this book does not focus on rights or activism, a majority of my interlocutors are and were involved in LGBT organizing. During my research, I interviewed members of Helem and Meem, the two most well-known LGBT organizations in Lebanon at the time.[18] Helem (2004–present) is a publicly visible, rights-based nongovernmental organization (NGO) working on LGBT rights in Lebanon; Meem (2007–2014) was a partially underground, grassroots group working for lesbian, bisexual, transgender, and queer women's empowerment and community building. Helem adopts an affirmative strategy of visibility, pride and coming out, albeit in a more cautious way than its Euro-American counterparts, by taking advantage of the ambiguities and discrepancies between the law and its irregular enforcement in Lebanon. Meem, however, adopted a strategy of relative invisibility, focusing on women's empowerment and community building while being critical of international human rights discourse. Both groups define and conceive of LGBT identities and communities by both simultaneously engaging with and contesting dominant models of Euro-American LGBT organizing. Even though at an international level Helem and Meem are similar in their focus on geopolitics and the multidimensionality of their positions and struggles, they are divergent in their LGBT organizing methods at the local level. Both call for sexual diversity and LGBT community empowerment in Lebanon but do so differently.

Prior to the development of Meem, a group of women who were members of Helem started Helem Girls, a support group for women, which was developed to open up a space for centralizing women's issues within the organization and derived its strategies from feminist politics ("Helem and Sexual Harassment" 2012). In a conversation with one of the former Meem coordinators, she told me that many women felt that Helem was very male dominated; Meem sought instead a space that centered on women's experiences. In addition, she claimed that, even though Helem Girls provided a space for some women, many remained unsatisfied with the affirmative and visible strategies of Helem and its hierarchical organizational structure. Hence, a group of women from Helem Girls started Meem in 2007 to create an alternative space that was not male dominated and had a different organizational structure and organizing strategies. Meem stressed the safety of members, and former Meem members stressed during interviews that the organization did not want to be as visible as Helem. They wanted an organization that was grounded in feminist issues and did not foreground fixed identity-based approaches to gender and sexuality. However, many women and gender-nonconforming and trans people remained in Helem but also joined Meem. (Chapter 5 goes into more detail about the history of LGBT organizing in Lebanon.) Meem's concerns about visibility and safety relate back to Sura's conception of what constitutes safety (or safer conditions) in "the situation." But in Beirut, living in *al-wad'*—a permanent state of precarity—what is seen as safer? What queer tactics are enacted to create safer conditions amid *al-wad'*?

Precarious Situations: Moving beyond Victims and Heroes

A book on imminent everyday-life disruptions and queer strategies is a book about precarity and precarious situations. While the concept of precarity has been used primarily to capture the reality of precarious labor conditions and practices (Bourdieu 1998; Standing 2011), it is also employed in accounting for the precarious nature of the human condition, particularly in a post–September 11 moment (Butler 2006, 2010). In *Precarious Life: The Powers of Mourning and Violence*, Butler (2006) contends that all humans are vulnerable because of the social condition of life.[19] Precarity, as a condition or state of life, produces feelings of precariousness, which are feelings of constant vulnerability and insecurity, including fear of violence and loss of human life (Butler 2006).[20] While this literature on precarity locates it as a global condition, because it focuses on a post–September 11 moment, it is still U.S.-centric. To consider precarious life only after a post–September 11 moment is also to disregard the myriad ways in which people of color, undocumented migrants, and immigrants and refugees have and continue to lead precarious lives in the United States and worldwide. As previously stated, this book is concerned with how queer theory fails in accounting for the precarious as a normative condition. The proliferation of scholarship on precarity uses Butler's (2006) work as primary for understanding the precarious nature of the human condition; however, scholars miss important work, such as that of Chicana feminist Gloria Anzaldúa. In the preface to *This Bridge We Call Home*, Anzaldúa describes the state of *nepantla*:

> Bridges span liminal (threshold) spaces between worlds, spaces I call nepantla, a Nahuatl word meaning tierra entre medio. Trans-formations occur in this in-between space, an unstable, unpredict-

able, precarious, always-in-transition space lacking clear boundaries. Nepantla es tierra desconocida, and living in this liminal zone means being in a constant state of displacement—an uncomfortable, even alarming feeling. Most of us dwell in nepantla so much of the time it's become a sort of "home." Though this state links us to other ideas, people, and worlds, we feel threatened by these new connections and the change they engender. (2002, 1)

Al-wad', like *nepantla*, is shifting and ongoing. Though *al-wad'* might seem to be a period of transition to those unfamiliar with everyday life in Beirut, it is experienced as a normative state of being for those living in it day in and day out. The state of *nepantla*—the bridges or liminal spaces—as decolonial theorist Walter Mignolo reminds us, "is not a happy place in the middle, but refers to a general question of knowledge and power. The kind of power relations inscribed in *nepantla* are the power relations sealing together modernity and what is inherent to it, namely, coloniality" (2000, 2). My reference to precarity and the liminal states that *al-wad'* is regularly (re)producing is not a romanticized gesture to the nature of the postmodern condition of fluidity (Lyotard 1984; Jameson 1990). Rather, it is about capturing the state of constantly living in uncertainty. While people remain uncertain about the present and the future, the affective state of uncertainty itself becomes familiar or known.

I propose that we think of precarity as a relational experience of vulnerability, since it does not affect everyone similarly. To do so, I draw and build on feminist geographer Lynda Johnston's argument that precarity and vulnerability are "embodied, contextual, multiscalar, and relational" (2018, 4).[21] Fractal Orientalism, like precarity, is also multiscalar, relational, contextual, and embodied: It simultaneously takes place on multiple scales, it can gain meaning only in relation and context, and it is embodied by individuals on either side and scale of the fractal. Here, I am not trying to include or account for the lives of LGBT people in war and its aftermath but am looking at what their experiences can tell us about everyday-life disruptions. That is, by using the lens of LGBT persons' queer tactics of everyday life, this book sheds light on the situation and everyday-life disruptions in Beirut beyond a framework of LGBT rights.

Methods

This book draws on three types of data: ethnographic observations; in-depth interviews in Arabic, English, and French; and textual analysis. I conducted ethnographic observations and twenty semistructured interviews with LGBT activists and individuals in Beirut during fifteen months in 2008–2009 and 2013–2014, along with shorter fieldwork stints in 2010, 2011, and 2012. In addition to my observations and formal interviews, I rely on a larger number of informal interviews and interactions throughout my fieldwork, particularly at social outings and gatherings with friends and acquaintances. Though I conducted research in 2008 and 2009, the main bulk of the book is on the research conducted from 2011 to 2016.[22]

It is over multiple conversations, meetings, and times spent together with my interlocutors that I gained insight into queer tactics in Beirut. I emphasize that I am writing about my interlocutors' *experiences and stories* rather than about *them*. Like queer studies scholar Jin Haritaworn (2015, 14), I refuse an "objectifying gaze" on LGBT people's lives. Instead, I gain access to my interlocutors' experiences through their stories and consider them to be knowledge producers.[23]

During the research and writing processes, I became aware of how I, too, was enacting and drawing on some of these queer tactics during my time in Beirut. Since I was able to leave "the situation" (and come back multiple times for research), I also became more aware (and reminded) of the times when I historically could not. In their article on "fugitive anthropology" and considerations of several dangers in the field, feminist anthropologists Maya J. Berry and colleagues remind us of the importance of decentering a disaffected, privileged researcher: "The intimacy with which terror invades our minds and bodies also poses a challenge to the idea of the researcher who is inherently privileged in relation to her field site or collaborators" (2017, 550).[24] Thus, I acknowledge not only my positionality but also my own feelings conducting ethnographic work in an intimate setting, where I grew up and lived, and the unease of having to manage "the situation."[25]

This book is not about generalizations or about merely including marginalized voices; rather, it is about specificity. Indigenous scholar Hayley Marama-Cavino (2018) asks us to rethink inclusion in social justice work and theorizing, as it erases the specificity of particular populations. Thus, I focus on the specifics of my interlocutors' experiences and the situation in Beirut rather than try to fit their lives into narratives of gay globality, discussed in more detail in Chapter 3. In a similar vein to the work of anthropologist Jafari S. Allen, this book attempts to "resist simplifying the complex" by accepting the shifting nature of my interlocutors' and (my) subjectivities and our experiences of precarity (2011, 9). It is about the specificity of precarious life in a *queer situation*. It tells the stories of multiple everyday-life disruptions of research and of people's lives and the queer strategies that they use to navigate violence and disruption. My fieldwork was disrupted multiple times by the situation in Lebanon. My interlocutors disrupt the dominant narratives of coming out, visibility, LGBT organizing, and modernity. And this book attempts to disrupt dominant representations of sexualities in Beirut and the Arab Middle East. I conducted this research not as a spectator or observer but as someone with familial ties and intimate friendships in the field. Finally, as Berry and colleagues remind us, for some "the field travels with us and within our bodies" (2017, 540). Though I do not currently reside in Beirut, *al-wad'* stays with me while writing this book, and I remain accountable to the "field" in a number of ways.

Overview of the Book

Chapter 1 critiques the projection of Beirut as gay friendly and suggests how such designations misrecognize conditions of economic and political inequalities. It unpacks transnational discourses of the gay friendliness of places by focusing on the representations of Beirut as gay friendly since the year 2005. It analyzes gay travelogues on Beirut and Euro-American tour guides from 2005 to 2016 and argues that categories such as "elite cosmopolitan gay subjects" and "Beirut as exception" are invoked to make Beirut intelligible as a gay-friendly city and tourist destination. Euro-American representations of gay life in Beirut employ narratives of linear progress, gauging improvements in the rise of tolerant attitudes and the growth of Western-style gay identities, gay-friendly spaces, and LGBT organizations. I argue that these representations produce and rely on "fractal Orientalism," which positions Lebanon and Beirut as exceptional in the Arab world. These distinctions, which are represented along a *seeming* binary, extend to divisions within Beirut and among the Lebanese. Fractals allow us to see how distinctions are mobilized at the levels of multiple scales (global, regional, and local)—distinguishing, for example, between "good" and "bad" Arabs and Muslims. These representations employ their understanding of Lebanese culture and religion to make the social organization of gender and sexuality intelligible to Euro-American audiences. I, however, am concerned with using material and geopolitical conditions to show how embodiments of race, gender, and class shape people's experience of gay-friendly Beirut.

Chapter 2 builds on the previous chapter's discussion of fractal Orientalism by considering how it operates at the everyday level and by examining how discourses of exceptionalism obscure exclusionary practices and disruptions of everyday life, or *al-wad'*, in Beirut. It draws on my ethnographic work and interviews with LGBT individuals in Beirut to show how concepts such as exceptionalism and elite cosmopolitanism are circulated and articulated among LGBT individuals in Beirut, while considering the material realities that these terms hide. Whereas discussions of cosmopolitanism tend to assume Western urban centers as reference points for understanding the category, my interlocutors have different referent categories. First, I illustrate that LGBT Beirutis create relational understandings of modernity and cosmopolitanism by situating Beirut in relation to other Arab cities rather than just Euro-American cities—a regional fractal Orientalism. Second, I unpack the multiple ways that Beirutis use narratives of cosmopolitanism, arguing that, in addition to being aspirational and instrumental (to attract tourists), the narratives are also affective. While for some, narratives of exceptionalism provide exuberance in times of despair, for others, they invoke anger at the classist and racist undertones that they express. Many individuals contest discourses of Beirut's exceptionalism and cosmopolitanism by drawing on experiences of gendered and classed exclusions, particularly regarding access to public and gay-friendly spaces and LGBT organizations. Beirut's seeming tolerance of middle- to upper-class gay and lesbian tourists—and not of groups such as Syrian and Palestinian refugees; migrant domestic workers; and gender-nonnormative, trans, and working-class people—becomes a sign of modernity and cosmopolitanism.

Chapter 3 moves away from fractal Orientalism to highlight *al-wad'*, a condition that fractal Orientalist discourses take for granted and ignore. This chapter analyzes my interlocutors' strategic uses of identity, arguing that they are also strategies of managing *al-wad'*. I contend that critical sexuality scholarship has replaced the older "coming-out narrative" with a what I call a "reconciliation narrative," which assumes that LGBT subjects need to reconcile what are represented as mutually exclusive aspects of their subjectivities, such as being Muslim and being gay. Similar to the coming-out narrative, the reconciliation narrative is used as a marker of the development of "universal" LGBT subjectivity. My interlocutors contest the framing of their experiences as narratives of reconciliation; that is, they do not present their lives or stories as harmonizing or resolving seemingly oppositional aspects of themselves. I show that my interlocutors resist reconciliation narratives, keeping their subjectivities separate and deploying them at different times as ways of simultaneously managing their multiple positionalities and *al wad'*. Unlike analyses that foreground reconciliation as a central organizing concept, my analysis shows how queer subjects in Beirut unsettle, trouble, and disrupt these frameworks.

Chapter 4 builds on the previous chapter's discussion of reconciliation narratives by focusing on LGBT visibility, which is often deployed in the fractal Orientalist accounts but is not a useful metric or tool to understand LGBT life in Beirut. The chapter examines LGBT individuals' strategies of visibility, which are based on gender, class, and sectarian visibilities rather than sexuality. It argues that one is always visible, since visibility is constantly shifting and contextual, particularly amid *al-wad'*. For example, in the context of *al-wad'*, Syrian refugees are treated as suspect and become "visible" by being racialized and criminalized, regardless of their gender, sexuality, class, or religion. I move away from an agential understanding of visibility toward visibility as it is experienced. I understand strategies of visibility not as manifestations of "closeting" but as complex strategies of maneuvering the city. The chapter argues that visibility is about (1) knowledge (something is assumed or known), (2) intelligibility, and (3) vulnerability. I touch on the role of LGBT visibility in Lebanese media and the ways that it reproduced the conflation between gender nonconformity and sexual nonnormativity. Finally, the chapter problematizes the tendency to focus on either gay activism or coming out, which presumes a desire for certain types of queer visibility.

Chapter 5 rethinks the notion of community and focuses on what my interlocutors call "the bubble," a metaphor for temporary sheltered spaces (metaphorical, physical, and relational) of retreat from both conditions of *al-wad'* and gender and sexual normativity. It presents the various ways that LGBT communities have failed a number of my interlocutors and how they use queer tactics such as the creation of bubbles. I conceive of the bubble as a shared sense of a public (including relations between people) that is best understood as a contradictory formation: It is an expression of both privilege and protection, critique and investment. Hence, it becomes both a strategy for the negotiation of life in Beirut and a part of the larger ideology of exceptionalism and progress. While the metaphor of the bubble has been employed in urban studies of inequalities, governance, and gated communities, I critique the concept by pointing out how bubbles abstract the material conditions through which they are produced.[26] I ask: Who has access to bubbles, and who can afford to create bubbles? Oftentimes coupled with everyday practices of denial of *al-wad'*, the bubble unwittingly maintains fractal Orientalist narratives of modernity and progress and of Beirut's exceptionalism.

The concluding chapter returns to and foregrounds the following questions: Why exceptionalism now? What does it serve? How do people feel and embody exception? In light of my question about what queer theory can do when disruptions are the conditions of everyday life, I suggest that fractals, as a theoretical tool of analysis, might be more useful than "queerness" in understanding the geopolitics of transnational sexualities. In addition, using the lens of *al-wad'* captures the everyday-life strategies of LGBT people in

Lebanon rather than frames their experiences through the lens of culture. Finally, while my fieldwork and interview process are discussed throughout the book, I highlight the importance of queer and feminist methods in navigating research where uncertainty and disruption are the norm. While not uniform, we are living in a precarious time when there is growing concern for researchers conducting work amid unexpected and unsettling disruptions. I propose moving toward "queer flexible methodologies" as an orientation that asks us to consider the constantly changing nature of the field, disruptions, and nature of access. A queer flexible methodology accepts that our methods are co-constituted by the field and are part and parcel of fieldwork. It requires a certain form of letting go and of being humble.

1

From Binaries to Fractals

"Glitter and Fears of Gay Life in Beirut"

Beirut sometimes looks like what you'd get if you put Paris, Miami, and Baghdad into a blender and pressed PUREE.

—MICHAEL TOTTEN, "Can Beirut Be Paris Again?"

In January 2009, the *New York Times* chose Beirut as the number-one travel destination for that year, specifically for the luxury it promised and the fact that it was "poised to reclaim its title as Paris of the Middle East" (Sherwood and Williams 2009). Later that year, the *New York Times* published another article, this time hailing Beirut as the "Provincetown of the Middle East," where "gay men and women from other Arab countries and the West are increasingly vacationing" (Healy 2009). "Paris of the Middle East" and "Switzerland of the Orient" are among some of the labels given to Beirut prior to the Lebanese civil war. More recently, however, Euro-American media have referred to Beirut as "San Francisco of the Arab World," "Amsterdam of the Middle East," "French Riviera of the Middle East," and "sin city" of the Middle East, specifically for its more liberal atmosphere and its thriving nightlife in relation to that of other neighboring Arab cities. Journalists depict tourists from Europe, North America, and the Arab world flocking to experience what many describe as Beirut's "glamorous nightlife, glitzy shows, nudist beach parties and gay clubs" (Yazbeck 2009). As noted earlier, following the assassination of ex–prime minister of Lebanon Rafic Hariri and Syrian troop withdrawal from Lebanon in 2005, there has been an upsurge in Euro-American journalistic interest in Lebanon, particularly in gay life in Beirut (e.g., see Zoepf 2007; Healy 2009; Teulings 2010; Totten 2013). These homo-orientalist representations create and codify Beirut as a new gay-friendly destination to be visited, discovered, and consumed by adventurous Western gay male travelers who are cosmopolitan, affluent, and willing to try a somewhat dangerous yet exciting destination. Homo-orientalism refers to essentialist discourses about the Middle East in which Western male writers describe the region as imbued with "homo-erotically charged encounters" with "natives" (Boone 1995, 90).

This chapter analyzes how Euro-American journalistic publications, gay travelogues, and an international gay tour guide represent gay Beirut from the period 2005–2016, especially in light of *al-wad'*, or everyday life disruptions and violence. It closely examines and analyzes seven articles and gay travelogues on Beirut and the 2009–2010, 2011–2012, and 2016 editions of *Spartacus International Gay Guide*. Five of the articles are targeted primarily to gay audiences since they are published in gay magazines (*Out Traveler* and *Winq Magazine*), and two address a more general public.[1] *Spartacus*, published in Germany, is examined because it claims to be the most widely read international gay guide (Alexander 1998; Puar 2002; Massad 2007). Since one of the primary means that gay destinations are presented and marketed is through international gay guides, having one such example is important for locating similar trends in these circulated images. As various scholars have argued, what makes *Spartacus* especially intriguing is that it "set[s] in motion an evolutionary narrative, where homophobia and heterosexism emerge as markers of cultural difference and act as a social border" (Waitt and Markwell 2006, 88; see also Alexander 2005). Given the dearth of contemporary gay travelogues on Beirut, the analysis also draws on more than twenty articles about tourism in Beirut since 2005.[2]

To make Beirut, Lebanese people, and "the situation" intelligible by and for Euro-American travelers, gay travelogues often trade in imagined "sexual utopias" and promise encounters in unfamiliar and exotic settings with other locals (Alexander 1998). At the same time that political and everyday-life disruptions are sometimes downplayed in these publications, they are also instrumentally foregrounded to present Beirut as a "thrilling" gay tourist destination. Everyday-life disruptions are used to mark Beirut as different from typical gay tourist destinations and are cited only to draw attention to the "exciting dangers" of Beirut as a travel destination. Rather than a deterrent for tourists, *al-wad'* is used as an attraction device to distinguish Beirut as a new option for adventurous gay travelers, a selective, even exclusive, audience. Furthermore, these representations use an understanding of disruptive situations as static even though everyday disruptions of *al-wad'* undergo various changes after 2005. Therefore, "the situation," in addition to Lebanon's multiconfessional political system and its liberal and laissez-faire traditions, is used to highlight a much-desired liminality and hybridity for travelers.

Travel writing has been historically used to produce different and racialized others, "as well as universal knowledge regarding the human body, desire, nature, history, and civilization" (Patil 2018, 4). The significance of this medium, alongside sexology and medicalized discourses of racial difference (Somerville 2000), is understated in documenting contemporary social-scientific understandings of transnational sexualities. Unlike medical texts that rely on medical authority, in travel writing, such as that analyzed here, the traveler gains authority and expertise based on his or her encounters with "the other." Since writing about other places and people entails a process of self-making and self-definition, these texts actively shape and construct relational images of Western gay tourists with the locals. The following discussion looks at how both tourists and locals are gendered, sexualized, and racialized in these accounts by considering the intersections of race, gender, sexuality, class, physical ability, and transnational mobility.[3] Ultimately, I argue that even though gay tourism is premised on disruptions of heteronormative spaces, these travelogues circulate and rely on essentialist and reductionist understandings of gender and sexuality and focus exclusively on flattened understandings of culture and rights. Such accounts emphasize Lebanon's exceptionalism in a region known for political and religious conflict and overlook political economies of gender, race, and sexualities, as well as patterns of exclusion based on race, class, gender, and immigration and refugee status. In addition, they end up (re)producing exclusionary spaces that can be accessed only by those with economic capital and those who are racialized as "proper" gay subjects.

Orientalist undertones and their reliance on discourses of discovery, exploration, and adventure present a certain notion of a gay identity premised on visibility, "outness" (openly identifying as gay or lesbian), transnational mobility, and racialized and masculinist assumptions of travel. I ask: How do the "queer other" and "other queer spaces" become conveniently defined and represented in these travelogues? How do these articles situate and characterize Beirut in relation to other Arab and Euro-American cities? How are images of potential gay tourists and locals relationally constructed? How is sexuality (specifically gay homosexualities) deployed and used in ways that rely on narratives of modernity and progress? How do neoliberal economic policies and their various formations on the ground in Beirut structurally shape and help foster dominant discourses and exclusions?

Fractal Orientalism and the "Fascinating" Middle East

European fascination with the mysteries of the Orient is a long-standing tradition, as Edward Said illustrates in *Orientalism*. The Orient, according to Said, "was almost a European invention and had been since antiquity a place of

romance, exotic beings, haunting memories, landscapes, and remarkable experiences" (1978, 1). By defining and locating an assumed homogeneous other,
Europeans were able to define themselves especially in terms of binary oppositional relationships between East and West, which mapped onto binaries of
self-other, civilized-uncivilized, and progressive-unprogressive. Said describes
Orientalism as "a Western style for dominating, restricting and having authority over the Orient," which renders it both voiceless and with no authority over
its own representation. The other in Orientalist depictions is defined strategically and conveniently to fit familiar and intelligible Western imaginings of the
East. The Orient is often described as unchanging and ahistorical and always
has a precedent, whereby "every writer on the Orient assumes some Oriental
precedent, some previous knowledge about the Orient, to which he refers and
on which he relies" (20). Hence, the citationary nature of Orientalism becomes
central to its existence and perpetuation, where the representations and images
described are often located within other texts (Said 1978). Orientalism, as
Said demonstrates, goes beyond mere description; it gave Europeans a form of
justification for colonial domination and ruling of the Orient.

Despite its various and shifting contemporary manifestations, Orientalism still exists today. For example, sociologist Asef Bayat calls today's Orientalism neo-Orientalism, which he rightfully describes as "more entrenched,
multi-faceted and harmful than its predecessor" (2015, 1). Today, powerful
institutions, think tanks, and experts do most of the knowledge production
on the Middle East and suggest that Middle Easterners are not only exotic,
different, and irrational but also dangerous, threatening Euro-American values and ways of life (Bayat 2015). This, as Bayat argues, has direct negative consequences on the Middle Eastern and Arab diaspora in Europe and
the United States. However, these Orientalisms do not affect all regions or
peoples of the Arab Middle East similarly; nor are they circulated only within
Euro-American contexts.

Departing from Edward Said and Asef Bayat, I argue that even though
these homo-orientalist representations are engaged in Orientalist and nativizing
discourses, they do not simply rest on the binary of East-West and Lebanese–
Euro-American, as in nineteenth-century Orientalism. These contemporary
neoliberal representations of Beirut use and rely on what I call fractal Orientalism, or Orientalisms within the Middle East. I suggest that fractals, or what
sociologist Andrew Abbott describes as "nested dichotomies" (2001, 9), serve
as a valuable metaphor to better understand how Beirut is presented as exceptional in the Arab Middle East. Fractal Orientalism employs neoliberal logics
and uses fractals instead of simple binaries to distinguish between parts of the
Middle East marked as "traditional" and "backward" and others marked as

"modern" and "progressive." Fractal Orientalism simultaneously operates on multiple levels: It represents the West as more progressive than the Middle East, Lebanon as more progressive than other Arab Middle Eastern countries, and Beirut as more gay friendly than the rest of Lebanon. These nested dichotomies extend to divisions within Beirut and between the Lebanese, where neighborhoods that are more predominantly Muslim are represented as less open than their Christian counterparts.[4] Moreover, secularists and Christians, more so than Muslims, become regarded as more appropriate gays.

Like neo-Orientalism, fractal Orientalism seemingly responds to criticisms of itself as Orientalist and Islamophobic and thus presents a more complex depiction of the Middle East. These fractal Orientalist accounts trade in neoliberal concepts of "gay globality" (Benedicto 2008, 317; see also Altman 1996; Benedicto 2014), which are global imaginings of what constitutes gay-friendly spaces and people. Thus, they celebrate and describe gay life in Beirut in terms of linear progress narratives, gauging improvements in relation to the rise of tolerant attitudes and the growth of Western-style gay identities, gay-friendly spaces, and LGBT organizations. Focusing on the Arab Middle East as a region, these nested dichotomies are multiscalar, producing regional and local distinctions to mark some spaces as queer(er) than others.[5] Depictions of Beirut gain meaning only through its geographical context in the Middle East and its relation to other cities in Lebanon and the Arab world. Beirut is positioned as a "better" option than other cities in the Arab Middle East, yet it still lags behind other cities in Western Europe and North America. Ultimately, transnational narratives of sexuality use fractal Orientalist notions of "openness" and "tolerance" to nonnormative gender and sexualities to market Beirut as a gay-friendly destination *in relation* to other neighboring Arab cities. Figures 1.1 and 1.2 visualize these fractals and distinctions and thus help clarify the workings of fractal Orientalism.[6]

Scale is crucial to understanding how these distinctions gain meaning at global (Europe–Middle East), regional (within the Arab world), and local levels (Beirut–other Lebanese cities). As this chapter demonstrates, these multiscalar distinctions occur simultaneously and gain meaning from one another. Though these narratives seemingly circulate outside Beirut, they are informed and made coherent by various local manifestations and articulations, such as the liberal economic policies of the Hariri post–civil war government in the 1990s. Beirut's exceptionalism is made possible by the interworking of neoliberal logics at these multiple scales. This chapter focuses on the larger geopolitical and transnational scales on which these discourses operate. Subsequent chapters discuss how these discourses travel and are articulated at the everyday level in Beirut.

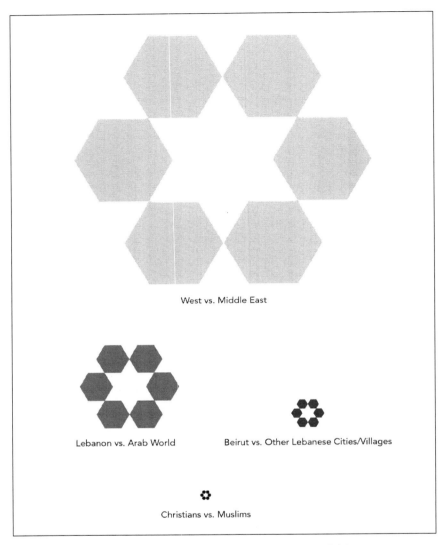

West vs. Middle East

Lebanon vs. Arab World

Beirut vs. Other Lebanese Cities/Villages

Christians vs. Muslims

FIGURE 1.1. Fractals. (Designed by Miriam Salah.)

Beirut and the "Exceptional Status of Homosexuality"

A primary way that Euro-American articles and travelogues promote Beirut and make it intelligible is by employing similes and metaphors to blur distinctions of the categories "East" and "West" (Dann 1992). Varied ways of labeling the city (e.g., "Paris of the Middle East") construct a Beirut that can be understood only by situating it in relation to both European cities and

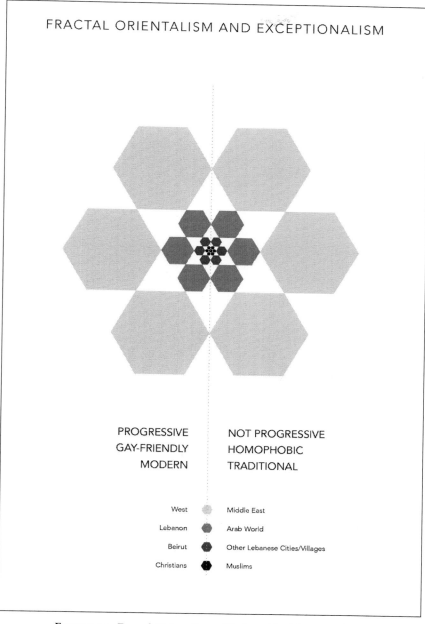

FIGURE 1.2. Fractal Orientalism. (Designed by Miriam Salah.)

cities in the Arab Middle East. This practice of fractal Orientalism distances Beirut from other cities in the Arab Middle East, making it exceptional.

To represent Beirut and Lebanon as exceptional in the Arab Middle East, fractal Orientalism relies on a number of erasures within Beirut, particularly those targeting women, trans persons, migrants, refugees, and working-class and LGBTQ individuals. Neoliberalism and gay friendliness work together to structurally shape and help foster dominant discourses and practices of exclusion in Beirut. The city is described as open and tolerant to difference and minorities without a mention of the existing racist, sexist, and sectarian realities and policies. Even though one might assume that the diverse makeup of Lebanese society, which consists of eighteen religious minorities with no sect in the majority, might make it easier for groups to accept difference, some argue that it is specifically "the sectarian makeup of its society," which "provides a breeding ground for divisions and intolerance" (M., n.d., 15, 5). In describing the experiences of white gay Western tourists in Beirut, the articles bring up *al-wad'* only as a reminder of the city's exciting dangers. They also do not discuss the rampant racism against Syrian and Palestinian refugees and migrant domestic workers from East Africa and Southeast Asia. Beirut's openness and acceptance are made possible by exclusionary practices against undesirable racialized and classed others, as Chapter 2 demonstrates. Acknowledging these exclusions and their neoliberal logics would collapse the nested or complex binaries that allow fractal Orientalism to function and replicate.

Some Euro-American articles describe Beirut as "the amazing and fascinating result of East meets West" in an implicit celebration of French colonialism (Lee Smith 2006; *Spartacus* 2009, 2011–2012). While the previous statement seems to collapse the binary of East-West, it actually reproduces it at multiple levels. For example, Beirut is hailed as "the largest city and the most liberal urban centre in the country, the last big city in European terms before the desert" (*Spartacus* 2011–2012, 578). Here, Beirut becomes familiar to Euro-American audiences, since it represents a "city in European terms." However, it is not *any* city, since it is described as the "last city" before the desert, where presumably cosmopolitan urban centers do not exist. Therefore, Beirut becomes legible as a cosmopolitan city only in relation to other cities in the Arab Middle East.

Labels such as "Paris of the Middle East," "San Francisco of the Arab world," "Amsterdam of the Arab world," and more recently "Christopher Street of the Middle East" serve as a means of situating the city as both exotic and familiar (Sherwood and Williams 2009; Zoepf 2007). Shifting localizations of Beirut demonstrate how the fluidity of its situatedness make it comprehensible and attractive to potential visitors. Comparing Beirut to various European and American cities, while still situating it as part of the Arab Middle East, is an example of how travelogues and guides rely on and create these fractal distinctions. Beirut's exceptionalism then, results from situating it as an urban center in the Arab world. Beirut is interchangeably and conveniently placed within the Arab world, the Middle East, and sometimes the "Muslim world" with few or no distinctions made between these geopolitical designations. In addition, situating Beirut as "a Mediterranean capital of night life" and invoking southern European and North African cities illustrates how it is conveniently considered a part of the Mediterranean region to make it more appealing to certain audiences (Healy 2009).

Such fractal Orientalist narratives are not restricted to Euro-American media. The Lebanese state, with its neoliberal policies, its Lebanese businesses, and its citizens, also employs fractal Orientalist accounts to highlight Beirut's exceptionalism and to distance it from the rest of the Arab Middle East—for example, in its tourist promotional materials. On its promotional website, the Lebanon Ministry of Tourism trades on the image of the Lebanese as "outward looking" and cosmopolitan and of Lebanon as combining both tradition and progressiveness:

> The cosmopolitan flair of modern-day Beirut, the gastronomic renown of the country's food and wine, and an educated and outward-looking population complement a country that is both traditional and progressive in outlook. For all the flavors of its storied past and rugged natural beauty, Lebanon is a well-kept tourist secret that begs exploration. (Lebanon Ministry of Tourism, n.d.)

In a similar vein to descriptions in gay travelogues, Lebanon becomes a "well-kept secret" that "begs exploration." These tropes are heavily used in inviting and calling adventurous tourists to choose Beirut as a destination. Whereas these discourses are based on nested binaries—though not as explicitly—Beirutis trouble and disrupt these narratives of exceptionalism.

However, even though Beirut is compared to major Euro-American cities, it is still distanced from them. It is represented as European and Western in its "glitzy nightlife" and facade, but not European because of its lack of cultural life. This becomes very apparent when *New York Times* journalist Patrick Healy (2009) claims that "the cultural life here is still in a stage of postwar development, with few museums or typical tourist destinations." This fractal Orientalist divide between Beirut and European cities represents Beirut as having some cultural life and thus presents it as progressing and not timeless, presumably unlike other cities in the Arab world. This progressive-ness is also explicitly invoked while talking about Beirut's emerging gay life.

Beirut's gay friendliness and exceptionalism result from a fractal Ori-entalism that mobilizes neoliberal concepts of tolerance and gay identities. Thus, Beirut is distinguished from other presumably homophobic cities in the Arab Middle East for what the travelogues refer to as the "exceptional status of homosexuality." Beirut becomes "the Arab world's most gay friendly city," promising to "represent a different Middle East for some gay and les-bian Arabs" (Healy 2009).

Even though same-sex sexual acts are technically illegal in Lebanon (since they are considered "unnatural" by Article 534 of the Lebanese Penal Code) and are punishable by up to one year in prison, all articles I analyzed charac-terize Beirut as a safer destination for gay Western tourists than other places in the Arab world. The articles claim that the Lebanese state has not been actively enforcing Article 534 or detaining people who are perceived to or do engage in same-sex sexual acts (Whitaker 2006; *Spartacus* 2016). However, the application of Article 534 remains highly discriminatory and is often and most commonly used against already-marginalized and vulnerable groups in Lebanese society, such as trans individuals and working-class and gay refu-gees, who are routinely harassed, arrested, and, until recently, forced to un-dergo the now-outlawed anal examinations by Lebanese authorities. Hence, the workings of transnational racial capitalism ensure that Beirut is a safe and gay-friendly space for (white) gay tourists, wealthy Arabs from the Gulf, and the Lebanese upper class.

In addition to representing Beirut as a playground, the articles present it as a safe haven for queer Arabs from other parts of the Arab world (Zoepf 2007). For example, as Healy claims, "But even more than the partying, Beirut represents a different Middle East for some gay and lesbian Arabs: the only place in the region where they can openly enjoy a social life denied them at home" (2009). Healy includes accounts of a number of gay Arab men whom he met in Beirut, including Mohammed, a gay Iraqi, who asserts that "Beirut is freedom. I can be every part of Mohammad here." For a U.S. audi-ence, invoking the freedom of an Iraqi gay man serves as a reminder of the "global war on terror" and the Iraq War in particular. Here, Beirut becomes safer than Baghdad, particularly for sexual minorities. Such accounts further the distinction between Beirut and other Arab cities but at the same time contextualize Beirut in the Arab Middle East, presenting it as good as it gets for LGBT individuals in the Arab world. In addition, the statement assumes the impossibility of Mohammad, a Muslim man, to be both gay and Muslim in Iraq. Therefore, the "every part of Mohammad" invokes that Mohammad is now able to reconcile his sexuality and his presumably Muslim identity. While Chapter 3 explores these "reconciliation narratives" that circulate in both travelogues and academic texts in more detail, it is important to note how fractal Orientalism plays into dominant narratives of the impossibility of the existence of gay Muslims.

Journalists use religious diversity in Lebanon as a marker of teleological progress, akin to what critical race scholar Jodi Melamed (2006) calls "neo-liberal multiculturalism." While Melamed uses "neoliberal multiculturalism" to refer to how the invocation of discourses of diversity and multiculturalism erases the centrality of racism to neoliberal projects in the United States, I use the term in the Lebanese case to show that discourses of Lebanese diversity and the coexistence of Muslims and Christians erase the inequalities between religious and sectarian groups. For example, it does not account for the historical and contemporary Islamophobia in Lebanon, including that directed at Muslim refugees and immigrants. Thus, discourses of Lebanese exceptionalism and religious coexistence present Lebanon as "leading the way for other Arab nations" through its "embrace" and tolerance of religious freedoms and diversity (Lee Smith 2006, 3).

In the article "Beirut Unexpected," journalist Lee Smith (2006) distances Lebanon from other Arab countries by employing the trope of Muslim and Christian coexistence, which remains exceptional to Lebanon. To further showcase how the Lebanese are distinct, Smith writes, "The Lebanese are descendants of the Phoenicians, a seafaring society that became one of the world's greatest civilizations precisely because they were open to new things" (2006, 3). By invoking their Phoenician heritage, Smith racializes the Lebanese as not Arab and attributes their openness to trying new things to their distinct heritage. He links the Phoenician ancestry to Lebanese Christians, more specifically Maronite Christians, who are then used to distinguish Lebanon from the rest of the Arab world. Thus, Beirut's presentation as exceptional in the Arab World relies on racialized stereotypes and an erasure of local structures and materialities of racial, class, and gendered inequalities in Beirut.

Discovering Gay Beirut

Fractal Orientalist accounts of gay Beirut consistently use linear narratives of progress and discourses of discovery. They rely on notions of progress, homophobia, and a neoliberal human rights discourse, which ultimately positions countries that are gay friendly as more modern and uses the "presence of Western-constituted gayness" as a marker of social progress and openness

(Waitt and Markwell 2006, 88; see also Hoad 2000). Therefore, in the case of Beirut, having nascent LGBT movements and the presence of gay- and lesbian-friendly bars and clubs marks it as more progressive and progressed than other Arab cities.

The elements of surprise and novelty are central in these articles, wherein journalists express their astonishment at Beirut's becoming a "new" gay-friendly destination in the Arab Middle East, albeit one that needs to be discovered. For example, Healy claims:

> Gay life in this city is still inching out of the shadows, to be sure, but it seems to have developed a steady forward momentum since the end of Lebanon's 15-year civil war in 1990 and especially in the calm that has followed the brief 2006 war between Hezbollah forces and Israel. (2009)

Healy's description of Beiruti gay life as "inching out of the shadows" presumes a slow-moving progression and something that has yet to come to light, that is, more visible. While Healy posits that gay life is steadily developing post–civil war, this sets in motion a teleological narrative that does not account for *al-wad'* and everyday-life disruptions. Furthermore, Healy's historicization of "the calm" following the 2006 Israeli war as a landmark for the continued progress of gay life in Beirut dismisses LGBT organizing efforts, which began in the late 1990s and early 2000s, were present during the Lebanese mobilization against the U.S. invasion of Iraq in 2003, and gained momentum during the 2006 Israeli war through their relief work with internally displaced refugees.

Almost all the articles I analyzed, including *Spartacus*'s section on Beirut, are premised on the notion of "surprise," where Beirut becomes a city that is constantly changing, to the extent that "even gay life is booming" (Teulings 2010, 102). The articles claim that the situation of gay men in the country has gotten better in the recent years, citing that "gay bars and clubs operate freely and an LGBTQ centre has been created to cater to all needs of the [gay] community" (*Spartacus* 2016, 482). This utopian image of a space for all LGBTQ people fails to consider those who do not have access to these spaces, such as women or transgender persons, or class and racial differences.

Fractal Orientalist depictions are not limited to gay travelogues but are also employed in a number of journalistic books, most prominently in journalist and author Shereen El-Feki's *Sex and the Citadel* (2013). El-Feki's book documents the changing nature of attitudes on sexuality in both Egypt and Lebanon, while focusing on the possibilities for change in the Arab world.

In her introduction, she states that "it took more than a thousand days to assemble these stories, and, like *One Thousand and One Nights,* these tales lead into each other in often unexpected ways" (2013, xviii). El-Feki employs Orientalist tropes by invoking *One Thousand and One Nights*—a collection of folkloric tales from the Middle East and beyond—to describe her research process. She likens the stories she collected from her interviews in Egypt and Lebanon to fictional tales, which also led her to surprising outcomes.

In accounting for the changing sexual lives and the possibility for progress in the Arab world, El-Feki claims that the Arab world is "like the West," albeit located at a different historical juncture:

> In broad strokes, this sexual climate looks a lot like the West on the brink of the sexual revolution. And many of the same underlying forces that drove change in Europe and America are present in the modern Arab world, if only in embryo: struggles toward democracy and personal rights; the rapid growth of cities and a growing strain on family structures. . . . Add to that greater exposure to the sexual mores of other parts of the world brought about through media and migration. (2013, xvii)

The explanations provided by El-Feki offer descriptions of Beirut very similar to those of the gay travelogues and tourism articles. To account for the changing sexual climate in the Arab world, El-Feki draws on what she perceives to be a singular narrative about sexual revolution in the West. She cites multiple forces that might be contributing to changes in the Arab world; yet she claims that though these forces might resemble those driving change in the West, they are not yet fully formed or are yet to arrive ("in embryo"). Further, her usage of "embryo" as a metaphor for progress is heteronormative and assumes a reproductive narrative that does not take into account LGBT models of social and cultural change. These explanations set in motion a linear progress narrative, which posits that Arab societies are on a linear Western liberal trajectory for women's and LGBT rights, even though they are lagging behind yet working to catch up. This fractal divide, which starts with her description of the West–Arab world, takes on similar distinctions at the scale of Lebanon–Arab world.

While El-Feki claims that societies have their own distinct trajectories for social change, she still situates the West and the Arab world in opposition:

> Development is a journey, not a race, and different societies take different paths. . . . I believe that a society that allows people to make

their own choices and to realize their sexual potential, that provides them with the education, tools, and opportunities to do so, and that respects the rights of others in the process is a better place for it. I do not believe this is fundamentally incompatible with social values in the Arab world, which was once more open to the full spectrum of human sexuality and could be so again. Nor need this irremediably clash with the region's dominant faith: it is through their interpretations of Islam that many Muslims are boxing themselves and their religion in. (2013, xvii–xviii)

Pointing to the fact that "development is a journey," El-Feki explicitly describes development in terms of a teleological journey. Arab societies are on the journey to development but are taking more time to arrive. She makes a distinction between Islam as a religion and Muslims' interpretations of Islam, which she describes as the obstacle to Muslim societies' progress rather than the religion itself. El-Feki's analysis assumes that there is a singular interpretation of Islam, without distinguishing diversity in the region (including differences between Lebanon and Egypt). By collapsing Arabs and Muslims, she purports that there are possibilities for change in the Arab world, despite what she describes as their failure, or falling behind. Religion and culture become the primary site of distinction between the West and the undifferentiated Arab world. Such claims fit with the journalistic accounts that also centralize a monolithic understanding of religion and culture in the Arab world to make the region and Lebanon intelligible to U.S. and European audiences.

Adventurous Tourists

Since gay nightlife in Beirut is described as new and flourishing, these articles are premised on notions of adventure and exploration. Thus, the tourist is presented as an explorer who is interested in individualized travel rather than part of a mass tourist culture. The assumed adventurous tourist in the articles is invited to discover Beirut and be part of the nascent, emerging, and flourishing gay life before the city becomes filled with mass tourists. For example, in the German article "Beirut: Hotbed of Vice of the Middle East," translated into English and posted on a *FlyerTalk* forum by the user Jimmy67 on June 8, 2005, tourists are encouraged to "check out Lebanon. A country—still—free of western mass tourists." New York–based traveler writer Michael Luongo (2010) echoes this in his "Lebanon Write Up" for the IGLTA familiarization trip to Lebanon: "There are about 2 million tourists who came to this country of 4 million during 2009, yet it never felt over-touristy. I think that is part of the magic—it's always good to visit places just before they become overwhelmed by those pouring in." In an introduction to "Bounce Back Beirut," by Dutch journalist Jurriaan Teulings (2010), reproduced on the website GlobalGayz, the site's Richard Ammon provides a summary of the article, in which he describes Teulings as an "intrepid Dutch reporter" who "ventures into the mixed-message country of Lebanon to experience the glitter and fears of gay life in Beirut. During his visit he discovers the fashionable avenues of Gemmayzeh and the tense streets of Dahiyeh (controlled by Hezbollah) yet finding gay life in both." Here, Teulings becomes a fearless risk taker who ventured into the mixed messages of Lebanon and ended up discovering that gay life exists in places where one would not expect.

Viewed through a Euro-American lens, "glitter and fears" are used to illustrate the mixed messages that characterize Lebanon. In an explicit use of fractal Orientalism, this passage distinguishes between the gentrified Christian neighborhood of Gemmayzeh and al-Dahiyeh, the predominantly working- and middle-class Shia southern suburbs of Beirut. The fractal distinction between Gemmayzeh and al-Dahiyeh echoes the descriptions by American journalist Michael Totten (2013). In Ammon's description, Gemmayzeh, a residential area converted into a hub of Beirut's nightlife, becomes associated with glitter and fashionable avenues, whereas al-Dahiyeh, which is also residential and a commercial center (though lacking the vibrant nightlife), is associated with fear and "tense streets." Teulings's article arrives four years after the Israeli war, which primarily targeted al-Dahiyeh. Yet the specters of this history are mistranslated into a sense of tension instead of accounting for the reconstruction and recovery that does not make al-Dahiyeh unlike Gemmayzeh. Spatial metaphors are central to understanding the fractal distinction produced. Gemmayzeh's avenues invoke space and openness, as opposed to the southern suburbs' tense streets, which offer less space. Despite juxtaposing these two areas, Teulings remains surprised to discover that gay life exists in both. Though it is still unclear what gay life is or how the journalist accounts for it, we are asked to trust Teulings's discovery of gay life.

Beirut becomes an exciting destination, specifically for its contradictions and the fact that travelers can discover gay life amid *al-wad'* and in a number of unexpected areas. Fractal Orientalism makes it possible to paint life in Beirut as exciting, liminal, and contradictory for the adventurous gay tourist, particularly in relation to European and other Arab cities. Whereas some tourists can avoid the disruptive effects of *al-wad'*, it is not possible at all times.[7] Everyday-life disruptions are sought after, as long as they do not pose physical threats or halt the tourist's experience altogether.

The gay tourist not only is constructed as an adventurous traveler but also is represented as a cultural persona who brings progress and openness to the country with his open lifestyle (Giorgi 2002). In the article "Beirut Unexpected," the gay tourist, who is likened to a "savior," is explained to have "empowered the country's gay and lesbian community [and] has made it the most liberal place in the Arab world" (Lee Smith 2006). Thus, the gay traveler's visit is also presented as being helpful to the gay and lesbian communities in the country. The image of the gay tourist rests on certain degrees of gender normativity, transnational mobility, possession of cultural and economic capital, commodification of spaces and places, whiteness, and physical ability. The person is described as an adventurous traveler (not necessarily tourist) who seeks to discover and introduce progress to the countries visited. In a manner similar to Beirut's description as contradictory and as embracing both East and West, the Lebanese are represented in terms of contradictions and racialized as ethnically mixed.

Lawrence (and the Gay Bears) of Arabia

Since these journalistic accounts are primarily written by gay-identified Euro-American men and circulate in Euro-American media, the consumers of the newspapers, magazines, and guides are assumed to be located in the West. The erasure (and impossibility) of women and trans individuals as travelers and as locals emphasizes the masculinist assumptions of this mode of travel and highlights that these representations are restricted to cisgender gay men. The image of the tourist also assumes numerous other exclusions.

Even though *Spartacus* claims to be international and promises to identify the gay promised lands to everyone who is part of the global gay community, it is far from inclusive. The quintessential international gay traveler is assumed to be cisgender, cosmopolitan, white, and an upwardly mobile consumer (Alexander 2005; Waitt and Markwell 2006). The "third-world gay man," however, is not considered a gay traveler. As M. Jacqui Alexander puts it:

> He is not expected to journey from home simply in search of sexual pleasure in the First World; he is to be encountered in the authentic local geography, imagined back into the "native" context in order to conform to and complete the terms of this colonialist fantasy. (2005, 85)

Therefore, third-world gay and nonheterosexual men are imagined only as locals that gay tourists encounter. These local men's presumed sexuality does not tell us much, since journalists report that even seemingly straight men engage in same-sex acts with Euro-American tourists. Journalists explain that this sexual fluidity (read as confusion) results from the lack of a clearly defined and developed gay identity.[8]

The advertisement of the 2010 international Gay Bear Arabia event co-organized by IGLTA and Lebtour circulates images of locals as "bears" and tourists as "discoverers." The "bear," simplified by Healy's (2009) definition as "a term used the world over for heavyset, hairy guys usually older than 30," is often invoked in these articles, most notably to discuss this event. The "bear" phenomenon, which associates gay men with hypermasculinity, may disrupt the links between male homosexuality and gender nonnormativity, specifically by "rejecting strict body norms (washboard abs and hairless torsos) that the broader gay community tends to value" (Slevin and Linneman 2010, 504; see also McCormick 2011). "Bears" instead embody more rugged and burly masculine physical traits. Hence, their rejection is not a rejection of gender norms but of "mainstream gay body norms" (Slevin and Linneman 2010, 504).[9] In the Arab world, in particular, men's facial and bodily hair is considered a sign of masculinity. However, the image of the bear, assumed to be hypermasculine and closer to nature, is often decontextualized in these articles and advertisements and employed in ways that confirm homo-orientalist and racialized stereotypes of hairy and seemingly hypermasculine Arab men (McCormick 2011).

In 2010, the IGLTA's website promoted the IGLTA symposium and FAM (familiarization) trip to Beirut with the heading "On the Steps of Lawrence of Arabia," which was followed by "Can you hear the Bears of Arabia roar? They are calling you to Beirut, Baalbek, Byblos, Jeita Grotto, Damascus, Amman & Surely the magnificent Petra. Don't miss out on discovering Lebanon, Syria & Jordan's hottest men!" The promotion went on to describe that the countries that "captivated Lawrence of Arabia and Indiana Jones" are now for the tourist to explore. The presumed tourist had the option of "reliving Lawrence of Arabia's adventure" by visiting historical sites in Lebanon, Syria, and Jordan with the gay bear Arabia group, Mister Gay Bear Arabia and Mister Cub Arabia,[10] as they hit the road from Beirut to Damascus, while promising to let "the refreshing breeze lift [their] hangover."

The image and figure of Lawrence of Arabia, or the "Blond Bedouin," has been described as epitomizing "the enduring myths of military manhood in twentieth century Western culture" (Dawson 1991, 113; see also Connell 2001).[11] However, at the same time, Lawrence of Arabia, who is assumed to have been homosexual by a number of historians, was not represented as always "conventionally masculine" but rather as performing both masculine and nonmasculine traits (Caton 1999, 200). The representation of Lawrence of Arabia in the media juxtaposes the image of the "soldier" (considered to be the most masculine of men) and a man "elaborately arrayed in flowing skirts," which denotes more "transgression of gender fixity" (Dawson 1991, 113).

The image of Lawrence of Arabia explicitly invokes notions of discovery, adventure, conquest, and individualism, with representations of the gay tourist as explorer and discoverer. In the advertised promotional trip, IGLTA promises potential tourists that they will walk "on the steps of Lawrence of Arabia." While there is more gender play in the representation of the image of Lawrence of Arabia in the 1962 Hollywood production, the circulated images of the gay male tourist by the promotional trip and travelogues presume gender and sexual fixity and rely on an out gay man who is both affluent and gender normative. Lawrence of Arabia's performance of both conventional and unconventional masculine traits, in that, despite being a soldier, he was soft spoken and displayed feminine mannerisms at times, illustrates more fluidity in masculine gender performances (Caton 1999). This, however, does not extend to the tourists themselves.

The traveler in most of the travelogues is presented as an out white gay man living in the West, looking for a vacation outside the West, and wanting to capitalize on the sense of adventure, discovery, and bravery involved in travel to a dangerous but thrilling place such as Beirut. Such travelers commodify danger and everyday-life disruptions so that they become thrilling and (sexually) appealing. While the tourist might get to experience some aspects of *al-wad'*, for his experiences to be somewhat authentic, he is also promised luxury. In addition, this traveler is not any gay consumer, since the invocations of Beirut as Paris, San Francisco, Amsterdam, and Provincetown assume that the presumed traveler has a knowledge and appreciation of these places. The traveler must embody the cultural and economic capital that gives him the access to properties and spaces in Beirut (and other parts of the world) that others do not have.

Since the traveler is presumed to be out and gay identified, these travelogues attempt to make Arab and Lebanese (gay) men intelligible by uncovering and explaining the impossibility of these men being appropriately or legitimately gay. Lebanese and Arab men are described as not out or necessarily gay identified in ways that the out traveler might be familiar with. Here, "outness" is used as another fractal distinction between the tourists and locals. That is, Lebanese locals are described as "not out" in relation to the "out" progressive gay traveler. Locals get essentialized such that only a few Lebanese activists, singers, and a travel agency are presented as out, while most men are not.

Closeted Arab Men

Lebanese men are made intelligible by drawing on homo-orientalist contradictions whereby they are represented as sexually available yet repressed, "closeted," and discreet yet overly sexual. By attempting to make homosexuality and gayness in Lebanon intelligible to Western gay audiences, these articles essentialize and homogenize both the gay tourist and gay locals, rendering invisible the complexities of gender, class, religious sect, and sexuality. These accounts are reminiscent of what anthropologist Kath Weston calls ethnocartography, the way that Euro-American anthropologists have historically looked "for evidence of same-sex sexuality and gendered ambiguity in 'other' societies" (1998, 341). In a similar way, these articles employ reductionist definitions of culture, which become a primary tool in explaining and representing the other without incorporating socioeconomic or material realities (Cantú 2002). In addition, ambiguity and contradictions become very central to explaining the lack of a proper development of gay identities. Rather than understand how Lebanese men negotiate their sexualities and how sexuality is co-constituted with gender, class, and religion, such reductionist depictions simplify Lebanese men's experiences and render these men voiceless. Even though most of the texts focus on Lebanese men, they also mention tourists' encounters with other Arab men from the Arab Gulf, Egypt, Jordan, and Iraq, such as Mohammad, the Iraqi gay man, referred to earlier.

Open gay identification becomes explicitly used as a marker of how modern a society is. The articles describe Lebanese men as sexually available yet at the same time closeted and not gay identified. This duality depicts the Lebanese as not quite modern since they are still not gay identified in public, despite their sexual availability in private. Such descriptions circulate the narrative that nonheterosexual Arabs tend to lead a double life, where they are closeted to their families and at their workplaces but open in LGBT circles.[12] The "double-life" narrative relies on using culture as a point of difference that is abstracted from context and political economy of sexualities. It resorts to Orientalist tropes about freedom and sexuality in the Arab and Muslim worlds. Nonheterosexual men are described as maintaining gender-normative and straight-acting fronts so they are not harassed by police officers or publicly ridiculed and possibly shamed. However, whereas the 2009 edition of

Spartacus explicitly mentions discretion by asserting that "gay people tend to be discreet, which minimizes police entrapment or prosecution," the 2011–2012 and 2016 editions do not (2009, 593). The newer editions omit the statement on discretion and instead claim that "legally homosexuality is prosecutable under article 534[;] however, this penal law [has not been] implemented [for] decades[;] however, affectionate behavior in public places is not advised" (*Spartacus* 2016, 482). Tourists are reminded of the presence of the penal code, even though it is not readily applied except to target already-marginalized populations.

Some articles credit Article 534 of the French Penal Code for introducing and familiarizing the Lebanese with homosexuality. In one instance, Michael Luongo explains that the Lebanese, unlike other Arabs who were not colonized or mandated by the French, are more "familiar with homosexuality" (quoted in Healy 2009). Familiarity with homosexuality becomes external to the Arab world, something that the Lebanese owe, as a form of cultural debt, to their French colonizers. Healy cites an interview with Michael Luongo, editor of the book *Gay Travels in the Muslim World*:

> What's interesting is that the Arab areas that were once controlled by the French, like Lebanon, are the ones with laws against homosexuality, because the French felt comfortable talking about sex, Mr. Luongo said, while the areas controlled by the British didn't have those laws because they didn't talk about sex. As a result, flowing from that French history is a relative familiarity with homosexuality in places like Lebanon. You have more gay life where the laws exist against it. (2009)

Luongo describes "familiarity with homosexuality" as a by-product of French rule. He claims that the "French felt comfortable talking about sex," which the Lebanese presumably did not. While this is factually untrue, Luongo uses this notion of openness and comfort of talking about sex as yet another sign of modernity. Luongo ignores the history of same-sex sexualities and homosexualities in the Muslim and Arab worlds and the fact that Europeans regarded the Muslim world as a region with uninhibited sexual experiences, where Europeans imagined they could indulge in sexual experiences unobtainable in Europe (Said 1978; Massad 2002; Waitt and Markwell 2006). Luongo credits France's introduction of a penal code that criminalizes "sexual acts contrary to nature" as giving rise to "more gay life" in Lebanon (quoted in Healy 2009).

Even though in the preface to *Gay Travels in the Muslim World* (which was mistranslated in Arabic to *Travels of a Deviant*) Luongo (2007) argues that a Western identity model cannot simply be applied to the Muslim world, other gay travelogues do not follow suit. Yet Luongo still relies on an essentialist understanding of culture, sexuality, and place. He argues:

> Within many of these cultures, to do is not to be, though clearly there are men who would be gay in every sense of the Western world. Homosexuality is something natural, something men do and enjoy with each other, yet it is not the basis of an identity as it is in the West. (2007, xxiv)

Luongo distinguishes between sexual behavior and identities in the Arab world. He claims that while same-sex sexual activity is "natural" in the Arab world, it is not a basis for a gay identity, as it is in the West. Luongo's assertion depends on an essentialist and fixed understanding of sexuality both in the West and the Muslim world. In addition, it assumes a white middle-class gay subject as embodying "proper gayness" and does not take into account the intersections of race, gender, and class in people's embodiments of sexuality.

Many accounts centralize the trope of the closet in the Arab world by reproducing the notion that most Lebanese men are closeted and lead a double life. These articles present a number of Beirut venues as gay friendly (but never gay), yet they still differentiate such venues from Euro-American ones by both their novelty and potential dangers and risks. Given that Beirut does not have a "gayborhood," the tourist is invited to visit and experience the number of gay-friendly spots, sites, and cruising areas (Healy 2009). Yet he is advised to be cautious and discreet in his sexual presentation and behaviors:

> While homosexual activity (technically, sexual relations that officials deem "unnatural") is illegal in Lebanon, as in most of the Arab world, Beirut's vitality as a Mediterranean capital of night life has fueled a flourishing gay scene—albeit one where men can be nervous about public displays of affection and where security guards at clubs can intercede if the good times turn too frisky on the dance floor. (Healy 2009)

Healy romanticizes Beirut's flourishing gay nightlife for tourists as exceptional in the Arab world, though not quite as it is in the West. By drawing on only one unnamed example of the now-closed nightclub Acid, he underscores the necessity for discretion to demarcate this difference with Western sexual culture.

In describing gay venues and clubs in Beirut, Teulings claims that these spaces are almost similar to those in Europe, with the caveat that Arab men are still mostly closeted:

> At the city's two main gay clubs, Milk and Acid, a mix of Lebanese, Syrian, Jordanian, Kuwaiti and even some Iraqi men disprove[s] any remaining theory of cultural relativism. That is to say, once inside people don't behave differently from any other gay club in the world—with the possible exception of the occasional male belly dance. But this being the Middle East, most of the men are closeted. (2010, 103)

While Teulings attempts to move away from using cultural distinctions to account for differences between men's behaviors in gay clubs in the Arab world and those in the West, he still uses culture as a central trope to reinforce difference—hence noting that although men in Lebanon belly-dance, they and are almost all closeted.

In the 2005 article "Beirut: Hotbed of Vice of the Middle East," Jimmy67 goes as far as to provide an explanation of why Lebanese men are closeted. He attributes their "not being out" to the fact that many have "internalized homophobia," where they try hard to be "straight acting and discriminatory." Despite not explaining this in more detail, the author reminds the tourist that he needs to inform gay Lebanese men that coming out and being gay in his home country (Germany, in this case) are not as easy as they might think. Hence, the tourist is invited to be empathetic and to educate Lebanese men about gay life in Europe.

Lee Smith also claims that even though people might seem to be traditional, this does not necessarily translate into their actions:

> Both Lebanon's Muslims and Christians are still ostensibly very traditional in their sexual mores, but there's more than an undercurrent of roiling passions. Sure, there are plenty of 30-year-old virgins, but Beirut is where the Arab world goes to let its hair down, party hard, and to be frank, have really good sex. (2006, 1)

In such statements, the travelogues seem to counter people's perceptions of the traditional mores of the Middle East by employing the homo-orientalist discourses of "hidden roiling passions" and using the dualist and "paradoxical view that the Orient is both the space of illicit and dangerous sex and the site of carefully suppressed animalistic sexual instincts" (Puar 2004, 526). In such depictions, Beirut becomes the playground where the Arab world lets it hair down and parties hard.

The lack of proper sexual identification among Lebanese men, in many of these accounts, signifies that Lebanese men are *more* sexually available and experimental. For example, a number of articles explicitly assert that men, whether in clubs or in public, are readily available for sex (Jimmy67 2005; Teulings 2010). Therefore, Lebanese and Arab men are presented as willing to engage in same-sex sexual acts, even though they do not adopt a gay identity. Jimmy67 (2005) writes that "having sex in Beirut, despite the fact that it is illegal, is very very easy." Teulings makes this point more explicit in the article "Bounce Back Beirut," in which he quotes Bertho Makso, the Lebanese owner of Lebtour, who claims that men from Western Europe and North America take his tours primarily to have sex with Arab men. "Come on," he said, "What do you think? They're not here for the food or the architecture; they're here to have sex with Arab men. You can just call out at them from your balcony and they will come" (2010). Suspicious of this Orientalist depiction of Lebanese and Arab men, Teulings was later surprised that his suspicions were unfounded when he experienced that for himself. He claims:

> But a few days later my cynicism was challenged when I was left rosy cheeked and dizzy with hormones after a wildly attractive construction worker—a real one, not the faux type that is actually a florist—chatted me up at Beirut's ocean front promenade and whispered a very indecent proposal in my ear. After him came another one. And another one. So maybe Mr Makso had a point. For one thing, there is certainly no shortage of lonely construction workers in Beirut. Still, I was loath to accept such a one-dimensional image of gay life in Lebanon. (2010)

Whether true or not, this account plays on the imagination and fantasy of travelers having local men available for them, in abundance, without having to actively seek them. This serves to illustrate the ease by which the presumed gay traveler can have access to a plethora of sex with locals. Painting such an image of being enchanted and aroused by the exotic Arab serves to highlight the fantasies of premodern licentious sexualities, in addition to Orientalist notions of sexual abundance and illicit sexual activities.

Teulings's invocation of the images of the authentic construction worker, read as working class, and real masculinity contradicts the image previously presented by Jimmy67, in which men in clubs are described as trying to act masculine. Even though class is invoked in these representations, class differences are never really accounted for. A closer analysis, however, shows that these articles promise the tourist interaction with men from diverse classes, where party and nightclub goers are assumed to be from the middle to upper classes and a "real" construction worker is assumed to be presenting a working-class Arab masculinity.

Travelogues and gay guides racialize Lebanese men by presenting them as ethnically mixed and hybrid, though more similar to Europeans than other Arabs. Thus, they are racialized as "almost the same, but not white" (Bhabha 1994, 128). The Lebanese become both familiar (European) and different (Middle Eastern), making them potentially more desirable. For example, *Spartacus* asserts that "because of the historical ethnic mix between European, Mediterranean, Middle Eastern groups and the whole spectrum in between, Lebanese men offer an appealing variety" (2016, 482). Race is used to commodify Lebanese men as offering an "appealing variety," suggesting that there is something desirable for everyone. Race in these accounts is not distinguished from ethnicity or culture; rather, it is used as an attraction device and as something to be *consumed*. In a similar fashion to how these travelogues market Beirut, Lebanese men—particularly Christians—are marked as familiar (safe) yet, at the same time, different (exciting and new).

Commodifying and consuming Arabs is an explicit trope in these articles. Even though the image of the bear is heavily used in the Lebtour and ILGTA advertisements of the gay Beirut tours as a marketing tool to attract tourists, Lebanese men are feminized in a majority of these travelogues. The invocation of the bear is used mostly in reference to the annual Gay Bear Arabia event rather than a totalizing description of Lebanese men or as a description of a specific bear subculture. Instead, these articles present a more diverse image, even though they focus excessively on facial and bodily hair in an attempt to racialize and physically describe Lebanese men. The article by Jimmy67 (2005) informs the potential traveler that if "[you are into] hairy and bearded men, then you [have] found your paradise, though other types are also there. . . . We crusaders left our traces also in Lebanon." This racialized statement of conquest is reminiscent of previous gay French tourists traveling to Morocco seeking "sexual self-discovery" by contact with others—in this case, previous colonial subjects (Cervulle and Rees-Roberts 2008, 198). Jimmy67 (2005) asserts that Lebanese men are "very hairy in general" and that their "well trimmed beards . . . complete the picture of the macho man" they are "at least trying to be." Lebanese men, according to

Jimmy67, become ultimately and always feminized despite their *attempts* for a masculine self-presentation.

As in other travelogues and tourism guides, the Lebanese people, like other "natives" in the articles, are described as "very hospitable and friendly," particularly to Euro-American gay men. "Any tourist in Lebanon, especially the Western ones, will experience an incredible level of hospitality and help. The Lebanese will do everything possible that you enjoy your stay there, does not matter what kind of activity you are up to" (Jimmy67 2005). Hospitality is an old Arab tradition that Lebanese people still follow, to the extent that it is described as "a national duty" for the Lebanese that the tourists enjoy their time.

The (Gay) City That Refuses to Disappear

This chapter examines how contemporary representations of gay Beirut as exceptional in the Arab Middle East are premised on what I call fractal Orientalism. Unlike Orientalism, fractal Orientalism better captures the complex ways that these distinctions circulate among people in the Middle East and by Middle Easterners in the diaspora who articulate it to distinguish between good and bad Muslims and Arabs and good and bad parts of the Middle East. By promoting Beirut as a gay tourist destination in the Middle East, these representations produce homogenized images of locals and tourists and reproduce gender binaries by essentializing gay masculinities while simultaneously erasing female homosexualities and transgender people's experience. They employ liminality and contradiction to attract potential tourists by presenting Beirut as safe yet dangerous, glamorous but war-torn. In addition, they represent Lebanese and Arab men as sexually available but closeted and discreet (in public) but sexually adventurous in private.

These discourses do not circulate only in Euro-American journalistic accounts and are not only textual. Rather, they are also taken up and used by local actors, including LGBT individuals, establishments, and social movement organizations. In addition, they have material effects on people's everyday lives. Commodifying Lebanese people and places and Hariri's governments' neoliberal economic polices make it possible to market gay-friendly Beirut and thus structurally shape discourses of exceptionalism and exclusionary practices. For instance, the marketing of gay-friendly spaces, such as coffee shops and bars in international venues, causes these places to become more expensive and therefore less accessible to lower-income locals. Often, local business owners benefit from the "pink dollar" and hence raise the prices of food and services. Naming cruising areas risks more policing and takes away public spaces from those who are less well-off and depend on these spaces rather than expensive bars and clubs.

Neoliberal narratives of Beirut's exceptionalism get in the way of recognizing the exclusionary and violent practices enacted by the Lebanese state and people, particularly against women, transgender individuals, refugees, and migrants. Chapter 2 highlights these exclusionary practices by examining how fractal Orientalist discourses are circulated and articulated by LGBT people in Beirut. It draws on my ethnographic fieldwork and interviews to focus on the various ways that discourses of exceptionalism are employed while exposing the inequalities and exclusions that these discourses mask.

2

"Because Lebanon Is Not Kandahar"

Beirut as Queer Exception

In mid-February 2014, topless calendar pictures of Lebanese skier Jackie Chamoun were leaked on Lebanese media soon after she had competed in the Winter Olympics in Sochi, Russia. Chamoun's photographs were taken three years earlier at a photoshoot for a German sports calendar. The Lebanese minister of youth and sports responded to these pictures by publicly proclaiming that Chamoun needed to be interrogated for what he described as an immoral and questionable act. This condemnation sparked an uproar among Lebanese youth, who saw this as an attack on personal freedoms and freedom of expression.

As a display of protest and solidarity with the Lebanese skier, they created the online social media campaign #stripforjackie, which consisted of Lebanese young people posting seminaked pictures of themselves, with their genitals hidden, on various social-media platforms. Individuals held signs describing their shock that this type of censorship would happen in Lebanon, which they regarded as distinct in the Middle East. In one image, a topless Lebanese woman tweeted her picture with a #stripforjackie sign, followed by this message: "Because Lebanon is not Kandahar and it will never be!" The woman asserted that Lebanon is a place of sexual freedoms, distancing it from Kandahar, the second-largest city in Afghanistan, where people presumably do not enjoy these freedoms.

While Afghanistan is typically included in the South or Central Asian region, its decontextualized usage by that image invokes fractal Orientalism, or the use of multiscalar patterns of distinction in the Middle East to mark some places as modern and others as not. In this case, the sign contrasts a country (Lebanon) in the Middle East and a city (Kandahar) in Central Asia—often mistaken to be in the Middle East—to showcase Lebanon as the more, if not most, progressive in the region. The sign presumably conflates Islam with the Middle East to make a point that Lebanon is distinct. The scale of comparison also plays on people's imaginations of what Kandahar is. Kandahar becomes imagined as a place that is near yet distant. Other individuals expressed their outrage by distinguishing Lebanon from Syria, Saudi Arabia, Iran, and Iraq, reaffirming that Lebanon is an exception.

This campaign also distinguishes the Lebanese people from their counterparts in the Middle East. The Lebanese are portrayed as liberal, tolerant, and exceptional in the region, suggesting that this type of censorship is "un-Lebanese." Chamoun, however, apologized for these images: "I want to apologize to all of you, I know that Lebanon is a conservative country, and this is not the image that reflects our culture" (Marquardt 2014). Whereas the solidarity campaign attempted to project Lebanon as unapologetically liberal and progressive, Chamoun's apology reinstated Lebanon as inherently conservative and presumably *not yet able* to accept such photographs.

The #stripforjackie campaign suggests that tolerance and a celebration of gender, sexual diversity, and visibility signify the cultural advancement of Lebanese society. Hence, Lebanon is imagined as more modern than the rest of the Middle East. This celebration of seminaked bodies is also linked to the incitement of discourses about gayness, coming out, and making oneself visibly queer that operate within global imaginaries and ideas of modernity.[1] However, these discourses are very contextual and historical. For example, in the mid-twentieth century, a shift occurred in how sex was used to determine who is and is not considered modern. Before the shift, Muslims were described as oversexualized in comparison to Europeans; since the shift, however, they are described as sexually repressive (Massad 2007).

A year following the #stripforjackie campaign, in May 2015, the Lebanese LGBT organization Proud Lebanon (founded in August 2014) released an advertisement for the International Day against Homophobia and Transphobia events in Lebanon. The short advertisement, first released on YouTube, featured a number of Lebanese comedians and TV personalities calling for an end to discrimination against homosexuality and for the abolishment of Article 534 of the Lebanese Penal Code. In this video, Lebanese celebrities and personalities invoke the Universal Declaration of Human Rights and call on Lebanese people to support the rights of all, including the rights of women, refugees, and gays and lesbians. They assert that individuals can support a cause (and be allies) even if they are not part of the group they are fighting for. For example, a male comedian says that someone does not have to be a woman to support women's rights, and another Lebanese artist claims that someone does not have to be a refugee to support refugee rights. The advertisement ends with a Lebanese actress stating that someone does not have to be gay to support gay rights, followed by all the other individuals repeating: "It is only enough for you to be a human being. Even if we are different, we shouldn't disagree."

LGBT activists and nonactivists alike shared, applauded, and/or critiqued this video on social media, particularly Facebook and Twitter. Activists I had spoken with and interviewed had many concerns about this new Proud Lebanon organization, particularly since it is headed by Bertho Makso, founder and owner of the Lebanese gay tourism agency Lebtour. Primarily because of Makso's involvement, the video did not get a lot of support from members of the queer activist networks I interviewed.[2] The advertisement used gender-normative, presumably straight men and women and relied on a politics of assimilation, stressing the fact that gays and lesbians (there was no mention of trans persons) are just like everybody else, except that they love someone of the same sex. Though many activists I interviewed were wary of this new initiative, it still gained popularity among other LGBT activist circles and nonactivists. In addition, it was popular on a number of Lebanese blogger websites and was mistakenly reported as "the first gay and lesbian campaign in the country." In one instance a Lebanese man posted the link on his Facebook account with the title "First step towards civilization #humanrights."

Explicit framings of linear civilizational and homonationalist narratives, such as the one just presented, reproduce Orientalist narratives of progress and ignore histories, inequalities, and exclusions that such a gay rights campaign propagates, particularly with regard to working-class, gender-nonnormative, and transgender individuals. Similar to the #stripforjackie campaign, this Proud Lebanon campaign in Lebanon relied heavily on discourses that depicted Lebanon as exceptional in the Arab Middle East yet lagging behind its Euro-American counterparts.

This chapter examines how these transnational discourses of modernity and exceptionalism get circulated and articulated by LGBT individuals in Beirut. While Chapter 1 examines how these discourses operate on the global, regional, and state levels, this chapter focuses on the ways that such discourses circulate at the everyday level. It pays close attention to the gap between discourses of Beiruti openness and the realities of exclusion experienced by LGBT persons. Focusing on unequal access to space, I ask: For whom is Beirut cosmopolitan and gay friendly? Many of my interlocutors contest claims that Beirut is exceptional and cosmopolitan by citing gendered and classed exclusions, particularly with regard to unequal access to public and gay-friendly spaces and NGOs. Thus, many collapse and disrupt fractal distinctions that make claims such as "Beirut as the Provincetown of the Middle East" possible. Beirut becomes gay friendly and exceptional only in relation to other cities in the Arab World and only to certain people, those with gendered and classed privileges.

Discourses of sexual openness and gay friendliness in Beirut (seen as markers of cosmopolitanism) are laden with a value structure informed by gender, class, and religion. Building on the notion that cities are sites of possibility and constraint (Hubbard 2012; Oswin 2015), I argue that "cosmopolitan Beirut" is accessible as a gay-friendly space to gender-normative, secular, and middle- to upper-class LGBTQ people. For example, English- and French-language skills are required to participate in certain LGBT social settings.

Exceptional Beirut

Scholarship examining discourses of cosmopolitanism in the Global South tends to depict the Global South as aspirational, using Euro-American cities as reference points and envisioning cosmopolitanism as a particularly urban Western phenomenon (Meijer 1999; Schwedler 2010). For example, scholars have framed cosmopolitanism in the Arab world and the Middle East in terms of progress narratives (Meijer 1999), as antinationalist projects (Seidman 2012), or as high-end and Western consumption patterns (Schwedler 2010). Historian Roel Meijer (1999) claims that cosmopolitanism and authenticity are at odds in the Arab world, arguing that Middle Eastern societies opt for "authenticity" rather than what he refers to as moving "forward" toward a European model of cosmopolitanism. Urban comparative methods, such as those used by Meijer, attempt to measure cosmopolitan progress using linear progress narratives that employ Eurocentric understandings of cosmopolitanism (Binnie 2014). It also homogenizes and neglects colonial histories of the Middle East. In addition to reflecting Eurocentric linear progress narratives, imagining that cosmopolitan discourses are only aspirational obscures the many ways that these discourses are employed. For example, while some discourses of exceptionalism are instrumental or influential, such as those intended to attract tourists, others are affective. That is, similar to the bubble discussed in Chapter 5, they create and reflect certain moods and sensibilities, making some people feel hope and others feel despair in times of constant disruption and violence. For some, these discourses have the affective potential of creating a sense of exuberance amid everyday-life violent disruptions.

Since the mid- to late 1990s, discourses on Lebanon's modern status point to several emerging social structures as signs of the country's progressiveness and cosmopolitanism, including the privatization of the media, sex tourism, gay tourism, and certain measures of bodily autonomy for women. In addition, these discourses mark Beirut as distinct and more Western than other Arab cities. Cultural geographer Ghada Masri's analysis of interviews with Beirutis reveals that this narrative often places Beirut's cosmopolitanism in opposition to traditional Muslim Arab values:

> The presence of Khaleeji tourists [from the Arab Gulf] during the summer months offends the sensibilities of many self-defined "cosmopolitans" residing in the city. Khaleeji men walking with their two or three wives and their children in tow through downtown Beirut fills many Lebanese with concern and threatens the perception of Beirut as a modern, cosmopolitan, city with a characteristic "Lebanese culture" and identity. (2010, 236)

This example illustrates how the Lebanese use fractal Orientalist distinctions, which are primarily based on sex and sexuality, to distinguish themselves from Khaleeji tourists. Thus, the Lebanese are able to imagine themselves as culturally different from and superior to what they perceive as a unitary and backward Muslim understanding of sex and marriage. Again, sexuality becomes the primary tool invoked in making fractal distinctions between the Lebanese and other Arabs.

LGBT Beirutis create their own definitions of cosmopolitanism in two ways, which also invoke fractal Orientalism on the regional and local levels. First, they create relational understandings of modernity and cosmopolitanism by situating Beirut in relation to other Arab cities rather than just in relation to Euro-American cities. Whereas discussions of cosmopolitanism tend to assume Western urban centers as reference points for understanding the category, my interlocutors have different reference points. Second, my interlocutors focus on gendered and classed exclusions that they and other people face, particularly regarding unequal access to public and gay-friendly spaces and LGBT organizations, which contrast with the narratives of Beiruti cosmopolitanism and exceptionalism discussed earlier. However, some disagree with the claim that Beirut is cosmopolitan and exceptional by pointing to its multiple exclusions. Middle- to upper-class women and men are more likely to highlight Beirut's cosmopolitanism, since their more normative gender and class positions allow them to experience Beirut as exceptional through shopping and access to high-end downtown spaces or wealthier neighborhoods that are not accessible to those who are nonnormative or less privileged.

Some interlocutors, for instance, reproduce fractal Orientalism, proving Beirut's exceptionalism by contrasting its religious diversity to more homogeneous Arab cities. For example, Samira, a twenty-one-year-old woman, states that Beirut is exceptional because of the diverse sectarian makeup of the city and its multiple feminist and queer initiatives. Samira identifies as lesbian and was born and raised in the Arab Gulf but moved to Lebanon to study at a private American university. Contrasting her experiences of Beirut with her experiences of the Arab Gulf, she believes that Beirut is exceptional in the Arab world:

> First, we are known as the most liberal. Technically, politically, we are the only Christian country in the Middle East. Second, we have so many different religions; not one dominates. We have different backgrounds. In Beirut, we all come together. In the city, your identity is lost among the masses. It's beautiful to see eighteen to nineteen different sects mash up in one city. At the end, everyone wants to live. After the civil war, people just want to live. Yeah, you still have the Shia area, Sunni, Druze, Maronite. Yes, this is Beirut; drop that shit outside, leave your religions in the villages, and come to Beirut and work.[3]

For Samira, Lebanon's being the "only Christian country in the Middle East" functions as the exception that proves the rule: the Christian country whose presence demonstrates the nonmodern, nonsecular nature of the rest of the Muslim Middle East. For her, leaving one's religious sect behind makes Beirut more diverse and cosmopolitan. Samira considers people to be "more open" to difference (and therefore more modern and cosmopolitan) in Beirut than in Lebanese villages. Invoking what Jack Halberstam calls "metronormativity" (2005, 36), or the assumed progressiveness of cities and urban spaces in relation to rural areas, Samira uses the same fractal distinctions between Beirut and other Arab cities to account for how Beirut is more modern than villages in Lebanon:

> In terms of gender and sexuality, people have expressed it in so many different ways and different spaces. It's fascinating, for example, how Helem and Meem started up as underground collectives that slowly

branched out to society. In terms of organizing, they organized and reached out. This *is* history. This is not like Jordan or the Gulf, where they prosecute you; here they didn't prosecute us. They didn't go out to look for gay people. I don't know if it's the nature of the government to just be careless, but we have freedom [here].

Contrasting Beirut to Jordan and the Arab Gulf nations, Samira finds Beirut to be exceptional. She contrasts the "history" in Beirut and Lebanon to the "timelessness" in other places. Using other Arab countries as reference points, Samira produces hierarchies of good and bad countries in the Arab world. In another instance of fractal Orientalism, Samira locates history in Beirut and Lebanon rather than in its Arab counterparts. Samira also suggests that even the Lebanese diaspora in the Arab Gulf is "less open-minded" and subscribes to more traditional values than do Lebanese people in Beirut. That is, the Lebanese living in the Gulf have become more traditional by virtue of the places where they live. For Samira, Beirut's exceptionalism helps her navigate *al-wad'* and feel a sense of hope and possibility. Her claim that "at the end, everyone wants to live. After the civil war, people just want to live" shows the affective dimension of these discourses. Even though Samira presents other places in the Arab world as ahistorical, she uses Lebanese history to contextualize her experiences of everyday disruptions. Though these discourses of cosmopolitanism are contradictory, they are productive in producing distinctions and meaning. Samira invokes histories of colonialism to account for Lebanese exceptionalism:

Now you can't deny the amount of people who came and took us over. We came out of the French Mandate; before that we had the Ottomans. We have a lot of societies that passed through us. It is fascinating, and the fact that we are the center of the trade, it's a huge part of our identity; we were never left alone to create our own identity. If our location wasn't that strategically important, we would have been like the Gulf, very conservative, very tribal; we are tribal but less so.

Here, Samira argues that because of Lebanon's history of occupation and colonialism, the Lebanese were never able to create a single unified identity. While she does not glorify colonialism, she does state that the strategic location of Lebanon and the influence of many cultures have made the country less conservative. Again, Lebanon becomes less conservative only in relation to other Arab countries. Samira uses fractal Orientalism, stating that while Lebanon is still tribal, it is not as tribal or conservative as the Arab Gulf. Scale is very important in how Samira contrasts Lebanon with other countries in the Arab world. She continues, "Beirut is very diverse because it's a major seaport on the Mediterranean [*pauses*] so I think that's why a part of us is so susceptible to change and to adopting different cultures and being open to new cultures. We have always had that in us." While Samira originally says that the Lebanese have no unified identity, she asserts that Lebanese people, especially Beirutis, tend to be open to change and other cultures. Samira invokes Beirut's location as a seaport on the Mediterranean as one explanation for Beirutis' developing a sense of openness to others.

Many male interlocutors' articulations of discourse on cosmopolitanism and exceptionalism also highlight the messiness and contradictions of these discourses. Like Samira, many contrast the exceptional gay life in Beirut to that in other places in the Arab world, mainly Saudi Arabia, Jordan, and the United Arab Emirates. Nonetheless, they still point to the difficulty of being openly gay and the gay community's exclusion of gender-nonnormative men. One example is Tarek, a twenty-seven-year-old, gay-identified man who is a Muslim medical doctor. Tarek lived in Beirut all his life until moving to Canada to pursue his postgraduate studies. In Beirut, he attended private schools and universities. Even after his move, he still spent significant time in Beirut visiting family and friends. Tarek claims that Lebanon is much better than other Arab countries:

> I am always comparing [Lebanon] to worse places: Saudi Arabia, Qatar, Dubai. As far as I know, there is no activism there. [*Pauses.*] I know friends in Qatar; they tell me that gay life is more underground over there, more so than [in] Beirut. Most gay men are married with kids and then resume their lives. . . . Lebanon has become an outlet for other countries in the Middle East to go out, have fun, let go of the repression. This applies to straight people as well.

When I ask him whether it is the case in all of Lebanon, he says,

> I am talking specifically about Beirut, not Lebanon. Lebanon in general you can see other women who are not veiled. Yes. To be specific, it is Beirut. Not Tripoli or Baalbeck. These are more religious cities, especially Tripoli; people have different levels of education. Education makes people more open.

Here, Tarek specifies Beirut as the most progressive city in Lebanon. He uses fractal distinction, marking Beirut as more open and progressive than other cities in Lebanon, where people are more religious (though he does not name religiosity, he is referring to Muslims because of the composition of Tripoli, a predominantly Sunni working-class city) and less educated. Tarek invokes the veil to explain that while other cities in Lebanon are not as open as Beirut, you can still see women without veils—making the veil stand in for conservatism.

Tarek's description echoes dominant discourses of Beiruti exceptionalism, particularly those that circulate in gay travelogues. Tarek considers Beirut to be exceptional in the Middle East yet lagging behind its Euro-American counterparts. He claims that Beirut is somewhat but not completely open. He insists that people in Beirut are "not as open-minded" as those in Canada, explaining that people in Beirut do not accept gay men and lesbians. He feels that there is no anonymity in Beirut and that everyone knows everyone else, so he prefers Canada because "he can do whatever he wants." To explain Beirut's openness and cosmopolitanism, Tarek distances it from both its Canadian and Arab counterparts. Both Tarek and Samira use fractal Orientalist distinctions between people, as well as places.

Most gay men find Beirut constraining and draw on their male privilege and gender conformity to navigate the city. However, like Tarek, many claim that Beirut is exceptional in the Arab world and consider it open, yet only to a certain extent. Male interlocutors, who were mostly middle to upper class, more often than other interlocutors express concern over the impact of legal restrictions on their lives.

Unlike findings from other research that suggest that Beirutis unreflectively reproduce narratives of Lebanese and Beiruti exceptionalism (Masri 2010; Seidman 2012), many interlocutors do not simply reproduce the claim that Beirut is cosmopolitan. Instead, many contest this claim by citing multiple exclusions targeting them and people they know. Souraya, a twenty-three-year-old queer-identified Muslim Lebanese woman who attended the public university, states that Lebanese gay life is "distinct" rather than necessarily better than that in other countries in the Arab world:

> I don't see things in Beirut as *better* than others. I find the conditions of Beirut to be different from the conditions in Jeddah or Riyadh. I don't necessarily see Beirut as open; in Riyadh there is nightlife, and it is all underground. There is no place that is completely cut off from anything, and then another place is more open or better. No, people always find their own ways to live, which are based on the conditions that are present in the city. Of course, inside Beirut, there are many differences; this does not mean that there is one area better than the

other. It means that the conditions in it are different, and people know how to negotiate them accordingly. I know how to negotiate the southern suburb more than I can Hamra. That doesn't mean that I feel safer [there]. Maybe I feel more comfortable, but safety is something else. Do you know what I mean?

Souraya does not think of Beirut as an "exceptional gay haven"; instead, she focuses on the different conditions that make gay life possible. Souraya decenters Western narratives of exceptionalism by indirectly suggesting that they are not useful. For example, instead of thinking of places in terms of being cosmopolitan and exceptional, she describes strategies that people use in navigating different social conditions, including those of *al-wad'*. In addition, Souraya asserts that safety and comfort have different meanings in negotiating the city. While she might feel safer in the southern suburbs, it does not mean that she feels comfortable.

Souraya questions the exceptionalism of Beirut by citing multiple exclusions that exist. She is attentive to how social and political economies produce developmental and linear narratives of progress in Lebanon, particularly concerning gender and sexuality. She is critical of those who do not consider the role of government policy in shaping these discourses that employ and reproduce fractal Orientalism. Souraya argues that narratives of Beirut's exceptionalism and cosmopolitanism are quite dominant because the Lebanese state and people use them to construct Lebanon as distinct in the Arab world:

All things have been worked on: in the government, politics and economics that Lebanon is exceptional. [*Pauses.*] Sexually, it is a sexual haven. The Arabs come here. [*Pauses.*] We have things that other Arab countries don't have, and our women are different. They wear swimsuits; other women in the Arab world don't. We have gay people that other places don't tolerate. But for me, this is all very superficial, of course, and we, the people who live here, know that it is very superficial.

By saying "all things have been worked on," Souraya suggests that the Lebanese state instrumentally works on its image as an open and exceptional place to promote and distinguish Lebanon in the region. She points to the state's active role in the commodification of difference and diversity, especially in its postwar narrative of Muslim-Christian coexistence, a commodification intended to attract tourism and foreign investments. Such a depiction shifts the focus away from *al-wad'* and post–civil war tensions, painting Lebanon as exceptional and diverse, unlike its Arab counterparts. In addition, this narrative suggests that the presence of Christians marks Lebanon as exceptional in relation to the rest of the Arab world. Even though Souraya claims that "the people who live here know that it is very superficial," Tarek's and Samira's cases illustrate that this is not always true. Souraya suggests that Lebanon's cosmopolitan image—created for self-promotion—masks everyday-life disruptions and many exclusions, particularly unequal access to public gay-friendly and LGBT organizing spaces.

Whose Gay Beirut? Policing Gender and Class

Racialized gender and class determine who gets to experience Beirut as cosmopolitan and gay friendly. The gay-friendly spaces of Beirut require certain performances of classed, normative femininities and masculinities, in addition to economic, social, and cultural capital (Bourdieu 1986; Skeggs 1997). Some interlocutors suggest that gay and lesbian normativity is highly racialized in Beirut. Souraya, for example, asserts that class, gender, and racial codes govern Beirut and that the people who are welcomed are those who can afford to live there:

> Beirut is welcoming to those who can pay, the people like me who can pay 850 U.S. dollars to live in Hamra. Beirut is very classist, very, very classist. We might not feel it as Lebanese, but I am sure people who are not Lebanese feel it a lot, much more than we do. Beirut's diversity is ruled by many codes, from nationality to skin color to societal status to class to the way that one looks. If she's a woman like me with short hair, she's not very welcome, and then they don't accept diversity/difference that much.

Souraya argues that non-Western (particularly nonwhite) foreigners are excluded much more than the Lebanese, pointing to the experiences of migrant workers from Southeast Asia and North and East Africa. However, she states that, as a Lebanese woman, she also feels unwelcome in certain areas because of her nonnormative gender presentation, particularly her short hair. Class privilege is central in shaping her access to and experiences of the city, which also makes her nonnormative haircut acceptable in certain spaces. Since class shapes gender performances, Souraya's gendered and classed position enables her to move safely between these areas of the city.

Sirine, a twenty-eight-year-old Lebanese Armenian genderqueer individual, argues that even though certain areas of Beirut seem "more open," they are not necessarily so. One needs economic and social capital (gained mainly through queer networks) to access private semi-LGBT-friendly places. Sirine compares her experiences of Beirut to those when she lived in France while pursuing her master's degree. She claims that if one can afford access in Beirut, one is welcome despite one's gender presentation and performances in private establishments. This, she feels, is not particular to the Lebanese case. Randa, a genderqueer Lebanese NGO manager in her early thirties, says that places become more expensive when they become labeled as "gay friendly," especially for tourists, and many Beirutis cannot afford the prices of gay-friendly places in Beirut:

> If you are poor, you are excluded; you can't pay in certain places. If you are from a prominent family, you can't go to these places. You will do things outside Lebanon. Also, women who can't go out at night, they are excluded. [*Pauses.*] If you can't go out, you are out of the loop because you can't join these outings.

Randa asserts that class limits people's access to gay spaces. Interestingly, she includes people from prominent backgrounds who have the means but come from well-known families so might prefer to go to gay spaces outside Lebanon for fear of being outed and compromising their family position. In addition, people's mobility also impacts who can access spaces. Individuals who live outside Beirut or in its suburbs and those who have family curfews are also excluded from gay spaces. These spaces, as many interlocutors recount, require not only economic capital but also normative gendered presentations and performances that embody cultural or social capital.

Sirine brings up her experiences in France to challenge the idea that LGBT individuals from Lebanon feel safer in Western contexts. She asserts that people never respond just to her gender presentation or sexuality but, instead, to a number of other positions she occupies, such as being a foreigner. Sirine says that she feels safer in Beirut than in France, precisely because she is not a foreigner. In France, she was not harassed only because of her gender nonnormativity but also because of her status as a noncitizen. Sirine experienced her first openly homophobic attack in France:

> Because of cable television and all that crap, I was like, of course, the West is much better to live in, you know. . . . It was not the first time I was hyperaware of my sexuality and gender nonnormativity on the streets; however, the first time I was harassed on the street by a homophobe was in France. So I thought that was very interest-

ing. . . . You go there, and you get spit at and shoved, and I am like, okay, interesting.

Sirine is often aware of her gender nonnormativity in both Lebanon and France, but she is surprised that her first blatant homophobic incident took place in Lyon, not Beirut, because people locate gay friendliness in the West. She continues to recount her assault:

> I was walking down to the Metro station, and there was this guy who was standing above a rail, like a balcony thing, and he ran after me, shoved me, and said, "You fucking lesbian," or something like that. And I was speaking in Arabic prior to that [*pauses*] so it is also because I dared talk in Arabic and all of that, you know? That was pretty much it. And I found it interesting all these notions you have about the West and that my first homophobic incident happened in the West.

In describing her story of being attacked by a presumably white French man, Sirine asserts that it happened because of her gender nonnormativity and presumed sexuality but also because she was speaking in Arabic. To understand her experience, she argues that all these subject positions that she occupied made her more vulnerable to being a target of harassment. Sirine does not glorify Beirut or France; rather, she points to the different ways that race, gender, and sexuality work:

> I was never scared for people to harass or attack me [in Beirut], and when they did it, it was—because it is my space, this is my city, I could retaliate. However, in other places you can't retaliate, not because of your gender identity but because you are a third-class citizen and because they have all these issues with racism and immigration. At a surface level, it starts off as if they are harassing you because they don't understand whether you are a man or a woman or the fact that it is a threat for them. But, in Beirut, this is my street. [*Pauses.*] If you harass me, I will curse you, and I will make a big scene.

Sirine felt less safe defending herself in France than in Beirut. She critiques both Orientalist discourses about the nonmodern status of Arab societies and fractal Orientalist discourses of Lebanese exceptionalism. For her, the narrative of modernity in both Lebanon and France is based on the tolerance of only particular groups.

Like Sirine, several interlocutors suggest that access to gay friendliness in Arab or Western cities depends on privilege. Thus, they refuse fractal Orientalist divides between Beirut and other cities in Europe and the United States, and between the city and village, suggesting that experiencing gay friendliness in cities depended on certain kinds of privileges that need to be acknowledged. For example, one must embody acceptable racial and ethnic makeup (as in the case of Sirine in France), gender, and class positions and be part of LGBT networks. Mays, a feminist and queer activist in her late twenties in Beirut, refuses the binary of thinking about Lebanon as modern in opposition to the traditional Arab world. Mays claims, "Clearly, this is an issue: to understand and define Beirut as progressive in comparison to Arab countries. Usually, Lebanon has all these oppressions: for example, the Dekwaneh incident. It is not true that it is better. We are just as bad." Like Souraya, Mays refutes the idea that Beirut is better than other cities in the Arab world by bringing up the multiple exclusions and oppressions that exist within the city. Significantly, she references the 2013 police raid and closing of the gay club Ghost in the predominantly Christian Dekwaneh neighborhood in East Beirut. During the raid, police detained, humiliated, and verbally and physically abused several gay and trans individuals (Marwan 2013).[4] Narratives of Beirut's gay exceptionalism rarely mention such incidents or, if they do, treat them as anomalies. However, these incidents illustrate how police maintain Beirut's cosmopolitanism by policing subjects who are treated as outsiders to cosmopolitanism. Police regularly harass and assault queer individuals who embody marginalized gendered and class positions. Most people detained at Ghost were both working class and gender nonnormative and included Syrian nationals and refugees. This homonormative and racialized classed and gendered policing constructs some queer formations as acceptable and others as not—what Mays means when she says "Lebanon has all these oppressions." Those deemed to be "less appropriate" queer individuals frequent spaces like Ghost, which many of my more-privileged informants distanced themselves from and framed as a "nasty" place. As in other global cities, Beirut's gay friendliness is based on policing classed and gendered boundaries and producing "others" who embody racialized and inappropriate sexualities.

Many interlocutors assert that having access to gay-friendly spaces and LGBT networks in Beirut requires having economic, cultural, and social capital. Therefore, networks (including activist networks) act as social capital, enabling access to safe(r) LGBT spaces. These networks also police class boundaries by granting people with economic capital access to the networks, while often keeping others out. In some cases, this type of social capital circulates globally. For example, Mays says that her queer activist networks primarily shape her experiences of cities, such as New York City and Cairo. Therefore, she argues that one cannot draw conclusions about gay life based only on one's experiences of a city without centralizing the role of the networks one is embedded in and relies on. For Mays, Beirut is not exceptional; instead, people who have access to Beirut's somewhat-quite-exclusive networks find the city easier to navigate.

For many, the presence of gay and lesbian places is less indicative of growing openness and tolerance than of neoliberalism and the profitability for establishments *becoming* gay friendly. Randa, like others, talks about the exclusivity of networks and private, gay-friendly places. She describes how private places in Beirut, such as privately owned bars, restaurants, and clubs, become gay friendly more readily than public spaces.[5] Randa insists that these places are "gay-friendly, not queer-friendly places," since most are transphobic. Hence, these places act as safe havens for some while excluding those most at risk for public harassment.

Gender normativity plays an important role in people's experiences of both public and private spaces in Beirut. Randa explains that people experience public harassment very differently, depending on their gender presentation and performance, and that trans women experience the worst harassment. Gay-friendly places in Beirut have also historically discriminated against gender-nonnormative men (Merabet 2014). In these spaces, classed and gendered presentations are still key to who is and is not welcome. Similar to Mays's and Sirine's discussions about accessibility and class, Randa states that gay-friendly spaces are also exclusive to those who have the means to afford them and are part of the "right" networks. For example, Randa says that Acid, the first gay club (now closed), was "money friendly" rather than gay friendly:

> If we think of the very fancy places, the one where you pay fifty dollars [for] entrance, people there don't care. I went to a place recently, to a gay friend's birthday. I usually go to an averagely priced pub. I don't go to very expensive places. They also require you to dress a certain way. I don't like someone to impose on me. I went there, and I saw a lot of people from the gay community I know. They were dressed—shirt and tie—and they paid the money. If you are going to pay money, no one says anything, unless you are going to make out or dance with someone of the same sex. It becomes a problem [for businesses] if all of them—[the] LGBT community—start going there, which is not going to happen, because they don't all have the money.

Like Sirine, Randa suggests that expensive places are less likely to discriminate based on gender presentation, since they are mostly concerned with profit. However, highlighting only economic capital risks omitting the multifaceted ways that class operates in conjunction with gender, race, religious sect, and sexuality. Randa notes that expensive places require particular gendered and classed presentations, such as her gay friends wearing ties and the expectation that she must "dress a certain way," reflecting a necessary embodiment of cultural capital as well as habitus (Bourdieu 1986).

Consumptive practices make for appropriate or desirable gay subjects. Even though gay-friendly places in Beirut historically have discriminated against gender-nonnormative men and continue to do so, the discrimination remains highly classed and racialized. For example, gender-nonnormative white men from the West and male tourists from the Arab Gulf are not harassed in the same manner because of their privileged class positions. Unlike the example of Ghost, these men are not penalized but upheld as proper tourists.

Souraya is the only one to address the antiblack discrimination in Beirut and, thus, complicates structures of stigmatization beyond gender and sexuality. Black people in Beirut are predominantly visible in the service industry or as migrant domestic workers from East Africa. In addition, Lebanese people also racialize South Asian workers as black. Souraya notes the exclusion of black people in the gay and lesbian scenes:

> What are the policies behind this? Even gay bars are not tolerant. Gay bars are very classist. If you have money, you can enter; if you are black, you can't enter. The only black people allowed are those who work in the place. You don't find a black person in gay bars in Lebanon.

It is not only class that determines access to gay-friendly places: Souraya makes an important point about the absence of black people in bars and restaurants, except as workers and cleaning staff.

Designation of spaces as "gay friendly" conceals the inequalities within LGBT communities. While interlocutors are critical of neoliberal conceptions of gay friendliness, they do not provide alternatives to the gay-friendly framework per se. Instead, they argue that concepts such as gay friendliness are not useful in determining if a place is welcoming and, hence, show that access to gay-friendly spaces remains exclusionary and depends on racialized and normative classed and gender performances. Even though they do not provide explicit alternatives, some express the need to make transformative spaces available rather than simply attempt to make gay friendliness more inclusive.

The need for transformative spaces for some extends to Lebanese LGBT organizing spaces, which many criticize. In recounting their experiences of gay and queer organizing spaces, many interlocutors show that such places presume middle-class positions and high education levels. For example, Rabab tells me, "Class issues are not discussed; they are *assumed*. We have a serious class issue [in the gay community]. People, including myself, have been shamed because of class." Rabab recounts that she has been made hyperaware of her class background and shamed for not being as proficient in English and French as others. In addition, her clothing style continues to be read as "hipster," though she does not identify as such. Being read as a hipster, a middle-class designation, signifies how other queers make her taste and style intelligible.

Queer Exclusions

Some consider normative queerness in Beirut to be gendered, classed, and raced. Queerness itself—as a radical position or project in relation to lesbian or gay—still reproduces normative assumptions and standards about what queer people should look like and how they should act and perform queerness. Rabab, for example, talked about how gender, class, and religiosity shape her experiences in queer and nonqueer circles. Rabab, who identifies as having a "bigender experience" (meaning she performs and experiences both genders), was in her mid-twenties at the time and, unlike most of my interlocutors, came from a working-class background. Having recently stopped wearing the hijab following a double mastectomy, Rabab recounts multiple incidents of harassment experienced when wearing the hijab in queer and nonqueer circles: "When I was wearing the veil," Rabab says, "it took me time to understand that people viewed it as an oppressive tool. I realized that when I was attacked for wearing it. I was treated differently." Here Rabab explains how appropriate queerness in a sense becomes defined in terms of being secular or at least not a pious Muslim. She recounts that the harassment is worst in private establishments and in what she calls "posh" places. These include most gay-friendly places, where, if she forgot she was wearing a hijab, people's stares often reminded her. She feels that she was most discriminated against when wearing the hijab presurgery: "I found out, at the end, that nothing tops the harassment that I got from the hijab [*pauses*], but then [after the surgery] I found myself content that people don't assume my gender, and I like that."

Rabab's working-class background informs her gender identification with a working-class masculinity. She plans on getting a forearm tattoo that she believes exemplifies that masculinity. She repeatedly expresses that she is different from the "other queers" for not attending private schools or universities and for having less access to Beirut growing up (she was born and raised in a southern Lebanese village). While Nadine Naber and Zeina Zaatari's (2014) research among LGBT and feminist antiwar activism in Beirut illustrates that after the 2006 Israeli war against Lebanon there was more awareness among these groups of the elitist nature of LGBT organizations, Rabab still points to the continued class elitism. She insists that cultural capital such as fluency in English or French grants people more access to Beiruti LGBT communities, circles, and spaces. These requirements are examples of how some queer activists and circles unwittingly reproduce exclusions that they claim to be critical of.

Rabab considers racism and classism to be directly linked to urban development and to cities such as Beirut: "Lebanon is a very racist country. Racism is also most common in urban areas such as Beirut, which is a by-product of urbanization and people thinking the space is open, diverse, and cosmopolitan." Rabab refers to racism toward nonwhite foreigners and to sectarian tensions, including against Shias, the historically marginalized religious sect who are often considered to be less modern than other sects (Deeb 2006). As Souraya's example demonstrates, gender and class remain determining factors in Shias' experiences of Beirut.

In this narrative of modernity, hierarchies of religious sect are mapped onto the possibility of being modern such that certain sects are considered as impossible sites of "modern queerness." Thus, some discourses focus on the impossibilities for Shia embodiment of modern cosmopolitanism and queerness. While this is deeply entangled with class politics and particular materialist histories of colonialism and religious sects, sectarian differentiations present themselves as "natural" distinctions (which become racialized) between sects. However, this is a particularly classed understanding of queerness, where it becomes a gendered and classed (even more so than sectarian) possibility.

Rabab does not agree with the claim that Beirut is more modern than villages in Lebanon. She recounts that, growing up in a predominantly Shia village, she had very different experiences of sex and sexuality from those of people in Beirut. Rabab disrupts Samira's binary about Beirut versus the village. She believes that her village, which is considered more traditional and conservative, is more open than Beirut, particularly since people there talked about sex more often than in Beirut. Her characterization of her village as more open than Beirut critiques the metropolitan discourses that construct Beirut as exceptional and open. Thus, Rabab disrupts elitist categories of the "cosmopolitan subject" by accounting for nonelite forms of cosmopolitanism.[6] Rabab asks, "How are we conservative? How are we traditional/uncivilized because we talk or don't talk about sex?" While disrupting the binary between urban and rural and redefining what "cosmopolitanism" means, Rabab still reproduces the idea that openness around sex and sexuality is a marker of progress and modernity.

Tolerating Cosmopolitanism

"You can tell a lot about society by the way it deals with its refugees and migrants," Yara, a twenty-nine-year-old Lebanese queer-identified woman, tells me. Many individuals, including Yara, recount the Lebanese state's racist policies and people and the Lebanese people's everyday racism, especially in how they treat non-Western foreigners. Given the surge of Syrian refugees and migrant domestic workers, open racist practices have become common, whether they are symbolic (discourses around refugees), are linked to access to resources (legal restriction on jobs and visa restrictions), or limit mobility. For instance, in July 2013, I came across banners on the entrances to some villages in Mount Lebanon ordering all Syrian refugees to register with the municipality and to follow a 7:00 P.M. curfew. Local government and municipalities justify such policies, which criminalize refugees, as necessary to curb the increasing levels of crime and other offenses linked to the surge of refugees. In January 2015, the Lebanese government introduced for the first time in its history a visa requirement for Syrians entering Lebanon. This suspicion of the other also extends to Palestinian and Sudanese refugees and to migrant domestic workers from East Africa and Southeast Asia. Othering in Lebanon takes on shifting manifestations depending on *al-wad'*. For example, Yara says,

> This whole propaganda of othering—the other becomes anyone, and it shifts. The Maronites can be the other of Palestinians. Now, Sunnis became the other of Palestinians because Shias support the Palestinian cause. So once a society is capable of othering and capable of creating these binaries [*pauses*], it keeps doing it.

Yara points to the shifting and contextual processes of othering in Lebanon and how it is deeply informed by geopolitics and shifting situations. This, again, presents another set of recurring fractals, since distinctions between groups of people remain, though the relations change. That is, othering does not happen only to distinguish between the Lebanese and non-Lebanese; rather, it also is an ongoing process of making distinctions among Lebanese people themselves.

Interestingly, claims of the progressiveness and cosmopolitanism of Lebanon deny internal distinctions between people. Particularly post–civil war, the Lebanese state's claim that Lebanon is built on the coexistence of Muslims and Christians is enacted to mark Lebanon as modern and cosmopolitan. These narratives of coexistence do not apply to migrants and refugees. Tolerance, as Wendy Brown reminds us, is "a political discourse and practice of governmentality that is historically and geographically variable" (2006, 4). Tolerance of only specific groups therefore is a characteristic of progress narratives (Brown 2006). The modern narrative of tolerance depends on not tolerating certain vulnerable groups (gender-nonnormative, trans, and working-class people, as well as refugees) whom it regards as nonmodern (El-Tayeb 2011).

Exceptional (Gay) Progress

Designating places such as Beirut as regionally exceptional, cosmopolitan, and LGBT friendly obscures multiple hierarchies and exclusions and the ways they shift based on *al-wad'*. Invoking urban cosmopolitanism limits our understanding of the lived experiences of marginalized communities. For example, Beirut's image as a safe haven for LGBT individuals and its seeming openness conceal a series of exclusions, particularly in relation to unequal access to space. Gender normativity and classism shape individuals' experience of cosmopolitan Beirut and gay life. These exclusions are reproduced in LGBT communities, particularly for working-class, trans, and gender-nonnormative individuals. Cosmopolitan Beirut is accessible as a gay-friendly space to gender-normative, secular, and middle- to upper-class LGBT people.

Marginalized queer Beirutis, particularly gender-nonnormative, genderqueer, and working-class individuals—among the people with the least protections and thus most impacted by *al-wad'*—are most likely to question Beirut's cosmopolitanism and to carve out new understandings of queer visibilities that challenge dominant understandings of modernity and progress. LGBT Beirutis rework what cosmopolitanism means by contesting dominant definitions and not centering Euro-American cities. Whereas discussions of cosmopolitanism tend to assume Western urban centers as reference points for understanding the category, my interlocutors have different reference points. For example, they create relational understandings of modernity and cosmopolitanism by situating Beirut in relation to other Arab cities rather than just in relation to Euro-American cities. Unlike research claiming that Lebanese LGBT individuals uncritically reproduce discourses of Beiruti cosmopolitanism (Masri 2010; Seidman 2012), LGBT Beirutis engage with this narrative and experience exclusions differently based on their gendered and classed positions. While they draw on these transnational discourses of modernity, progress, and cosmopolitanism, they do not uncritically reproduce them.

Transnational discourses on sex and sexuality are used as markers of progress for places and people. When used in Lebanon, they promote two claims about progress: first, that modern homosexuality and gay rights are signs of state progress; and second, that Lebanon is the most developed nation in the region. These narratives do not attend to *al-wad'*, its shifting disruptive and violent manifestations, and its uneven effect on populations. Also, such narratives obscure race, gender, and class-based exclusions operating in Lebanon, such as the dehumanization and racialization of Syrian refugees, which reproduce different valuations of life. Beirut's seeming tolerance of middle- to upper-class gay and lesbian tourists—and not of groups such as Syrian and Palestinian refugees; migrant domestic workers; and gender-nonnormative, trans, and working-class people—is considered a sign of modernity and cosmopolitanism.

My interlocutors focus on racialized gendered and classed exclusions that they and other people face, which contrasted with the narratives of Beiruti cosmopolitanism and exceptionalism. Many assert that Beirut is not cosmopolitan, precisely because it remains highly exclusionary. Following feminist sociologist Beverley Skeggs (1997), this chapter suggests that we must think about how gender and class coproduce certain types of cosmopolitan queer individuals, to which the fractal Orientalist narratives of Beirut's cosmopolitanism do not attend. Instead of reflecting humanist attitudes toward others (Plummer 2015), cosmopolitanism becomes an elite category reserved for those who are deemed "appropriately queer" and *deserving* of gay-friendly space. Chapters 1 and 2 illustrate the ways that fractal Orientalism works at the global, regional, and everyday levels and exposes the multiple erasures and exclusions it makes possible. The following chapters, however, use the lens of *al-wad'* to consider the materialities of queer life in Beirut, which fractal Orientalism obscures. They focus on a number of queer strategies that LGBT individuals use in their everyday lives to navigate both *al-wad'* and gender and sexual nonnormativity in Beirut. Moving away from cultural explanations, the chapters use the political economy of gender and sexuality, which explains the queer strategies that LGBT individuals employ.

3

Against Reconciliation

"People congratulated me when I took off the hijab, both in my [new] neighborhood and within queer circles," Rabab tells me. Rabab, who is briefly introduced in Chapter 2, is in her mid-twenties, identifies as having a bigender experience, and was okay with both masculine and feminine pronouns but not gender-neutral pronouns.[1] At the time of the interview, she preferred the pronouns "she" and "her."[2] While it may seem that the pronoun "they" is appropriate in Rabab's case, Rabab refuses it, as it does not capture the ways that she conceives of her gender experience as bigender. She describes herself as having been a "paid activist" in gender and sexuality politics in Lebanon. Rabab had recently stopped wearing the hijab, following a double mastectomy undergone a few months before we met. She had also recently moved from the southern suburbs of Beirut, a predominantly Shia area, to a predominantly Christian neighborhood. Rabab is frustrated because people congratulated her after removing her hijab, since they assume that she has become liberated, secular, and for some, more legitimately queer. She had become more intelligible *as* queer after removing the hijab. The reactions to Rabab as a queer hijabi are unsurprising given the global war on terror, which draws on imperialist and racial logics that cast Islam and Muslims as regressive and not "accepting" of sexual freedoms, to the extent that an LGBT Muslim becomes hard to imagine. These fractal Orientalist discourses, while originating in a post–Euro-American 9/11 moment, circulate globally as well as in the Middle East. Rather than represent the Middle East and/or people in the Middle East as homogeneous, fractal

Orientalism distinguishes between parts of the Middle East that are *better* than others. Still, the veil in all its forms became a stand-in for the oppression that Muslim women face.

Rabab had decided to stop wearing the hijab because it was a clear gender marker of womanhood rather than because she felt it contradicted her queerness: "I only took the hijab off because I did not want to be viewed as a woman at all times. For me, it depends on the context." Removing the hijab meant that Rabab could have more freedom in deciding her gender presentation. She could now easily experiment with clothing: "I don't like unisex clothing; I like either to wear men's stuff or women's stuff, but I don't like unisex." Rabab challenges some segments of Beiruti LGBT activists' understandings of the gender binary and experiences of transgender identities. She is aware of hegemonic understandings of LGBT identities, which expect people to identify themselves along a gender binary and along binaries of the closet and outness. She rejects the idea held by many in her new neighborhood and queer circles that the hijab is oppressive and "not queer," arguing that it has saved her at various times because it helped her fit in in certain places and contexts. The hijab is something she strategically uses when she finds fit, particularly when visiting family in the southern suburbs of Beirut.

I met and interviewed Rabab in the midst of the increasing ISIL terrorist attacks in Beirut. While our discussions were meant to focus on queer life in Beirut, our exchanges focused more on the anxieties and increasing instability and violence of *al-wad'*. Following more than a dozen suicide attacks on civilians and army checkpoints in the summers of 2013 and 2014, the Lebanese army set up more checkpoints in various parts of Beirut, including its suburbs, and throughout Lebanon for precautionary and added security measures. These checkpoints were intended to inspect vehicles entering residential neighborhoods, malls, and shopping centers. As anthropologist Kristin Monroe's (2011, 2016) careful ethnography of everyday mobility in Beirut illustrates, class primarily determines how people's mobility changes, particularly with regard to security measures taken by instituting checkpoints and road alterations. While the primary suspects/targets for such checkpoints were usually younger working-class men and suspect foreigners—particularly Syrian and Palestinian refugees—people's everyday mobility became more restricted. Mopeds, the chosen mode of transportation for many working-class younger men and queer persons, were among the vehicles routinely targeted by these checkpoints, since such types of vehicles were used in a number of suicide attacks.[3] A growing number of queer individuals (primarily women and transgender men) had started using scooters in Beirut for their ease in navigating a congested city and their cost-effectiveness; they also allowed these people to avoid sexual harassment that takes place on shared public and private transportation.

Rabab used a moped as her primary mode of transportation and for what she referred to as her "office boy" work. During the summers of 2013 and 2014, she was routinely stopped at checkpoints, especially when visiting her family, most likely for being read as a working-class man. These checkpoints were particularly heightened at all entry points to the southern suburbs of Beirut since they were primary targets for ISIL bombings because of the large population of working- to middle-class Shia Muslims residing there. She told me of the extreme discomfort she felt while being searched and patted down and recounted that she would assert to male officers that she is a woman so that she would not be searched. Rabab tells me that she strategically identified as a woman to safeguard herself from being inappropriately touched and not upset her mother for having taken off her hijab. Encounters at the checkpoint in Lebanon are always emblematic of the larger geo- and sociopolitical context: from the civil war's Muslim and Christian militias' checkpoints, to Israeli and Syrian checkpoints. While geopolitics is often treated as a backdrop for studies on gender and sexuality, here I show that geopolitics has an intimate relationship with gender and sexuality. For example, Rabab's encounters show how the entangled embodiment of gender, race, class, and religious sect inform the experiences at the checkpoint.

This chapter analyzes the everyday tactics and strategic uses of identity among LGBT individuals in Beirut and examines what it tells us about experiences of everyday-life uncertainties, disruptions, and violence. *Al-wad'* is used to describe the context of precarity and as an analytical tool to better understand the queer strategies enacted by my interlocutors. The chapter draws on interviews and life stories of six interlocutors and highlights the queer materialities by attending to lived experiences of nonnormative gender and sexualities in Beirut. This and subsequent chapters flesh out how these strategies, which seemingly have to do only with gender and sexuality, can also shed light on how people deal with the realities, anxieties, and disruptions that *al-wad'* produces and normalizes.

Using *al-wad'* as a critical theoretical tool, the chapter analyzes and emphasizes the strategies of everyday life rather than LGBT subjects themselves—decentering rather than consolidating a "gay subject." Rabab, like many of my interlocutors, disrupts dominant Euro-American understandings that assume a gay, lesbian, or trans subject who is either out or closeted and who aspires to certain forms of visibility. These narratives assume that open identification with lesbian, gay, bisexual, or trans identities and marking oneself as such are examples of acceptance and a "developed" LGBT identity. These narratives are used to mark some places as gay friendly, and thus modern, and others as not. While there is a robust critique of the closet and linear coming-out narratives in the field of Euro-American queer studies (Sedgwick 1990; Seidman 2002) and queer migration studies (Manalansan 2003; Guzman 2005; Cantú 2009; Decena 2011), this chapter looks at the queer strategies of my interlocutors and the productive nature of refusing reconciliation.

Analyzing the queer strategies of reconciliation (or antireconciliation) of different aspects of selfhood and subjectivity, this chapter argues that living amid an already *queer situation* means that everyday-life strategies of survival in Beirut are *queer*. While "queer strategies" here refer to the experiences of my LGBT interlocutors, these strategies are not enacted only by LGBT people. Rather, they are a lens to show how people manage everyday-life anxiety and disruptions in Beirut. Queer strategies are not simply rational or calculation based; rather, they are embodied and affective experiences. Negotiating queer subjectivities, much like managing *al-wad'* in Beirut, occurs in complex, nonlinear, and often contradictory ways. Questions around whether individuals are out or visible or whether they identify as LGBT are less central. The multiple and often contending ways by which individuals negotiate and experience sexuality are always constituted and constitutive of geopolitical contexts, gender, and class. By examining the strategic negotiations of queer subjectivities, I ask the following questions: How can queer strategies disrupt yet help people navigate everyday-life disruptions? Since queer visibility is often linked to assumptions about open and modern LGBT subjects, how does that affect our understanding of queer subjectivities that do not rely on mainstream strategies of coming out and visibility? What does a political economy of coming out look like? How does embracing seeming contradictions help us better understand the uses of queer strategies?

Moving away from cultural explanations, this analysis highlights the political economy of sexuality, which focuses on the centrality of structures and structural dimensions of experiences rather than performativity alone (Cantú 2009). A political economy of transnational sexuality sheds light on social structures, networks, and institutions that shape people's experiences of gender and sexuality. Therefore, questions such as those raised in Chapter 1—for example, Can people in Beirut be gay? or Is Beirut a gay-friendly city?—obfuscate the central role of geopolitics, gender, class, resources, support networks, and family arrangements.

There are multiple ways of understanding Rabab's reality. Her experiences are particular; however, they are not necessarily exceptional. One could argue that Rabab's story is a (linear) narrative of how individuals in the Arab

Middle East come to accept their nonnormative gender and sexual identity. My goal is not to reproduce simplified narratives of LGBT individuals' lives that rely on flattened understandings of culture, religion, and identity. Rather than simply critique the neoliberal narratives of the closet and coming out, my aim is to provide an analysis of Rabab and other LGBT people's experiences that foregrounds political economies of gender and sexuality. I move away from an analysis that assumes that LGBT people from or in the Global South must either reject or accept white Euro-American conceptions of nonnormative sexualities. Accounting for the multiple queer strategies of everyday life, I focus on the intersections of gender, class, family, and household structures as well as people's relation to activism.

Queer Strategies

LGBT individuals in Beirut use three distinct yet interrelated queer strategies in negotiating subjectivity and access to space amid *al-wad'*. This chapter presents three analytically distinct queer strategies that are quite intertwined in people's lives on a daily basis. To account for their interrelation and how they inform one another, I do not make clear-cut distinctions in my analysis. Therefore, I use the "messiness" (Manalansan 2014, 99) and seeming contradictions as productive to highlighting the everyday-life strategies that *simultaneously* disrupt and navigate disruption.

First, my interlocutors refuse to frame their experiences in terms of what I call "narratives of reconciliation." Here, I borrow the term "reconciliation" from postconflict societies to refer to the act of resolving/harmonizing/uniting multiple parts of oneself that might seem oppositional. Reconciliation, according to the *Oxford English Dictionary*, is "the action or an act of bringing a thing or things to agreement, concord, or harmony; the fact of being made consistent or compatible."[4] To reconcile is to make compatible or consistent. Euro-American narratives of reconciliation assume a Christian Catholic tradition of confession and penance and the necessity for individuals to be in harmony with multiple aspects of themselves. Euro-American media depict LGBT Arabs and Muslims as always having to reconcile what are assumed to be mutually exclusive categories of sexuality, religion, and culture (e.g., LGBT, Muslim, Arab). Whereas narratives of reconciliation uphold binaries (on multiple scales), my attention to everyday experiences of rejecting reconciliation disrupts binaries and fractals and thus renders them flat.

Reconciliation lenses assume and uphold binaries such as out-closeted, visible-invisible, and religious-secular. Coming out, then, is considered an act of reconciling one's sexuality with other aspects of one's identity. To assume that subjectivities need to be reconciled is to take for granted that sexuality is incompatible with other aspects of the self rather than part and parcel of our lives. To reconcile is to not accept the mess and disruptions that constitute and are constitutive of our everyday lives and subjectivities. My interlocutors do not present their lives or experiences as reconciling seemingly oppositional or inharmonious aspects of themselves. This disrupts the dominant framework that posits Arabs and Muslims and queerness to be incompatible. My interlocutors embrace and make use of seeming contradictions in their lives, understanding that contradictions in part result from the multiple positions that they occupy and the possibilities for individuals to occupy more than one position in different contexts (even if others regard the positions as contradictory). Though these positions are not experienced as oppositional, they are regarded as oppositional by society, usually along lines of normativity, especially reflecting gender binaries (man-woman), sexuality (straight-gay), and religiosity (religious-secular).

Second, related to their refusal to embrace narratives of reconciliation, my interlocutors do not adhere to a dominant gay or lesbian coming-out narrative that necessarily privileges sexuality. They disrupt coming-out narratives that focus on LGBT identities and instead consider the political economy of coming-out processes. Thus, they center their relationships in regard to family members and what sexual-identity categories make possible (or not). Even though they might be tacit about their sexualities, my interlocutors use selective disclosure and are vocal and explicit about other personal and political aspects of their lives that highlight their anti- and nonnormativity. For example, taking a personal or political stance that might be unpopular with one's family marks one as different. Moments of not explicitly verbalizing are not to be understood as moments of concealing. There are parallels between how people speak of the nebulous nature of *al-wad'* and sexuality. Both need not be explicitly verbalized, yet that does not deny the ways people experience them.

Third, in many cases, my interlocutors employ gendered strategies to highlight their nonnormativity, which is also a way of embracing contradictions and resisting reconciliation. In a similar vein to what anthropologist Jafari S. Allen (2011) shows among LGBT and nonheteronormative subjects in Cuba, it is not so much homosexuality that is problematic; rather it is normative presentations of gender, class, and race. In the case of Beirut, gender, class, and sect become prominent in people's conceptions of sexuality. Coming out for my interlocutors becomes about the strategic and contextual nature and embodiment of gendered sexual subjectivities and experiences. Thus, gendered experiences confound the coming-out model, which is primarily focused on sexuality.

Against Narratives of Reconciliation

A primary queer strategy that my interlocutors employ is disrupting and rejecting narratives of reconciliation: the claim that queer individuals, mostly from the Global South, must reconcile their culture and often their religion with their sexuality. Narratives of reconciliation are not only employed while describing LGBT life in the Arab Middle East; they have become common tropes in accounting for sexuality among religious and ethnic minorities in the Global North and Global South, including immigrant populations. Such narratives assume that one needs to reconcile or harmonize multiple parts of oneself to be legitimately queer.[5] This assumption drives the notion that Muslim queer and/or feminist identifications are antithetical, to the extent that LGBT persons must reconcile these seemingly oppositional positions. Interlocutors such as Rabab disrupt and reject such narratives and instead adopt a *queer* approach to subjectivity, one that embraces and makes use of seeming contradictions in their lives—they regard contradictions to be common or even necessary aspects of their life in Beirut. For example, they understand that despite everyday-life disruptions and imminent wars, Beirut still gets represented as a new gay touristic destination.

LGBT subjectivities in Beirut are about a classed and gendered fashioning of the self that is strategic in its response to both context and issues of safety amid precarious situations. Rabab recounts on more than one occasion that she does not like approaches that assume that Muslim LGBTs and LGBT people from the Middle East must always reconcile their sexual identification with their faith and culture. "I do not like this idea of reconciliation," Rabab says and further explains that reconciliation assumes that queerness and the practice of Islam are mutually exclusive experiences and positions. Rather than frame her life in terms of binaries of the closet and outness and religiosity and secularism, she recounts her experiences with strategic uses of identity and the importance of gender, class, sexuality, and social context. For example, she does not see her hijab as being antithetical to her queerness.

Rabab's embodied experiences get lost when people attempt to make them intelligible by describing her story in terms of linear narratives of moving from an oppressive to a free (read as modern) expression of herself. Rabab expresses her discomfort with how some might narrate her story in terms of "unlikely combinations" of Muslim, queer, and bigender, as this misrepresents how she views herself. For her, the multiple positions she occupies are not contradictory. Instead of reconciliation, Rabab embraces and uses what she refers to as contradictions in her life: "There is nothing wrong with being contradictory. [*Pauses.*] The hijab helps me fit somewhere, and being gay helps me belong in a certain place; they both help me in different aspects of my life." Even though she tells me that others might see her life as contradictory, she explains that these seeming contradictions are highly contextual.

Throughout our conversations, Rabab does not refer to or talk about her surgery as much as the hijab, which highlights how others around her (mis)understand the symbolic nature of being a queer hijabi. While I do not wish to use Orientalist tropes of veiling/unveiling in the Arab world as signs of modernity and secularism, I focus on this example to illustrate how Rabab *queers* the hijab by using her experiences with queer visibilities, intelligibility, and queer normativity in Beirut.

While people embrace their own complexities and the role of context and the multiple positions they occupy, many interlocutors express that their lives and experiences are misunderstood and essentialized, particularly by academics and Euro-American journalists. Media and some scholarly representations of Beirut often treat class, gender, and sexuality as independent of one another rather than as interrelated. For example, people's experiences of faith and religious sect are treated as independent of gender, gender as independent of class, sect as independent of class, and sexuality as independent of class and gender. A political economy of transnational sexualities, however, asks us to pay attention to how these different positions have material consequences on people's everyday lives and embodiments of gender and sexuality. Culture alone is not useful for explaining LGBT people's experiences.

(Un)Necessary Outings: Selective Disclosure and Family

It is well documented that individuals have various experiences and processes of coming out based on intersections of gender, class, and social networks.[6] However, Euro-American understandings of coming out presume living a public life where out persons disclose their sexuality to family and friends (Seidman 2002). While some of my interlocutors discussed their experiences of coming out, they do not talk about outness and the closet as binary experiences. Not being out, in the dominant sense, does not mean a lack of acceptance of one's gender and/or sexual expression, experience, and identity.[7] This is another way they embrace the complexity of their multiple positions rather than attempt to unify the apparent discrepancies through reconciliation.

Recounting their experiences of coming to terms with and accepting their sexualities, many interlocutors described their experiences in nonlinear and nonoppositional ways. That is, they did not regard outness and the closet to be oppositional experiences or linked to particular forms of concealment and visibility. To understand how my interlocutors define their experiences, I did not explicitly ask about coming out but asked individuals to describe what they consider to be central aspects of who they are. In some cases, individuals brought up processes of coming out during the interviews, but at other times, it was not even mentioned. Rather than employ liberal definitions of such constructs, I privilege my interlocutors' understandings, embodied experiences, and ways that they make their lives intelligible to themselves and others.[8] Therefore, I use the term "coming out" as it is used by my interlocutors, and since not everyone shares the same definition of "outness," I explain it as it came up in interviews.

Tarek, introduced in Chapter 2, makes a distinction between what he calls "Western" and "non-Western" understandings of coming out. Tarek was raised in Beirut and lived there with his parents all his life until moving away for two years for his studies. He had been living in Canada for the past two years to pursue his postgraduate studies. Tarek feels that his life is more restricted in Beirut than in Canada, particularly because he is afraid that his parents would "come to know" about his sexuality through other people. In Beirut, Tarek tells acquaintances that he dates women. While in Canada he feels less anxious about his parents' finding out. He feels frustrated that his understanding of coming out is not shared by many of the men he meets and dates there:

> I am not out in the Western definition, you know: out to your parents, everyone in society can know. Mainly [in Canada] if you're not out to your parents, you are not considered out. I know this from people I have dated—they probably never said it directly, but they take a step back [when they find that I am not out to my parents]; they say, "He isn't out yet." My definition is more derived from Arab culture; coming out in Lebanon does not mean telling parents. People who go out to the [gay] places don't tell their parents, so they are not hiding it. I am not closeted.

Given his interactions and dating experiences with predominantly white men in Canada, Tarek makes a distinction between his conception of and a Western definition of coming out. A Western definition of being out, for him, implies that one comes out to "everyone" one knows, including (and most important) one's parents. However, since he is not out to his parents, he feels that many men assume that he is closeted. Tarek insists that he is not closeted but says that he is "out" in certain contexts and that his decision to not tell his parents is a strategy meant to preserve what he considers central familial ties. Tarek adds that his understanding of coming out is "cultural." Though he uses culture to distinguish his experiences as a gay man in Beirut from those of his Canadian friends, his narrative is more complicated. Like other gay men, Tarek fears that by telling his family that he is gay, they will think less of him "as a man." Thus, he focuses on his normative gender performances and presentations as key to his sexuality. For Tarek, gender, family, security, and selective disclosure are central. While he turns to culture to explain the different conceptions of coming out, in Lebanon, Tarek's concerns remain more about social and familial networks than culture itself.

Tarek brings up his parents as the main reason for why he chooses not to disclose his sexuality to acquaintances in Beirut: "I don't tell people who might tell other people and then tell my parents. [*Pauses.*] If I had told my parents from the start, then I don't care about what other people say. I would tell a straight person who is homophobic, but I don't [*pauses*] only because of my parents." When I ask him to expand on what he means by coming out, he says, "Coming out is not necessarily adopting a Western level of comfort; it is a different level of comfort. With time the definition might change if people become more open-minded; developmentally, we improve." Tarek situates his definition of coming out as neither Western nor Lebanese, unwittingly collapsing fractals and binaries in understandings of coming out and non-normative sexualities. However, at the same time, he uses a linear narrative of progress, which assumes that, with time, Arabs, like their Western counterparts, will be able to accept and tolerate or, in his own words, "become more open-minded [and improve] developmentally." To make sense of his different experiences in Beirut and Canada, Tarek utilizes contradictions and essentializes culture, framing one as being more "progressive" and "open-minded" than the other. Though Tarek mentions that gay Canadian men assume he is not out since his immediate family does not know, he feels that being a gay Arab Muslim man plays no role in his interactions with other white gay men.

Like Tarek, Rabab fears the potential backlash on her immediate family from extended family in the form of cutting ties. She compares the act of removing the hijab to the process of coming out; she conceives of both as relational processes that involve a great deal of caution, especially if they might jeopardize her familial networks and ties. However, she explains that the process of coming out differs from one person to another based on the person's support networks and positions. "My mother is scared of people," she explains, "so she didn't want me to take off the hijab."

Others refuse to identify in terms of LGBT categories and understand these identifications as Western imports that do not work for them. Though many argue that they do not use Euro-American categories, they still rely on feminist and queer theories to deconstruct LGBT categories. Mays, who had been involved in Lebanese and international feminist and queer activism, openly resists these identifications, both in her activism and personal life. Mays, who is working on her master's degree in the arts in Beirut, tells me, "The problem is how these categories and identifications are used. The problem is importing discourses, when they are not the only categories you fit in. [The problem is] when it becomes your only identity. [*Pauses.*] There are other aspects that are as central." Despite being active and involved in local and international queer activism, Mays says that she is not out to her parents and explains that there is much more to her than being lesbian. She expresses that she feels uneasy to speak from the position of "a lesbian," as it obscures the multiple positions she occupies. For her, context and nuance are very central.

Mays insists that queerness is not an identification.[9] By refusing cultural explanations, Mays disrupts fractal distinctions that set in motion linear narratives of progress. She says that she tried coming out to her heterosexual friends, for example, by telling them that she dates and has sex with other women, and it did not make her feel better or safe:

> I tried it, and it made me feel vulnerable, and I felt I needed somebody else's acceptance. It is as though the validity of my feelings had to come from someone else, and I felt like it was imposed and not organic. I wasn't comfortable at all. There are situations when I might talk about my sexuality where I would want to share; however, I do it in a much more subtle way. I do it in a way that doesn't require anyone's approval.

Coming out, for Mays, is a relational process in which she feels that she is seeking someone else's approval. This makes the experience less validating for her. Mays prefers selective and subtle disclosure, which makes her feel safer. For example, Mays talks about how she had subtly brought up her sexuality with acquaintances. She recounts a story about being with a group of heterosexual women who were talking about men. She told them, "If you think men are difficult, try dating women." For her, this was an example of how she could subtly bring up sexuality. "You test the waters, in a way," she says. "Also, being subtle feels much more intimate." For Mays, being subtle means that she can experiment, feel safer, and anticipate people's reactions. While Mays describes her unease with LGBT identifications, she still uses Euro-American queer theory, such as insisting that queerness is not a sexual identification, to explain her apprehension with sexual-identity categories. Mays is not necessarily resisting Euro-American conceptions of LGBT identities or queerness; rather, she is working through them, precisely by employing feminist theory to deconstruct them.

Some individuals reject LGBT categorizations because they find them too restrictive. Yasmine is in her mid-thirties and while currently based in the United States, she visits Beirut twice a year. She had been living in the United States for ten years, since she moved to pursue her graduate studies at the age of twenty-four. Yasmine comes from an upper-middle-class background and was educated in private American schools in Beirut. She considers herself quite gender normative. When I ask her about what she considers to be central aspects of who she is, she explains, "I see my identity as that of a woman who likes comfortable clothing. Sexuality-wise, I know that I am gay, but I don't present myself as gay. I feel like with the way I am I can fit in everywhere without people knowing. I like the fact that my sexuality is not obvious."

Yasmine is comfortable with the fact that she does not embody her non-normative sexuality or that her "sexuality is not obvious." This makes her feel safe and gives her the opportunity, or more accurately, *the power*, to fit anywhere. Yasmine is referring to her normative gender practices and performances, which she claims signals to people that she is not necessarily lesbian. Gender performances become central to how Yasmine conceives of and experiences her sexuality.

Yasmine disrupts coming out and reconciliation narratives by recounting that after coming out, she felt she had become more restricted because she has to identify herself in "one box." With coming out, there was the expectation that she had to "consolidate"—or what I call "reconcile"—these aspects in a way that makes her fit an already-established "box" of "lesbian." Yasmine describes coming out as moving from one box to another, which she feels is as oppressive as not being able to talk about it in the first place. She recounts that in Beirut, she inhabits a "nonbox." Her use of "nonbox" is yet another queer strategy of refusing reconciliation and making use of contradictions.

Yasmine describes the nonbox as enabling and giving her the space to express her various performances and practices. In Beirut, the nonbox clearly signals Yasmine's nonnormativity without having to name it. She finds this practice to be more comfortable than having to explicitly come out:

> In Lebanon, when I say I don't want to get married, which is what many queer women say, or even if a straight woman didn't find the appropriate person to marry, these things are still shut down. [They tell you,] "Don't say this." There is this "don't talk about it." You can't express this type of preference. Coming out is similar, in the sense that you can't directly say [it].

Yasmine considers coming out to be almost always tacit in the context of Lebanon.[10] By openly stating that she does not want to get married, she indirectly signals her nonnormativity. This strategy enables individuals to claim nonnormativity without explicitly verbalizing their sexual experiences and preferences.

Yasmine prefers inhabiting the nonbox in Beirut, which she finds is not understood by LGBT people in the United States. She compares her experiences in Beirut to those in the United States:

> I don't know if it's better; it's just different. I feel more comfortable in Lebanon because I didn't go into another box. I feel better because I am in a box that I had revolted against. People know that I am outside the box; however, they don't know where I am. So my family says, "This is the one who isn't married; she studied too much; maybe she is overqualified," so they wonder and try to find what box I am in, but I am in the nonbox. Even for my family who doesn't know. So I am somewhere where they might reject, but it's not rejected like being gay. For example, they might say, "She should have married; wouldn't it have been better than this Ph.D.?" Whatever, but I am in a nonbox.

Yasmine's experiences the nonbox as a position of power that she inhabits only in Beirut. Her description of the nonbox is highly relational. That is, her inhabiting a nonbox must be read and understood by her family and others around her *as* nonnormative. From her description, it is clear that her family tries to make sense of this nonbox by assuming that she is probably too educated to want to settle down and marry a man. At the same time, Yasmine understands that while she might be rejected by her family for her nonnormative outlooks on life, at least she is not being rejected for "being gay." Thus, Yasmine feels that the nonbox makes it not only more comfortable but also safer for her, as she is able to be "whatever she wants to" without necessarily defining herself, which feels less empowering.

While in the urban spaces of the U.S. Northeast, Yasmine feels she can be more public in displays of same-sex affection; the feeling of being "boxed in" makes her less comfortable:

> The difference in the U.S. is that I can have a girlfriend, walk on the streets, and hold her hand, maybe kiss her; maybe people would look at us funny, [but] there is no danger, no fear; there isn't this type of experience. I can't say one is better than the other, but there are advantages and disadvantages to both. In the U.S. I feel more boxed in.

Yasmine, like Tarek and Mays, considers herself out, though not directly or openly claiming a lesbian identity to her family so she can preserve familial ties.

During the Lebanese civil war, people's last names were used to identify and distinguish between Muslims and Christians and to determine who belonged and had access to which areas of the city and hence ensure and maintain partition. Christian and Muslim militias would inspect people's identification cards at checkpoints on the demarcation line between East and West Beirut to allow or deny access and in many cases murder people for their religious background. Today, however, last names are still used to determine people's religious sect, which often serves as a proxy for their political affiliations. Choosing not to identity, or be in a nonbox, as Yasmine does, can also be seen as a strategy of responding to *al-wad'* and society's historical and contemporary mobilization of violence that stems from the need to identify and enact violence against "the other." Both Mays's and Yasmine's discomfort with coming-out processes and embodying sexual-identity categories are queer strategies that complicate our understandings of dominant LGBT identifications. While LGBT identifications, as Sara Ahmed points out, are "shaped by their refusal of public comfort" (2013, 151), queerness suggests that individuals still can feel uncomfortable *inhabiting* them. Given the unease and anxiety produced daily by the situation, a refusal to *situate* oneself along sexual-identity categories is not about closeting but about opening up possibilities. Inhabiting a nonbox is also an example of a queer strategy that responds to *al-wad'*. In a post–civil war city where one's last name signifies the individual's religious sect—and in many cases class background—and boxes the person in, Yasmine's discomfort and rejection of sexual-identity categories is a queer strategy that enables her to hold on to power and seeks to deconstruct, rather than embody, what she refers to as "boxed" categories.

Yasmine finds a sense of community among queer activists in Beirut who also reject these boxes, something lacking in her life in the United States:

> I feel more similar to members of the queer community in Beirut [than to those in the United States]. I didn't move into any box; I am comfortable in Lebanon with my identity because I am not in a different box. I am in the box of "queer" with my queer friends, which is very broad, because most of them are activists, and being in this similar space, people think of these topics, think of boxes. They rejected the same box that I did, so they wouldn't put me in boxes. I was very happy in this community because I connect better with it than I do with LGBT people here [the United States]. They created new boxes here; they put themselves in this box. Even the lesbians don't like bisexuals; there is still discrimination against trans individuals; the boxes are very clear.

Yasmine expresses her affinity to her friends in the queer community in Beirut because they resist boxes as much as she does. However, in the United States, she argues, people are so invested in boxes and identity categories that it makes her feel she has to constantly mark herself. She says that creating all these boxes in the United States leads to fewer alliances between diverse groups of LGBT people.

My interlocutors recount their experiences of coming out in ways similar to the queer of color theorist José Esteban Muñoz's concept of disidentifications. That is, they draw on and engage with dominant Euro-American understandings of coming out, queer visibility, and gender transgression and work through them rather than simply reject or adopt them and, therefore, produce new understandings and embodied experiences. As Muñoz argues:

> Disidentification is the third mode of dealing with dominant ideology, one that neither opts to assimilate within such a structure nor strictly opposes it; rather, disidentification is a strategy that works on and against dominant ideology. Instead of buckling under the pressures of dominant ideology (identification, assimilation) or attempting to break free of its inescapable sphere (counteridentification, utopianism), this "working on and against" is a strategy that tries to transform a cultural logic from within, always laboring to enact permanent structural change while at the same time valuing the importance of local and everyday struggles of resistance. (1999, 11–12)

My interlocutors' engagements with coming out and queer visibility disrupt dominant coming-out narratives and are examples of what queer studies scholar Fatima El-Tayeb calls a "'failure of identification,' that potentially opens a moment of disruption and reorientation" (2011, xxxiv). While El-Tayeb makes this argument in reference to organizing strategies of queer immigrants of color in the Netherlands, here I employ it to show how it is used as a queer strategy in Beirut. That is, even though queer Beirutis do not employ affirmative coming-out narratives, they do not necessarily position themselves against them; rather, they proceed through a "third mode" of dealing with these dominant middle-class, white Euro-American concepts. In most cases, individuals work through concepts of coming out and seek to transform them through their experiences of *al-wad'* and its local everyday disruptions.

Though Muñoz's concept of disidentifications is useful, it does not account for contexts or situations where disruption is the norm of everyday life. While disidentification focuses on "failures of identification" that seek to disrupt, LGBT Beirutis have to already manage everyday-life disruptions. Instead of reorienting these disruptions, LGBT Beirutis make use of strategies that embrace contradictions, disruptions, and "mess" (Manalansan 2014, 97) that are already constitutive of their everyday lives amid *al-wad'*. To add another geopolitical dimension, a number of my interlocutors understand dominant coming-out narratives as "Western constructs" that do not necessarily apply to their lives. In those cases, they see disruption to coming-out narratives as active resistance to Western constructs. However, despite this resistance, a number of the university-educated and LGBT activists use queer and feminist theory to make sense of their experiences. They do not necessarily adopt or reject but disidentify.

LGBT Beirutis' queer strategies and disidentifications disrupt fractal Orientalist representations and distinctions that rely on normative understandings of LGBT outness and visibility as signs of modernity. If the presence of an out and visible LGBT community is used to gauge signs of gay life and exceptionalism, then rejecting binaries disrupts such distinctions that produce Beirut as exceptional in the Arab world. While the narratives presented here show how my interlocutors reject LGBT identifications, they still have to make themselves intelligible to those around them.

Another strategy that my interlocutors employ is selective disclosure, a relational process in which individuals disclose a nonnormative aspect of their life that may or may not directly relate to sexuality. In addition, many of my interlocutors assert that it is not necessary to come out to one's family. They stress that directly articulating their sexuality is neither necessary nor important, since parents can already assume and accept without their having to verbalize their sexuality or the parents having to verbalize acknowledgment.

Many consider that speaking about their sexuality can possibly cause more harm than good.

Concealment and disclosure play a central role in reproducing and resisting normative understandings of queer visibility. LGBT Beirutis navigate processes of coming out in ways that are similar to queer studies scholar Carlos Decena's concept of "tacit subjects" (2008, 340).[11] While Decena uses "tacit subjects" in reference to how queer Dominican men in New York City negotiate knowledge about their nonheteronormative sexualities with their families, I build on this concept in the Beiruti context. Being tacit about one's sexuality feels like the safer option for sustaining family relations and networks. Despite being tacit about their sexuality, many still make clear statements about their nonnormative gender presentations and performances and/or political views. For example, some explain to their families that they are feminists or simply working on women's rights, which seems like a safer option to preserve their household and family ties. Making such assertions is a queer strategy in which one expresses nonnormativity without directly addressing sexuality. Even though some do not openly talk about or explicitly identify as LGBT, they *do* openly talk about other aspects of themselves that are non- or antinormative. What does it mean to selectively disclose, and how is this a queer strategy?

Some individuals find it unnecessary to share information about their sexuality with their family. While Sirine, introduced in Chapter 2, openly discusses her sexuality with her mother, she still argues that coming out to one's family is unnecessary:

> My family matters a lot, and just as much as it is hard for me to understand what I am going through as queer or whatever, I just don't believe these people who need to come out. [*Pauses.*] It took you seven years to accept yourself, [so] you expect your mother to accept you in a second when she has been building all these expectations? Snap out of it; have a little bit of empathy. I am not talking about the case where people come out and their parents beat them, but a bit of drama is okay.

Sirine frames the decision not to tell one's family as a way of empathizing with family members and a means of maintaining family ties. She argues that people need to see coming out as a process, and just as it takes individual people years to "come to terms with their sexuality," it will take their family time. Despite minimizing the importance of verbalizing and talking about one's sexuality, Sirine recounts how she told her mother about her sexuality and how they maintain their relationship:

Not everything needs to be verbalized. However, I verbalize every-thing to my mother; this is how I came out to my mother [*pauses*] drama [*pauses*] crying; I was crying more than her. She said, "Oh, everybody is bisexual." I said, "No, you don't understand." She then said, "The only thing I am worried about is your safety; I have known for the longest time. I have known." I then spent two hours crying, and she was laughing at me, and now it's a running joke. For example, when my aunt is trying to set me up with the next hunk, she [my mother] gets a kick out of it. When there is a cute girl, she makes a gesture to me to check her out, and two weeks ago she asked me how is my love life, so I said it is dry. She said we should set you up, and I am like, do you have anyone in mind? It is funny. This is the relation-ship I have with my mom.

Though Sirine says that "not everything needs to verbalized," she explains that her relationship with her mother is built on openness. Sirine finds it eas-ier to use humor as she discusses her love life with her mother. Not needing to verbalize everything is yet another strategy that people use in speaking about *al-wad'*. As stated previously, experiences of *al-wad'* bring people together because it does not have to be explained in detail for others to understand.

In addition to talking about her experience of disclosure to her mother, Sirine contrasts the relationship with her mother to that with her father, where she feels she does not need to or does not want to verbalize everything. Though she never told her father about her sexuality, she has a feeling that he assumes and knows:

Now with my dad, I never really came and told him [*whispers*], "You know, Dad, I like girls." [*Pauses.*] Me and my dad, we talk a lot about the world, about politics. We argue a lot. We are a family when, once a week, I visit; we sit and talk for hours and hours about everything except our personal lives. So my dad understands what I like; he has seen me grow up; he has seen what I wear [*pauses*] and he has never objected.

Sirine recounts specific incidents when she had used selective disclosure and humor to point to her gender and sexual nonnormativity to her father and felt he was very accepting:

There were these little moments when we were growing up, and I was going to a baptism. And I was wearing this skirt—because I felt like wearing a skirt; it wasn't forced at all—I was going for the secretary look. And then he was like, "Oh, my god, I have a daughter," and I was like, "No, you have a daughter and a son and something in between," and he laughed. And I didn't feel I needed to say something more than that. I was sixteen or something like that.

Telling her father that he has "a daughter and a son and something in between," though humorous, is an example of how Sirine signals her nonnormativity. She does not directly tell her father that she is genderqueer and attracted to women, but she does selectively disclose her nonnormativity. Sirine describes another incident when she was watching television with her father and the topic of civil marriage in Lebanon came up. Her dad asked what her thoughts on the civil marriage debate were:

I said I don't believe in marriage. I had just come back from work, and I was tired. [*Pauses.*] And I said, "Dad, I don't give a shit about marriage; I don't find it to be an interesting institution." And then he said, "Is that it, or is it because you like girls?" And then I said, "I am going to go take a shower; I am not going to talk about this."

Rather than directly address her sexuality, Sirine told her father that she does not care about marriage and chose not to respond to his question about her attraction to women. At the same time, Sirine recounts that her girlfriend would come over to her family's home, and Sirine suspects that her father knew and tacitly accepted:

My girlfriend would come home, and he would sit with her, and I never needed to tell my dad, "You know what? I am gay." And sometimes when he watches gay pride on TV, and he says that he doesn't really understand why they need to be so flamboyant, et cetera [*pauses*] and he says it in front of me. He says, "Sometimes I do question whether this is the natural order of things." He says it in front of me; he questions all of these things, but then he knows, come on. [*Pauses.*] He doesn't ask me about my ex anymore. [*Pauses.*] She doesn't live with us anymore. [*Pauses.*] It is obvious that he knows there was a breakup.

Sirine is convinced that her father knows and to some extent, accepts, though he does not directly acknowledge it. For example, though he had met her ex-girlfriend and knew that they were "good friends," he never followed up or asked about her after she stopped showing up at their family apartment. Thus, this illustrates that even though he knows, he does not initiate a direct conversation about it. Similar to Katie Acosta's (2013) focus on context rather than preconceived notions of culture in the family negotiations of Latina LBQ women in the United States, my interlocutors' narratives demonstrate that their gendered strategies cannot be understood without centralizing class and context.

Selective disclosure is a relational process that is not necessarily initiated by the individuals themselves. Tarek recounts an incident similar to Sirine's. Even though Tarek told me on more than one occasion that his parents do not know about his sexuality, he says that his father suspects. He describes a time when he was watching a Lebanese satire TV show with his father, and when two gay characters appeared, his father looked at him and said, "Look, it's your friends." Tarek laughs and says that he thinks this might mean that his father knew and that was a tacit way of letting him know. Both Tarek and his father use humor to bring up his sexuality without specifically addressing it.

Many assert that generally people do not often discuss their sex lives with their parents, which makes discussing sexuality that is outside cultural, religious, and class norms harder to do. Sirine, like many others, says that one of the reasons she does not discuss her sexuality is that she simply does not discuss her intimate and sexual life with her father. In addition, Sirine points to the tacit knowledge around her sexuality; she makes it clear that, even though she would never talk to her dad explicitly about her girlfriend or her sexuality, she assumes that he knows. When her father asked her briefly while they were watching TV whether she liked women, she felt uncomfortable. However, she recounts the previously discussed incidents to illustrate that her father might know and assume and seems to be fine with it. Sirine also gives the example of the interactions she has with her grandmother:

> When I go visit my grandma and my girlfriend is with me, I don't go like, "Hey, Grandma, this is my girlfriend." I say, "This is Tania." I love the interaction that they have; my grandma loves her. She probably assumes, she probably knows, but whatever, I am not going to do that: "Yes, I am gay and I am proud and we are going to have so many babies and whatever." No! I am just glad you have welcomed her into your house; you are both having a meal together, having fun together; you both love each other.

Sirine disrupts coming-out narratives that presume outness, visibility, and a discourse centered on pride. She does not feel the need to come out to her grandmother yet enjoys the relationship that her grandmother and girl-friend have and the fact that they can all spend time together without neces-sarily verbalizing or clearly stating that Sirine and Tania are in a romantic relationship.

Activists and those who have had experiences with LGBT activism in Beirut describe their disillusionment with the process and promise(s) of com-ing out. While many had grown up with Euro-American discourses of gay and lesbian liberation and the importance of coming out for one to feel lib-erated and true to oneself, they questioned this narrative because it did not capture their lived experiences. Yara, introduced earlier, disrupts dominant coming-out narratives by focusing on the numerous effects it can have on people's livelihoods. Yara used to consider herself an activist when she was involved in a number of LGBT activist groups and initiatives in Lebanon; however, she had been traumatized and says she is not an activist anymore. It is unclear whether her traumas are linked to the Lebanese queer activist cultures. Yara, who became disillusioned with the promises of coming out, describes her coming out humorously:

> I came out to my family. [*Pauses.*] I actually got *dragged out of the closet*. My mom saw my girlfriend, who is more obvious, but she had her doubts. [*Pauses.*] But we [activists] had that dream of coming out; if we all come out of the closet, society will change. We will all be kicked out of our jobs; we will all take up fights that we can't handle. Now, when my friends tell me that they are going to come out to their families, I feel like, okay, is there something so important and pressing that they need to know about you? First, are you hurting your family? Sometimes—not all the time—some people would have a better rela-tionship with their family because there is something stuck, and it's no longer stuck, and it becomes more transparent. But some people don't need to. If your parents are seventy years old, why do you want to give them a heart attack; why, just to come out? What is coming out, really?

Yara, similar to others, focuses on familial networks and empathy. She rejects liberal coming-out narratives that focus solely on individual identification and self-actualization. Instead, she privileges a relational conception of the self, which relies on networks and material conditions—the political econ-omy of familial kinship relationships. A political economy of coming out, unlike liberal narratives of coming out, is concerned with reproducing and maintaining ties that are essential for one's survival. Having been active in LGBT rights groups and activism in Lebanon, Yara had previously imagined that coming out would have collective positive impacts and that it would "change society," particularly with changing people's attitudes toward homosexuality. Currently, however, Yara questions the process of coming out and the necessity of telling one's family. Given her and her friends' experiences, where they either did not choose to come out or faced backlash from their families for doing so, she asserts that sometimes it is not useful to tell family members. Here, Yara extends political economies of queer sociality by thinking about people beyond her immediate family. Yara stresses that not telling family members does not equate to one not living one's "true life" or that one is hiding; rather, many parents, she explains, are not able to understand the experiences of lesbian, gay, and/or bisexual subjectivities or desires in the first place. However, she also says that if one chooses to come out to one's family, the process should be selective and done with caution.

Gendered Strategies

In many instances, gender identities and experiences become more central than sexuality. Various interlocutors negotiate embodied gender performances in response to popular conceptions in Lebanon and elsewhere that link gender nonnormativity to sexual nonnormativity. While gender normativity gives some individuals a sense of security, for others, gender nonnormativity and transgression are central for carving out space and feeling empowered. In many instances, gender becomes the primary experience that is negotiated and that confounds the reconciliation and coming-out models. For example, this pattern is common with family members: Individuals openly tell their family that they are not a "typical woman or man," which in many cases is an example of selective disclosure. Many individuals make it clear that they feel comfortable marking their antinormativity, whether it is through clothing, self-presentation, or referring to themselves as "not typical," without necessarily being explicit about their sexuality. Many LGBT Beirutis contest normative expectations of gender and sexuality by presenting themselves as antinormative in various aspects of their lives that are not limited to sexuality. Gender presentation and performances become more central than sexuality, since they are the aspects that make many people visible and thus, the part of their lives that they need to defend and negotiate the most.

Randa, who identifies as genderqueer, says that her gender performance is the opposite of that of normative Lebanese femininity. She works full-time as the manager of a Lebanese NGO dealing with sexual health and LGBT health awareness and had been active in the activist LGBT community in Lebanon since it started as an underground movement in the 1990s. Born and raised in Beirut, she rarely leaves the city, even on weekends. This is considered unusual in Lebanon, where individuals tend to leave Beirut on the weekends, especially in the summer to go either to the mountains or to the beach in the north or south of the city. Randa tells me that she loves Beirut, especially Hamra, and feels that this is her space. In describing her experiences of gender nonnormativity, Randa says,

> I look different from the typical Lebanese woman, and I have looked this way since I was young. Since I am different—the way that I dress is different, and my hair is different, and the piercings I have are different—these things allow people to make fun of me. They find the way that I look strange. They allow themselves the freedom to laugh at me or tell me vulgar words. [*Pauses.*] That part really annoys me, and this butting in—first they start with a look, and then a person comes up to you and talks to you and asks you, "Why did you do this to yourself?" to which I reply, "It's none of your business."

Randa's gender-nonnormative presentation make her susceptible to ridicule. She uses this as an example to show how people's personal spaces are not respected in Beirut, the aspect she hates most about the city. Souraya, a twenty-three-year-old queer activist, echoes Randa's concerns about life in Beirut: "What I don't like about Beirut is that I have no place to be private about myself. Wherever I go, I feel I am being watched. People are talking about me, asking about me; maybe I am paranoid. I don't know." Souraya feels the weight of everyday-life surveillance of living in a small city, where "everyone knows everyone," especially surveillance of nonnormativity.

Randa's gender identity is of primary importance to her and has shaped who she is:

> Even before I was a teenager, I didn't feel like I am a girl, but that I would rather be a boy. That shaped my personality, the way I had to defend why I dress that way, or cut my hair that way; from that sense it shaped my personality. Maybe if I like women or even if I felt like a boy, or even when you are taught this is what men do and women do [*pauses*] even if I felt like I wasn't a girl, but I had no problem with wearing a dress and having long hair, I don't think my gender identity would have been that important for me while I was growing up. I didn't have a choice. I was either going to be destroyed, or I had to stand up for myself and defend the choices that I make, the way I live my life.

Randa's gender presentation and performance are the aspects of herself that she needs to defend the most, as they mark her and make her visible. She distinguishes between sexuality and gender by attributing her strength and resilience to her gender nonnormativity. In addition, she says that she had to develop sarcastic humor, another queer strategy, to stay strong. Unlike Yasmine, who feels most comfortable with her gender normativity, Randa's gender performance and experience empower her, making it possible for her to confidently navigate and feel at home in the city.

Even though she is harassed because of her gender nonnormativity, Randa argues that being a woman has provided her with some "privileges." For example, when her mother found out that Randa is sexually attracted to women, she did not kick her out of the house, because she is a woman. Randa recounts that she was "pushed out of the closet" by her mother, who suspected that she was dating a woman. While they were on a vacation outside Lebanon, her mother had asked her whether she prefers men or women, to which Randa responded that she liked women: "What do you want me to say? Lie to her? I won't. I don't like lying. So, whatever, I am like that; I won't change. She said, 'Yeah okay, I know, but I just want to check.'" Randa's mother followed up by telling her that if she were a man, she would have disowned her and kicked her out of the house. Here, Randa laughs and tells me that "patriarchy saved her," since her being a woman provided her a safety net. Since her family believes that they need to protect their daughter, Randa's humorous use of the paradox of patriarchy to save her is a queer strategy that embraces contradictions. Though jokingly, she shows that patriarchy afforded her resources and kept her familial relations intact.

Randa recounts that her mother had pressured her to marry a man, especially after her sister got married and had a baby. Her mother, Randa describes, had suggested that she marry a man, have children, and then divorce: "She wanted me, no matter how, to just make babies. So then I bought her a dog. Now she's happy with the dog," Randa says laughingly. However, given the pressures she was facing from her mother, Randa had seriously entertained the idea of marrying her gay best friend so she could have children, but that never happened.

Unlike others, Randa is critical of those in queer circles in Beirut who treat the process of coming out lightly:

We were all there; we all went through it. Now because it was ten years ago and we read so much about it, do we now just forget it? It is important because at that time it was very central to us and it shaped the way we are today. So I am against biting the hand that fed us.

For Randa, individuals who dismiss the centrality of the coming-out process are choosing to forget how it shaped their experiences. Here, Randa distinguishes between queer and gay activists in Beirut. As explained previously, those such as Mays who work in queer organizing take a more deconstructionist approach to sexuality (Moussawi 2015). By referring to people who "have read so much about it," she is referencing people who reject the coming-out narrative and, according to her, forget about their own coming-out experiences.

In addition to being bullied for her gender presentation, Randa recounts that queer and radical feminists bully her and sometimes talk to her in condescending ways, since they see her as having liberal rather than radical politics. For example, Randa participates in pride events. However, her previous experiences of being bullied make her stronger:

> Now, because I had to stand up for myself before, I feel that I became more equipped to voice and defend my opinion. It also made me accepting of other people. If you reflect on yourself and take a step back, you would see that [self-examination] made me more open to other people's differences. From that perspective, I can say that my gender identity influenced my personality or shaped it a lot.

Randa uses and embraces contradictions as a source of empowerment. Though her gender nonnormativity is a central aspect of herself that serves as a source of personal empowerment, she feels she can get away with more because she is identified as a woman.

Genderqueer individuals, such as Randa and Rabab, are more likely to point out their gender nonnormativity as a source of empowerment. Men, however, seek to maintain their privileged status and hence define themselves in opposition to gender-nonnormative men. In addition, men are less likely to bring up feminist issues or class- and gendered-based discrimination.[12] The majority of the men I interviewed are concerned with maintaining a gender-normative front, even though they do not explicitly frame it as such. They distance themselves from feminine masculinities and think of themselves as gender normative. In addition, many men feel they *are* inherently masculine rather than just *acting* masculine. Men are less likely to see their gender behaviors as performances that they enact; rather, they talk about such behavior as something indicative of who they are. Therefore, for many, enacting gender-normative or masculine behavior means that they are "real men." They express normative masculinities to hold on to their privileged status as men in Lebanon.

Unlike genderqueer and trans persons, cisgender men's discussions of sexual nonnormativity is mostly concerned with same-sex desire and relations between other men. In some cases, this was very evident and explicit. For example, Tarek, who considers himself "naturally masculine," perceives that it is easier for women than men to have same-sex sexual relations in Lebanon. "Women are more likely to be accepted," he says. "Not many people accept gay men or lesbians. Maybe lesbians are accepted more than gay men. Lesbians are more accepted in the world in general." When I ask him about the reasoning behind his claim, he responds:

> One, you see them in movies; they refer to lesbians more. [In] any movie production lesbians are more represented. Straight men accept lesbians more than gay men. Why? Because they find it attractive; they are not threatened by it. They are afraid a gay man might be attracted to them and want to do something to them. I don't want to generalize, but you can see a lesbian couple in Lebanon holding hands; no one says anything.

Tarek argues that it is easier for women in Lebanon to exhibit same-sex relations (such as holding hands in public) than men, since straight men tend to feel threatened by gay men and women are not perceived as threatening. I ask Tarek if he had actually seen women holding hands in the streets of Beirut, to which he replies, "Yes, I have, more than once." I ask him how he knew they were lesbians, to which he answers, "I just assumed, based on the fact that they were holding hands and walking, or hugging." Tarek feels that female public homosocial (or even romantic) behavior is more accepted in Beirut than that between men, suggesting that it is easier for lesbians than gay men to live in Beirut. In his explanations, he does not account for various gender presentations, contexts, or class. Rather, he makes a generalization that it is harder for gay men in Lebanon, as he feels he is personally more policed, especially in public. While the gay travelogues do not account for same-sex relations between women in Lebanon and render them invisible, Tarek intervenes in these fractal Orientalist accounts, arguing the opposite. For him, women have much more leeway than men, as men have to maintain gender-normative fronts.

Tarek's viewpoints are not shared by any of the women or genderqueer individuals I talked to, who point to the prevalence of lesbian invisibility. Men, however, are not as vocal about gender, as they perceive homophobia to be more directly related to sexuality than to gender performances, class, ethnicity, migrant status, or religious sect. However, even though the majority of men do not mention the importance of gender, they still rely on the concepts of masculinity to distance themselves from gender-nonnormative men, a point discussed in more detail in Chapter 4.

Constitutive Contradictions: Beyond Coming Out and Reconciliation

Despite important advances in critical transnational studies of sexuality (Allen 2011; Cantú 2009; Carrillo 2017; Decena 2011; El-Tayeb 2011; Guzman 2005; Manalansan 2003; Puri 2016; Vidal-Ortiz 2014), sociological and anthropological scholarship still downplays political economies of transnational sexualities. While critical sexuality and transnational sexuality scholarship attempts to move away from hegemonic coming-out narratives, some studies have replaced it with what I call a "reconciliation narrative." Reconciliation narratives assume that LGBT subjects need to reconcile what are represented as mutually exclusive aspects of their subjectivities. Reconciliation narratives abstract political economy and context and, therefore, rely on flattened understandings of queerness, religion, and culture. Similar to coming-out narratives, reconciliation narratives are used to gauge the development of global gay and LGBT subjectivity in some places, particularly in the Global South. However, a majority of my interlocutors do not necessarily want to take part in the "gay globality" discussed by a number of LGBT and queer studies theorists (Benedicto 2008, 317; see also Altman 1996; Benedicto 2014). Many LGBT individuals are aware of the multiple exclusions that gay globality is built on and are not necessarily working toward being included by engaging with global gay cultures or movements. Instead, they actively form, practice, and embody conceptions of queerness that centralize context, gender, class, and religious sect.

Both reconciliation and coming-out narratives reproduce binaries and fractals to make intelligible the levels or degrees to which people, places, and cultures are accepting (read as modern) of LGBT identities. Reconciliation narratives are prominently circulated in Euro-American media, such as the travelogues discussed in Chapter 1. While people from the Global South and people of color are particularly represented in these reconciliation narratives, Arabs and Muslims are overrepresented. Arab and Muslim LGBT people are often portrayed by Euro-American media and studies as needing to reconcile their faith and culture with their sexuality.

This chapter focuses on my interlocutors' queer strategies of everyday life and thus shows the limits of reconciliation and coming-out narratives. It moves away from analyses that conceptualize LGBT people as a discernible category and minority and that assume that queer subjects in the Arab world are always in the process of resisting and/or adopting Western conceptions of LGBT identities. My interlocutors do not situate their lives along the lines of this rejection-adoption dichotomy: They do not simply adopt LGBT identities; nor do they really attempt to fit their lives within the dominant Euro-American LGBT framework. This chapter also moves away from a narrative that uses culture as the main lens to explain LGBT people's experiences to one that centers the political economy of sexuality and coming out. While I look at three distinct yet interrelated strategies, I show how these strategies embrace contradiction and are both contextual and shifting. Subject positions, which are informed by larger social contexts, can seem paradoxical and are always shifting. Therefore, the shifting nature of how we inhabit multiple positions makes it harder for us to fit people's lives within intelligible narratives. In the discussion of strategies and shifting subject positions, I do not intend to privilege rationality or claim that these strategic moves are simply by-products of individuals' rational thinking, but they do point to the negotiations of subject positions, social context, and, in many cases, individuals' embodied experiences and feelings of safety. As previously stated, these three strategies are presented as analytically distinct; they are not easily separated when accounting for the everyday. For example, individuals reject narratives of reconciliation while embracing contradiction and disidentifying at the same time. By *disidentifying*, my interlocutors resist and trouble a narrative of modernity, which upholds binaries and fractals in understanding the self, queer subjectivities, and linear understanding of modernity.

Individuals strategically make use of contradiction in their lives to manage gender, sexuality, and everyday-life disruptions. For example, while the hijab for Rabab does not seem contradictory to her position in queer activism, others in her queer networks assume that it is. For Rabab, it was the hijab as a signifier of womanhood that is restrictive rather than its religious connotation. A feminist activist stating that patriarchy saved her is another example of strategic use of paradoxes. A third example is that of Yasmine, who reveals that she feels more comfortable in Lebanon because she does not necessarily have to, as she puts it, "leave a box and enter another." It is precisely this ambiguity that provides her with the security necessary for her to feel comfortable. These examples illustrate the complexities, contradictions, and ambiguities in the strategies that inform experiences of coming out. Thus, they disrupt linear coming-out and reconciliation narratives.

While queer strategies can be understood as related only to LGBT life, they are routinely employed in negotiating everyday life in Beirut. First, individuals use selective disclosure in navigating identities that are not welcome in certain neighborhoods, such as religious sect or gender identities, as Chapter 4 shows. Second, gender becomes very pronounced in how people manage mobility and movement across the city. For example, during moments of constant violence and disruption men's mobility becomes more restricted than women's. Racialized and working-class men particularly become suspect and are stopped and searched more often. While one can understand people's navigation of *al-wad'* through cultures of resilience, the following chapters argue that we must look at the political economies and embodied and affective dimensions of these strategies.

4

Always Visible

"Visibility is not a choice, we are all visible bodies on the streets, we are all making political statements, [and] we are all actively presenting ourselves," Souraya tells me. While some choose to use visibility strategically or purposely to make a statement, we do not always have a choice about whether we are considered marked (nonnormative) or not.

Liberal understandings of coming out contend that it is an integral aspect of LGBT visibility, since it is assumed that when people come out, they are choosing to take ownership by presenting themselves as authentic gay and lesbian subjects. In addition, global rights–based LGBT organizations and homonationalist understandings of gay identities use LGBT (in)visibility as a barometer of the progressiveness of places and people. As discussed previously, fractal Orientalist representations in Euro-American media gauge LGBT life in various parts of the world by relying on the presence of visible LGBT people, neighborhoods, organizations, and establishments. While this approach is useful for understanding affirmative coming-out and visibility strategies of LGBT people and organizations, it assumes linear developmental understandings of time and sexuality. That is, this approach considers LGBT visibility as a manifestation and outcome of (healthy) coming-out experiences and development of LGBT identities. In addition, such an approach takes for granted a normative undisrupted baseline of everyday life. Given the ways that coming out and closet narratives are always contextual as well as racial, classed, and gendered, how does one account for LGBT visibility in Beirut?

This chapter takes up another aspect of *al-wad'*, particularly as it relates to issues of visibility, and asks, In what ways does *al-wad'* open up critical queer strategies of visibility? Thus, I consider *al-wad'* to be a tool of queer survival that makes possible radical reimaginations of queerness, subjectivity, and politics. I consider both conditions and contexts of visibility and the way that visibility is used as a queer strategy of everyday life in Beirut. Drawing on my interlocutors' experiences of everyday-life disruptions and visibilities, I argue that one is always visible, though in various ways, depending on shifting conditions of visibility and legibility and what has been deemed as marked or unmarked categories in certain historical periods, contexts, and situations. While in some cases visibility is about gender, sexuality, and/or ethnicity, it is ultimately about power. The analysis builds on political scientist and queer studies scholar Cathy Cohen's (1997) work on queer politics in the United States and sociologist Jyoti Puri's (2016) work on the role of the "sexual state" in India by conceiving of visibility as always tied to relationships of power, control, and surveillance. As Cohen argues, queer politics needs to take into account the role of the state in defining which populations are defined and marked as suspect and which are not. Similarly, Puri argues that in the applications of the antisodomy law in India, the Indian state actively racializes Muslims as oversexualized and deviant and thus ends up applying antisodomy laws to Muslims, immigrant populations, and LGBT populations. The analysis centers the state as the main site of control and shifts attention to what queer strategies of visibility tell us about geopolitics (which identities and visibilities gain meaning and in what contexts). In addition, it shows how centering the geopolitical flattens fractal Orientalist accounts of gay life in Beirut that rely on mainstream understanding of gay or lesbian visibility as a lens to account for LGBT people's experiences.

Queer strategies are never solely about sexuality, but they are relationships of power that are also used in managing everyday-life disruptions amid *al-wad'*.[1] As already noted, *al-wad'* and shifting everyday-life disruptions in Lebanon contest assumptions of everyday-life normativity. To understand visibility amid *al-wad'*, we cannot grant sexuality primacy or master status. My interlocutors use visibility strategically to negotiate their daily lives in Beirut and to access various public and private spaces. Thus, I consider the tensions and frictions of simultaneously considering context and individual and collective strategies of visibility that are informed by *al-wad'*.

To say one is "always visible" is to move away from an agential or "voluntaristic" understanding of visibility, which sees it *only* as a conscious choice or *solely* an LGBT strategy of empowerment. My interlocutors employ queer strategies of visibility in which they recognize that what is considered visible or marked in a person is not necessarily a personal choice. However, they are able to use such strategies deliberately in navigating everyday life. Instead of thinking of visibility as a manifestation of outness or closeting, I ask that we think of it in terms of complex strategies of maneuvering subjectivities and the everyday disruptions of the city. In disrupting developmental and linear narratives of sexuality, my interlocutors use visibility *as* a queer strategy by attending to what particular moments or situations demand of them. Context, instead of the binary of visibility-invisibility, becomes central—in some instances people need to highlight or downplay certain aspects of themselves, including gender, religious sect, and class, that are not necessarily about sexuality.

This chapter broadens how we define and conceive of queer visibilities by focusing on how conditions and strategies of visibility can be utilized in navigating cities and accessing space rather than visibility as solely an expression of identity. It considers the political economy of visibility, which centralizes individuals' gendered and classed positions and their access to various spaces. Political economy of visibility, rather than identity, provides a framework for understanding how one's markedness grants or denies a person access to networks and spaces. Ultimately, this chapter argues against using mainstream gay visibility as a barometer of freedom of expression and a sign of national/cultural progress of places and people on a global scale.

Understanding queer visibilities as being constantly negotiated at the intersections of multiple (and often shifting and contending) sites of presentation and recognition helps us better get at the slippery nature of visibilities. Thus, I redefine visibility along these three main components: political and productive effects in the world, relationality, and conditions of vulnerability.

First, while visibility is not always about a person's choice or intention, it can be used politically and thus produces something in the world. As geographer Andrew Tucker (2009) reminds us in his work on queer visibilities in South Africa, visibility can and does sometimes involve a choice and intention of making aspects of oneself known to others, such as those that they consider to be political. For many of my interlocutors, especially those active in queer organizing (as opposed to LGBT), to be political is to focus on aspects other than sexuality.

Second, visibility is relational and contextual. What is or what becomes visible has to have shared meaning to people around an individual. For example, two men holding hands in some parts of the Arab Middle East is a sign of homosociality, not homosexuality. The act of holding hands or other particular forms of intimacy has to be intelligible as either homosocial or sexualized for it to have a particular meaning. In Lebanon, working-class migrant Syrian men hold hands as a form of homosocial kinship. Thus, this act becomes about a classed and racialized understanding of masculinity.

Third, visibility creates conditions of vulnerability. Visible aspects of one's self, particularly with regard to what is considered nonnormative, have the potential of making a person more vulnerable to possible harassment, microaggressions, acts of symbolic violence, or outright exclusion and violence. Safety becomes a key issue, since many individuals attempt to highlight parts of themselves or experiences that might be considered safer to express. Taking seriously that queer visibility is constituted by and constitutive of race, class, gender, and religious sect, I ask the following questions: How do people use various queer strategies of visibility in navigating personal and familial networks, as well as city spaces? How do constant everyday-life disruptions create conditions for shifting visibilities and vulnerabilities? How do experiences and strategies of visibility better help us understand everyday-life experiences of disruption?

Visibility as Situation

Visibility, like finding oneself in "the situation," is not necessarily about choice. *Al-wad'* creates conditions in which people have to deal with everyday-life disruptions as a sort of "business as usual" (Fadda-Conrey 2010, 160). Thus, people are carving out spaces based not only on their sexuality but also on gender, class, and religious sect. Amid the shifting conditions of *al-wad'* individuals' visibilities gain new and various meanings based on who is marked and in what contexts. For example, the war in Syria and the displacement of refugees into Lebanon make Syrians a newly marked category in Lebanon by the state and the Lebanese people.

Al-wad' does not follow linear conceptions of temporality. Similar to how the shifting conditions of *al-wad'* demand people's immediate attention, different contexts call on people to manage visibility differently. Queer strategies of visibility disrupt linear understandings of sexuality and time by attending to what a particular moment demands. Therefore, my interlocutors emphasize what particular moments in the present *demand* of them. In this way they illustrate that, like *al-wad'*, visibilities are volatile, highly contextual, and almost always about multiple and intersecting factors. Describing their experiences as gendered, classed, and sectarian subjects, they *queer* visibility by continuously doing what "the situation" already does, which is to disrupt, contest, and reinscribe boundaries. Here, *al-wad'* becomes a creative strategy to reimagine understandings of queer visibility and communities.

While gender normativity affords some people a less marked status on the streets of Beirut, queer visibilities still involve a set of strategic choices that are not solely about gender or sexuality. My interlocutors describe their experiences of visibility with regard to their class, political commitments, standpoints, and values. For instance, some individuals talk about the expectations that they hold certain political views that are in line with those of their religious sect, others focus on religiosity, and many talk about their gendered performances. By focusing on "other" aspects of their lived experiences, they reframe and trouble linear narratives of queer visibilities, particularly those employed by the Euro-American fractal Orientalist representations of Lebanon.

The following sections examine the three aspects of visibility outlined previously: political, relational, and vulnerable. My interlocutors distinguish between two types of queer visibilities. The first relates to personal or individual visibility in terms of whether individuals are visible as LGBT, how they perform queerness, and whether others could tell that they are queer. The second understanding relates to collective queer visibility, including LGBTQ organizing, gay and lesbian spaces, and media representations of LGBT communities.

Visibility as Political

Conditions of daily life and politics in Lebanon challenge understandings of queer visibility that rely solely on gender and sexuality. Yara, who is in her late twenties, lived in Lebanon all her life, except for a year abroad to pursue her graduate education. Yara is of a middle-class background; lived and grew up with her family in Achrafieh, a predominantly Christian neighborhood of Beirut; and then moved to another predominantly Christian city north of Beirut. She moved back to Beirut in her early twenties and now lives on her own. When I ask about her religious background, Yara tells me she is a "full-time atheist," pauses, and then jokingly says, "I am sorry; I am Maronite Christian; I apologize," and then laughs. But then she says, "You know, you have to acknowledge your history." Yara situates yet distances herself from what is considered to be a historically privileged religious sect in Lebanon. Some Maronite Christian parties had a major role, alongside Israeli forces, in the 1982 Sabra and Shatila Palestinian massacre in Lebanon, which led to the death of more than a thousand Palestinians and approximately one hundred Lebanese (Traboulsi 2007).

Yara's political views, especially her commitment to and solidarity with the Palestinian cause, are of primary importance to her. Interestingly, it was easier for her family to accept her as lesbian than accept her support for the Palestinian cause:

> Sometimes people can accept you more if you are queer than if you support the Palestinian cause. Let's consider the context of Maronite—very cultivated, educated [*muthakkaf*]. [Educated Maronites] might . . . accept [you] as a queer person, and they will clap for you, and they will tell you they love you, and they will say look at France . . . but the moment you say you support the Palestinian cause, you get into trouble; you will start arguing. [*Pauses.*] So yeah, visibility about what? Outness regarding what? Sometimes, I feel I need to be out to my family that I support the Palestinian cause more than the fact that I am gay. Because there are whole different sets and levels of reactions.

Lebanese racism against Palestinians trumps Yara's family's homophobia. Yara particularly draws on the image of what she calls a "cultivated" Maronite Christian, who looks to the West as a reference for modernity and progress. Using France as the exemplar, Yara's family reproduces imperial and racialized narratives of progress, locating metrics of modernity in the former colonizer of Lebanon, France. This emulation and reproduction of imperial narratives of progress posit Muslim and Palestinian refugees in Lebanon as undesirable. Here, Yara disrupts the fractals that posit Christians as being more open to LGBT people and frames it contextually. That is, instead of assuming that Christians in Lebanon are simply more open to sexual nonnormativity, Yara recounts that her family is more accepting of coming out as lesbian than of her supporting the Palestinian cause. Acceptance here is contextual.

For Yara, like other interlocutors, the experience of visibility is about the need to make public (embody or verbalize) something that is considered potentially unfavorable or nonnormative. In the context of Yara's family, visibility and coming out have to do more with voicing support for Palestinians than sexuality:

> My family and I, we had a problem, a fight. Now when we talk about queer issues, we have a small argument. They make fun a bit, they're a bit scared of me, so they shut up. But when we talk about Palestinians, we start arguing, and now, it's Syrians. [*Pauses.*] I feel like I need to come out and be visible as supportive of the Palestinian cause and support the revolution in Syria.

Al-wad', as Yara describes, creates new conditions and forms of visibility as well as shifts conditions of vulnerability. Given "the situation" and the rampant racism against Syrian refugees, she feels the need to express and enact her own solidarity. Yara asserts that this issue is not specific to her, since people in "leftist circles," as she calls them, "are coming out as supporters of the Syrian revolution and, thus, get bullied, and vice versa." Yara stresses that she needs to be visible in terms of what are considered unfavorable political opinions within her family circles and some of these leftist circles.

Yara does not organize with LGBT people who do not share multiple viewpoints and political perspectives beyond LGBT issues. She describes her LGBT circle as primarily feminist and inclusive and one that shares values beyond LGBT concerns:

> If you want to talk about a queer circle, how I define my queer circle, [*pauses*] I define it as one that is inclusive of everything. [*Pauses.*] I am queer, and you're queer, and that's the only thing that we have in common. [*Pauses.*] This is not the queer circle I belong to. [The one I belong to] cares about the Palestinian cause, cares about class issues, migrant workers, cares about queer issues, feminist issues as a first obsession; this is the queer circle I belong to. Not only I am a woman; you are a woman; we are both gay; we get together. No! This stopped a long time ago.

Yara seeks transformative LGBT communities and organizations that are rooted in and derive their priorities from *al-wad'* rather than simply LGBT rights. Coming out and being visible as a supporter of Palestinians and Syrian refugees in Lebanon are intertwined with her self-presentation as a feminist. An LGBT community, for her, must be attentive to inequalities beyond sexuality and gay rights, including refugee, feminist, and class issues.

Yara describes how she had looked for a queer(er) community that shares common visions regarding LGBT rights. However, with time, cliques formed within the larger LGBT circle, and she became drawn to people who share transformative political beliefs beyond LGBT politics:

> First, the meeting point was a lesbian community that includes transgender people; then the cliques happened accordingly. If you are a lesbian and you support the Phalanges Party, you and I can't sit in the same place and talk. [*Pauses.*] There is this history where you have killed thousands of people. Not just because you sleep with women,

I am going to accept to talk to you and debate with you politically. [*Pauses.*] It's not that I want to kill and get rid of you, but if you are not open to accepting my point of view, and I am not open to accept what your history has allowed or how you are also brought up, [*pauses*] people are a package that they come with.

The Phalanges Party is a Maronite Christian Lebanese political party believing in Lebanese nationalism and Phoenician rather than Arab heritage and was involved with Israel in the massacre of the Sabra and Shatila Palestinian refugee camps in 1982 (Traboulsi 2007). Yara specifically uses the example of this party to illustrate her refusal to organize with someone who holds political views incompatible with hers.

While discourses around war-torn areas assume that there is a dichotomy between survival and LGBT activism, as anthropologist Nadine Naber and researcher Zeina Zaatari (2014) argue and as Yara illustrates, this is a false binary; the two can and do coexist. Yara believes in queer organizing that acknowledges *al-wad'* and recognizes people's histories and positionalities, and thus organizing is about changing society as much as it is about LGBT issues. Yara does not think that it is possible for her to organize with individuals who do not acknowledge their histories and who hold opposing views on issues fundamental to her, such as the Palestinian cause. As a supporter of the Boycott, Divestment, Sanctions (BDS) movement against the state of Israel, Yara had decided to boycott the concert of Belgian band Placebo, who had recently played a show in Israel. She comments that people say that "I am not civilized because I support the Palestinian cause." This echoes what Naber and Zaatari show in their research on LGBT and feminist antiwar activism in Beirut, where "anyone critical of the United States or Israel" becomes regarded as "a supporter of Hezbollah and therefore a terrorist" (2014, 106). Yara contests definitions of what being civilized entails, asking, "What is civilized? To kill half the people who live in this country because they have a Palestinian identity? They didn't come here because they love you; they came here because they were kicked out of their country." Here, Yara is speaking to the racialization of Palestinians and anti-Palestinian racism, which is taking forms similar to those of anti-Syrian racism. As noted earlier, visibility is largely based on the state's power to define certain populations as marked and nonnormative. For example, with the influx of Syrian refugees, Syrians (particularly men) have become racialized as prone to crime, as sexual predators, and as an undesirable population.

Al-wad' redefines what political acts mean. While for some, queer spaces allow the possibility to openly verbalize their political positions and feel safe, for others, these spaces are regarded as not political enough. Sirine, introduced earlier, feels that she does not have enough space to speak in Armenian in LGBT spaces. Sirine had already graduated from an Armenian school in Lebanon, but since her mother is not Armenian, she does not have as many opportunities to interact and speak in Armenian. However, she has one friend in the queer community whom she can converse with in Armenian in her daily life. She recounts how much she enjoys conversing in Armenian and feels that it is her way of reappropriating queer spaces. Sirine, like Yara, defines a political act as one that highlights aspects of oneself that are not necessarily about sexuality. This becomes especially important for her when other LGBT people tell her that it is rude to be using a language that not everyone understands. For her, given the history of the Armenian genocide, speaking Armenian is a political act, and she argues that LGBT spaces need to be more political:

> This space became a place where I am rediscovering myself. I am making a point of speaking because it's a reappropriation of this space by speaking my paternal tongue. Another racial group tried to annihilate you and your language, so speaking it becomes a political act, and you telling me to shut up is you silencing me. Maybe in another place or context you might want me to be a bit more respectful because you don't understand the language. If I was with my grandmother and she tells me not to speak the language because not everyone understands it and it's rude, then yes, I get it. In another context [such as a queer space] you trying to tell me not to speak is you silencing me because you don't understand that historically this language was supposed to be dead. And me speaking it is a political act; it took me ten years to understand that. Before that I would silence myself and would refuse to speak it.

While Sirine's last name already marks her Armenian heritage, she makes a strategic choice to speak Armenian around other LGBT people as a way of marking a space for herself. Her visibility in LGBT circles is not about gender or sexuality but about highlighting her ethnic background and language. One form of visibility (speaking Armenian, in this case) is a political act, which for her is also an act of survival (communicating in a language that was supposed to become dead). Sirine makes the distinction between what she calls queer and nonqueer spaces; she feels more silenced in queer spaces, since she expects people in these spaces to be more political and potentially self-aware. However, Sirine explains that she is at the point where she feels that ethnic identity is as socially constructed as her sexuality, so whenever she wants to identify herself, she goes back to cultural traits, things that she loves, her upbringing and her language, rather than her sexuality. While she does not attend Armenian pride festivals, she prefers to appropriate spaces in more subtle ways, such as speaking the language in non-Armenian spaces. Speaking Armenian enables her to be a "fuller" version of herself or to express important aspects of herself that she might not be able to in Arabic, French, or English: "It's just a form of expression of the different backgrounds that I find within me. What I find fascinating is that when I speak a different language, a different character would come out; this is why for me everything is about expression."

Clearly, context is very central to Sirine, since she focuses on her experiences of visibility and being political in queer spaces. Similarly, as discussed earlier, Rabab's identification as Shia is also a political response to "the situation" and erasures within Beiruti LGBT circles. While Rabab previously did not necessarily identify as Shia, she says that given the racialization of Sunni-Shia divides and conflicts in the Arab world, including Lebanon, she now more readily identifies as Shia.

Visibility is central for people who in particular contexts hold nonnormative or unpopular political beliefs or standpoints. Similar to Yara, Souraya, who had also been active in LGBT, queer, and feminist movements in Lebanon, states that visibility is important for all people expressing their political position, particularly if it is a marginalized standpoint. She asserts that this could be applied to someone wearing the Palestinian *kufiyah* (a headdress signaling solidarity and support for the Palestinian cause), a rainbow flag, or a religious symbol such as a cross. Souraya believes that people mark themselves and thus become visible when they use these symbols in an attempt to convey their political and/or religious beliefs. However, at the same time, she asserts that visibility is not necessarily a conscious choice. Like the questions raised by Yara, Souraya troubles what we think of as visible by making a distinction between how people define normativity and LGBT visibility: "I don't think visibility is a choice. Why would we call this form of expression visibility, and the women who wear heels and walk in a very feminine way, we call it normativity? They are both visible on the street. Why do we call one visible and not the other?" In line with her argument that we are all visible, she argues that whether one is normative or not, the individual's presence has an effect in the world. By bringing up the example of women who perform "normative Lebanese femininity," Souraya asks why we do not consider them as visible as people who are nonnormative in their presentations. Both, according to her, are visible—yet with varying implications and experiences of gender embodiment:

I think everyone is making a political statement when they walk. Even the woman who doesn't think that she is performing a political identity when she is being very normative, she is still making a political statement of normativity in how society understands her. For me it's not a major issue. I would personally not wear a rainbow flag or something, but there are guys from Helem who I see wearing rainbow bracelets, and for them it is a political statement. For me the *kufiyah* is a political statement; I wear it all the time [in Beirut and other cities in Europe]. Sometimes I feel I am overdoing it, but I feel safe.

Souraya asserts that everyone is visible and making political statements in the ways they choose to be visible, whether they are aware or not. She considers normative presentations, which are viewed as "unmarked," as almost always a way that people also mark themselves and thus become visible. Asserting that everyone is visible, albeit differently, Souraya does not take into account the different positions of power that people occupy and the ways that certain forms of visibility can be safer, based on the context one is in. For example, a rainbow flag (when intelligible) is less safe than wearing a Christian cross on the streets of Beirut. However, wearing a *kufiyah* might be safer in Beirut than in London, where she is currently pursuing her master's degree. Visibility, however, is not only a matter of personal choice. Therefore, while my interlocutors recount their experiences of visibility, it is important to keep in mind that they are also responding to national and geopolitical conceptions of populations (beyond sexuality) as marked in relation to others.

Visibility as Relational

"What is visibility?" Sirine asks. "When I walk on the streets, I don't make an effort to say, 'Hey! Look at me. I am queer.' However, people automatically assume that because I don't have the characteristics that they stamp on a straight person." Sirine recognizes that visibility is not always about an individual's personal choice, arguing that it is largely based on people's perception of what counts as normative. Her queer visibility becomes highlighted only in relation to characteristics associated with straight female femininity, such as long hair, makeup, and tight-fitting clothes. Visibility is relational and intersubjective. For something to be marked, it has to gain meaning in relation to what is deemed normative or unmarked.

Yara echoes Sirine's argument, pointing to how visibility gains different meanings based on shifting contexts:

What is normative [for a woman]? To be thin or to have long hair?
It is to be in this box of "I am a woman," and I am supposed to walk
and sway and put [on] ten kilograms of makeup, and I wear things
that women wear. [*Pauses.*] What do I know? These are things that
are very shallow in gender identifications for women. If you want to
go deeper, even in sexual practices, things get complicated, you know
[*pauses*] butch/femme, et cetera. All these are part of one's gender
identity; if you are this, then you are like that. [*Pauses.*] You know,
everything else disappears from the spectrum, of all the shades of
what you can be, and what you want to be *now* and what you wear.

It is tricky to think about visibility only in terms of gender nonnormativity, as
definitions of normativity are always shifting based on context. Like Souraya,
Yara believes that we are always visible, asserting that gender-normative presentations also make people visible in particular moments and contexts. She
questions the construction of categories of normativity and the shifting nature of what counts as marked or unmarked gender presentations or performances, arguing that the available gender and sexual categories do not
capture the diversity of gender experiences. Similar to Yasmine's unease with
"boxes," discussed in Chapter 3, Yara suggests that definitions of gender and
normativity obscure the multiplicity and various gender enactments possible.
This is most clear when she says, "You know, everything else disappears off
all the spectrum, of all the shades of what you can be, and what you want to
be now and what you wear." By focusing on "now," Yara suggests that there
is not a single decontextualized understanding of visibility. She takes into account that individuals might want to present themselves differently in various
settings, and thus, she, like others, focuses on what particular moments demand of individuals rather than talks about visibility as something static that
elicits similar reactions and/or meanings in different settings and contexts.

Mays also asserts that there are no strict normative codes of masculinity
and femininity in Lebanon. Mays pushes back on the notion that there is
one normative conception of Lebanese masculinity or femininity. Questioning what counts as normative gender performances in Lebanon, she draws
on the example of her father to illustrate that even if one is "not traditionally
normative," one's sexuality is not necessarily questioned. "My father has a
very feminine masculinity," she says. While Mays does not go into detail into
how her father is nonnormative, she asserts that while people can broadly
detect diverse nonnormativities, they do not necessarily mark one as sexually
nonnormative:

In our society, nonnormative gender expressions are not so outside the ordinary. What we make of these expressions [is] where the points of tension are. When you say, "I identify as a gay person," what becomes an issue is taking this up as an identity. Growing up, we had gay men in my life, [and] people were hush hush about it; everyone knew, but the idea is that people acknowledge that there are gay people living among us but . . . that when you make it about who you are, this is when people would say, "What the hell."

For Mays, Lebanese society accepts a wide range of nonnormative gender expressions. However, it is the identification with gender and/or sexual non-normativities that becomes illegible for people who are not LGBT. Mays distinguishes gender nonnormativity from gay identification, arguing that the act of taking up a nonnormative identity is what non-LGBT people might find hard to understand. The majority of gay men I interviewed, however, do not agree with this claim, as they feel most targeted for their gender non-normativity and thus use it as a primary strategy to feel safe and gain access to spaces while navigating the city.

Although there is no consensus on what gender normativity entails, gen-derqueer and trans persons already have to navigate visibility as nonnorma-tive people on a daily basis. Sirine, who grew up as a "tomboy," as she says, has gotten used to being made fun of and being the "odd one out." However, she tells me that decisions about visibility are contextual and are also about compromises, the queer strategies that she enacts. Sirine does not like to wear dresses or makeup. When she was invited to her cousin's wedding, she entertained the idea of attending in drag. However, in instances involving her parents, such as family occasions, she refrains from wearing a suit to safeguard her parents from potential harassment from her extended family. "I don't want them to go through that crap, so I compromise," she said, "and it's okay for that matter." Sirine's statement reflects yet another facet of the po-litical economy of gender. Sirine is okay with making this concession, which reflects an implicit exchange or transaction, to preserve and maintain her kinship and familial ties. She compromises her gender presentation, which is distinct from her gender identity and experience, to safeguard her par-ents from being stigmatized or harassed by extended-family networks. Here, Sirine is not negotiating her gender identity; rather, she is responding to what the moment asks of her and thus compromises her gender performance. By attending to present moments rather than the past or future, queer strategies disrupt linear narratives of visibility and coming out. Queer strategies, such as those enacted by Sirine, centralize context instead of decontextualized notions of visibility and coming out. These strategies are also used in navigating *al-wad'*; people do what the moment demands of them.

Sirine draws on her experiences in France to further highlight the relational nature of visibility:

> I don't want to fall into the stereotype, but once when I was in France, I was at my friend's in a Moroccan neighborhood, and I was leaving her place. I was trashed, and I was walking home, and I had my laptop, and it was three A.M. This guy starts approaching me and telling [me] I am a whore for walking this late at night. I had very red hair at the time. Because I picked up on the fact that he was North African, it was the first time I felt I could stand up for myself, so I cursed him in Arabic, and then he turned and he said, "Tu es Arabe?" [Are you Arab?]. Then he told me, "Sorry, sister; excuse me, sister."

In France, as Sirine notes, both her gender nonnormativity and ethnicity marked her. However, given that she was harassed by a North African Arab man, she felt she was able to respond in Arabic and thus strategically use her "Arabness":

> Yes, I was saying about this Algerian guy who was harassing me, and then I spoke to him in Arabic—suddenly I am his sister, right? "Ma soeur, ma soeur, désolé ma soeur" [My sister, my sister, I am sorry, my sister], but because I am very white looking, in a sense, because he thought I was French, and he was a foreigner and he was harassing me, yet I was more foreign than him.

Sirine highlights the nature of relational visibilities and how she was able to use her foreignness in this incident to mark herself so she could feel safe, which is not the case with her interactions with other white French people. Queer strategies here respond to both relational understanding of visibility and to what particular moments demand of people.

Visibility as Vulnerable

Visibility produces conditions of vulnerability that call for various queer strategies of safety. Yasmine distinguishes between LGBT visibility in Lebanon and the United States: "Visibility doesn't have to be important. In Lebanon, it is less important than in the [United States] just because of the nature of the culture. I feel in Lebanon you are safer when you are not visible. In Lebanon, it is a lot about safety. Safety takes priority over visibility for me." While she explains visibility in terms of Lebanese culture, she is implicitly referring to the political economy of safety. Preferring to feel safe does not mean that Yasmine is not out even though her narrative may make it seem so. Her strategy is another manifestation of responding to what she needs to do in a particular moment:

> When I was with my ex in Lebanon for years, we weren't visible, but our relationship went well. Our relationship wasn't affected by the visibility. We acted like straight people. In Lebanon, it's okay for a woman not to date men, so that helped a lot. That's why visibility is not important; you can say that "I don't date; I want to get married." You can go with this virtuous image. There are many heterosexuals who go out with guys in secret, because they can't go out with them. [*Pauses.*] Everyone has sex, but no one talks about it. So visibility just wasn't part of the culture of being in a relationship, even when I dated a guy.

While she prefers to hold on to privilege and thus be regarded as straight in family contexts in Beirut, Yasmine asserts that heterosexual men and women have to also negotiate visibility, as they do not want to disclose their dating relationships to their parents. Yasmine draws on her own experiences as an upper-middle-class woman whose family expectations are marriage rather than casual dating. Like Sirine, she negotiates visibility by not disclosing her relationship to her family to preserve familial ties. This negotiation is a facet of the political economy of visibility and disclosure. She wants to keep her relationship with her family intact and wants to preserve her and her family's status as upper middle class by not disrupting the norms too much.

Visibility, or signaling your sexuality to others, is important in setting boundaries with other people. Yasmine argues that heterosexuals also do not openly discuss their sex or dating life: "Even the straight couples are not visible. So for us, it wasn't that 'oh, because we are gay, we can't be visible'; it's because you can't be visible in [casual] relationships in Lebanon to start with." When Yasmine says that "straight couples aren't visible," she means that casual dating even among straight couples who are middle-upper class might remain hidden from family members, since the family expectation is to get engaged and married, often to someone from a similar socioeconomic and religious background. Thus, people might conceal their heterosexual relationship if it is with someone from a different religious or sectarian background or class. Responding to the moment, Yasmine prefers not to be visible as lesbian with her family; however, she chooses to be visible when she tries to set boundaries with straight men: "Whether I am in [a] straight or a gay relationship, visibility is important just for being able to set the boundaries of other people."

At the collective level, Yasmine believes in the importance of LGBT visibility as an activist strategy for social change. However, she finds that for LGBT visibility to be successful, it has to be done in a particular manner: "Visibility is important, but I think it has to be smart in a marketing way." She continues:

> To have someone famous come out is more important than me coming out—someone who is respected, who is a thinker, who is educated. [*Pauses.*] It is the people who don't go to protests who should be going. The people who are there are people who are "more out." Others will say, "Look at these freaks!" I think part of it is to show them that [gay] people are similar to them. It's like you [designate] a spokesperson to speak to people. I know it's very mean, but it's what works best. It breaks the stereotypes of gay people but adds the stereotypes of expected gender identity. It's not a straightforward answer, but as a marketing tactic it would work more in *our* favor.

Yasmine draws on her experience as a business marketer and argues that it is important to have celebrities and intellectuals come out. She is primarily concerned with educating the public by having gender-normative individuals and what she assumes the public will view as "respectable" gays and lesbians represent the movement. She echoes a strategy that is in line with politics of assimilation: "We are like you, just gay." Since she worries about safety, Yasmine finds that an approach that highlights similarities to the norm is more effective and less harmful for LGBT individuals.

Yasmine's understanding of public visibility is focused on a collective visibility centered around LGBT positionalities that can present themselves as normatively gendered. However, as Naber and Zaatari (2014) illustrate, during the 2006 Israeli war against Lebanon, members of Helem and other visibly queer activists were able to be primary actors in relief and humanitarian work. Helem, for example, first became publicly visible as an active participant in working with internal refugees and people fleeing areas under attack (Naber and Zaatari 2014). Helem's antiwar activism was public— it provided resources and offered its center as shelter—and it retained its identity as an LGBT organization. In this case, Helem and other queer and feminist activists' civic engagement in times of crisis led them to be a visible group that was doing primary relief work. Their work and visibility became tied to geopolitical issues, such as the war against Lebanon.

Yasmine worries about safety and argues that discrimination within LGBT circles, even for marketing perspectives, is not good:

> I think [LGBT visibility] is important, but it is very limited in Lebanon; some people will pay the price. That's why people are visible, present physically in certain spaces that are safer. Being able to be yourself and be trans there, being present and treated with respect is important. [*Pauses.*] I think, like, feminist movements [*pauses*] they distanced themselves from lesbians in order to grow.

In Beirut, feminist and sexual health organizations have had to distance themselves from LGBT groups to grow and gain publicity, and Yasmine does not consider this to be a fair strategy.[2] Yasmine sees the merits of visibility at a collective level but desires caution at the individual level, arguing that women's safety trumps any other experience:

> Physical presence is important; however, I think of it as secondary compared to women's presence—all women: gay, straight, trans, because their physical presence is attacked. I don't feel safe walking in shorts in Hamra, so I don't feel this is my physical space. At the university, I only used to feel safe when I entered campus, and I felt unsafe when I went out. It's like a different world, a gated community.

Yasmine has always felt less physically safe in Beirut and is anxious about possibilities of harassment and cat-calling on the street. This makes Beirut feel less "her space," and consequently she feels safer in the gated community of one of the two major American universities in Beirut. In the United States, she feels physically safer, even though she does not feel that she belongs:

> In the U.S., I feel safer physically; I can wear whatever I want. [*Pauses.*] I feel much safer, though, not politically safer. In Lebanon, there is no single time when I walked on the streets that I wasn't cat-called. There is this threat that [men] have the right, that they have the power; I always felt weaker. I love Beirut, but all my life I had this

constant background fear, fear of a lot of things—people know—I was afraid of visibility if I was smoking or drinking or wearing a short skirt. There is always a fear of someone saying something to me, of someone [raping] me, someone [saying] something to my parents.

Yasmine recounts that Beirut's streets are controlled by men. As Chapters 2 and 5 discuss, genderqueer persons enact strategies that make public spaces, particularly streets, their own. Yasmine's anxieties, like those of Tarek and Rabab, are often linked to fears that their parents would learn about their sexuality or that their immediate families would be harassed by extended family: "People learn to ignore fear, but I felt it all my life because I was against everything my parents want me to do in so many ways. I had so many experiences that I was always afraid." Prioritizing feelings of safety, Yasmine strategically comes out as nonnormative rather than lesbian.

Yara, like Yasmine, expresses that visibility and safety are continually being redefined based on multiple and shifting contexts:

Visibility in terms of being queer: Sometimes it's easy; sometimes it isn't. Sometimes it poses a danger and threat to your life, and sometimes it's okay. [*Pauses.*] When you are talking politics and you are taking a political side, there are a lot of "coming outs" to do. But in general, coming out as a gay person might make you lose your job, lose your family, go to jail. If we want to dig deeper, there are political fights you can come out to, or even coming out as an atheist, and these can cause you a lot of trouble.

In the context of *al-wad'*, individuals have a number of coming outs and situations to deal with alongside their sexuality. The situation creates particular conditions of vulnerability and visibility, and since it is constantly changing, vulnerability and safety also constantly take on new and shifting meanings. Yara's focus on the centrality of context and her multiple positionalities disrupts the framing of questions around LGBT visibility and safety that focus only on sexuality and gender. Though not explicit, she centralizes *al-wad'* by comparing the dangers of being visibly queer in certain areas in Beirut to the dangers of expressing undesirable political viewpoints in some neighborhoods. She says that in Lebanon, as elsewhere, there is always some issue to be wary about, whether it is sexuality or political opinion, and people often have to go through processes of strategic concealment and speaking up as a form of coming out. Yara sees her experiences of coming out as lesbian to be less exceptional in relation to other forms of coming out, such as political opinion or religiosity (in her case, atheism). *Who* and *where* people choose to say or share their political opinion is central to how it is received.

Classed and gendered performances are also used strategically. Yara, like many interlocutors, uses shifting gender performances as a key to safety and security in certain situations:

> How important is my performance? It is really important actually, my gender performance. Definitely. In certain areas, if you were going somewhere and you are performing your gender as a woman, sometimes it complicates stuff, but sometimes it's easier because you can get what you want easier. Sometimes being a woman and performing gender as a feminine woman, it makes things more complicated because you get harassed, so it depends really what you want to get out of this performance.

Yara, like Rabab, contends that performing femininity as a cis woman can either help or make situations more complicated. Both Yara and Rabab recount their experiences of selective gendered performances, centralizing the role of audiences and people with whom they interact. Since gender performances are relational, *how* people respond to and engage is as important as the performance and experience of gender itself. Even if one chooses to perform normative femininity, it is not always received as such because of the ways people process and interpret performances rather than take them at face value. Yara understands gender performances to be continually shifting based on context:

> You play with it; it's just a game; it's a theater where I want to be a normative woman today; I go to a [business] company; I don't know. [*Pauses.*] Sometimes they greet you better, or something like that, or while if you were a dyke with a shirt and going to a company, they would look at you like, why did she do this to herself?

Yara regards gender as something that one can play with and likens it to a "game." The political economy of gender, as she points out, illustrates how certain gender performances can potentially be utilized to access space. Her description highlights the relational and transactional way that she conceives of gender, wherein gender performances become symbolic capital, allowing one access.

Yara, however, does not account for unintentional visibilities and trans experiences. Many of the men I spoke with emphasize the importance of normative gender presentations as a key for safely navigating the city and gaining access to space. Being associated with feminine-acting men meant that one could be assumed to be gay or queer and therefore more vulnerable and prone to possible harassment. While Yara and other queer women conceive of gender as something that one performs, men, such as Tarek, see gender as indicating something internal to a person—being a man is not about performance but an internal part of oneself.

As already discussed, gendered and sexual visibility are vexed and are best understood based on context. For Mays visibility is never about one aspect of a person's social location. Even though global mainstream gay organizing tends to make LGBT visibility solely about sexuality, Mays insists that gender, class, and racialization play central roles, where the visibility of some people happens at the expense of others. In addition, aspects of one's gender presentation and performance are marked and therefore visible only in a particular context. She describes her experiences of attending a young Arab feminist meeting: "Most people told me this is against religion. In such spaces, it made me extremely uncomfortable, but I had to speak from a position of a lesbian. It depends on the space; it is about context. In other contexts, it is simply a detail." Not only is context central to understanding how bodies and people become visible, but visibility is always a relational process with possible consequences. For example, in the workplace, one might be discriminated against and possibly kicked out of a job for being nonnormative:

> It always comes at the expense of others; the more racialized, nonhomonormative, these are the visible. It is a conscious choice—I think that it is—if you are visible in your workspace, everybody accepts you and it's great, and if not, then you change jobs? What are you going to do? It is something you negotiate all the time. I think people can detect whatever isn't normative.

For Mays, visibility can be a choice for gender-normative people. Given her experiences in LGBT and then feminist and queer organizing, Mays believes that visibility should never be the end goal of an LGBT community, particularly since certain bodies—gender nonnormative and racialized—are always marked and, hence, more visible. Mays and Randa both agree that people can "detect whatever isn't normative," though they don't explicitly define what normativity entails.

Randa distinguishes between gay, lesbian, and trans visibility. For her, it is very important to avoid lumping people's experiences together:

Gay visibility is different from lesbian visibility from trans visibility—so typically, the clothes, the gym (gay men), the brands, expensive clothing. However, lesbian visibility—she has short hair; she walks and talks like a man, even though this is a very old stereotype—and now the picture is changing in Lebanon. For example, if people see two women together all the time without men, they would start understanding that they are not simply best friends; these are a couple; they are always together.

According to Randa, the concept of visibility is also changing; gay and lesbian visibility is no longer only recognized through the prism of gender nonnormativity. She says that people are more able to pick up on lesbian and gay couples if they see a same-sex couple spending a lot of time together. She recounts that once people would mostly rely on gender nonconformity, but people can now "guess" someone's sexuality by relying on other or different cues. Though the media relies solely on exaggerated gender nonnormativity in its depictions of gay and lesbian characters, Randa asserts that Beirutis are smarter than that. She continues: "This visibility is changing not only for women, for men too. People are more clever now, so now they know if someone is gay even if he is not *typically* gay." This changing conception of visibility and greater awareness beyond gender nonnormativity increase conditions of vulnerability for queer and LGBT individuals.

Visibility and the Lebanese Media

In March 2014, FutureTV aired an interview with a random Lebanese woman, Amal Hamadeh, about *al-wad'* in Lebanon. In what became a viral three-minute video, Hamadeh, in her late thirties, describes how the escalating situation and violence in Lebanon are causing people so much anxiety that they are no longer leaving their houses, not even to celebrate events such as Valentine's Day or Mother's Day (which in Lebanon is on March 20). Hamadeh mentions that she is single because of *al-wad'* and because "men in Lebanon are extinct": "They have been taken to war," she says, "but also, they have all become gay. Wherever I go, I meet gays." Hamadeh's statement "men are extinct" went viral, to such an extent that she became an internet celebrity, routinely interviewed by TV stations about topics ranging from the status of men in Lebanon, to the garbage crisis and corruption, to celebrity gossip. Hamadeh's following, until her sudden death (from a stroke) in November 2018, was largely Lebanese gay men—she became a Lebanese gay icon of camp in the short period of three years. "Men are extinct" became a viral meme and, along with other of her statements, the phrase was mixed with Arabic music in gay dance clubs. Her statement provides an unprecedented visibility: By jokingly invoking all men in Lebanon as gay, she broke the stereotype that gay men can be visible only through their gender nonnormativity. At the same time, by saying that men are extinct since they have all become gay, Hamadeh equated "a man" as straight by definition. Her conflation of manhood and straightness is a common stereotype perpetuated by the media that many of my gay male interlocutors negotiate.

Media and social media representations, as sociologist Imogen Tyler (2013) points out, are components of everyday public life, including the street. Local Lebanese media representations of LGBT characters are mostly focused on gay male characters and trans women. Gay male characters are always centered on gender nonnormativity, hypersexuality, and the image of the *tante*—the French term for "auntie." *Tante* is used among many Lebanese to refer to nonheterosexual men who are both feminine acting and are generally interested in gossip. Even though people are "smarter," as Randa says— since they understand that gay men and lesbians can be gender normative— she points to the Lebanese media continuing to use exaggerated portrayals based on gender nonconformity, most notably gay femininities, to represent gay characters. Viewers are also more likely to accept cartoonish images of gender-nonnormative men rather than representations of gay men who embody working-class masculinities. The political economy of representation is central to the various ways that Lebanese gay men are depicted and how these representations shift based on venue and audience. Whereas the gay travelogues analyzed earlier are more likely to represent gay men in Lebanon through the image of the bear and as possibly more buff and hypermasculine, local Lebanese TV represents gay men as overly feminized. The gay travelogues show the men as discreet, while Lebanese TV depicts them as flamboyant, with an emphasis on their overly feminine self-presentations and obsession with sex. These representations are part of the global femme phobia and transnational circulations of caricatures of gay men.[3]

Though Lebanese media's representations of local gay characters rely on overexaggerated images of sex-crazed and overtly feminine men, Randa argues that this still has the potential to introduce the general public to gay people. Speaking of the importance of collective LGBT visibilities, Randa says, "It is very important. For people, it is like a strange-looking thing that you get used to with time; this is how important it is. If you look at all the comedy shows, they all have a gay character, but represented as repressed sexually and obsessed with [the] penis." Though it is no surprise that abject figures are usually represented in cartoonish manners (Tyler 2013), these images are meant to be entertaining while invoking revulsion and disgust in audiences. As Tyler argues, media representations of "the abject" aim to produce images that are both recognizable and affective (2013, 9).

Randa describes a Lebanese soap opera about a rich father who refuses to give his son an inheritance because he is romantically involved with another man:

> There is another show—I forgot its name—but it is about a family with money. There is a scene on the terrace. The son, a bit of [a] *tante*, and his boyfriend live there. His father comes in, and the boyfriend says, "I am going to go get stuff from the shop," while pouting his lips. It's good that they show this action, that they show a gay character like that. The gay man is chubby; he talks in a feminine way. Now you still can't show a mechanic who's very masculine and gay, even though you should, but people don't accept that yet. No one has shown this yet.

Gayness and nonnormative masculinities are classed attributes. Not only are gay characters portrayed as overly feminine, but they are also represented as middle to upper class. Representing working-class gay masculinities, according to Randa, would make people uncomfortable, as these depictions contradict people's stereotypes of gay men and, thus, become unintelligible.

Randa also asserts that stereotypical images have the potential for and actually do end up empowering some men who appropriate these representations and identify with such characters. Since gender-nonnormative men are hypervisible in daily life and more prone to harassment, these representations can be empowering:

> What's nasty is that there's a large part of the community that is, like, overly feminine, and they are the ones who are most visible—the highest visibility—that's what changes the formula, because when you are *that* gay and really like Majdi and Wajdi, some people you can't help but notice that the way they act is different [overly feminine, for example]. Their sense of difference translates to the way they act. But if people see it more on TV, it will make them get used to it more. For some, they just become secluded; others become extroverts. If you are an extrovert, you become empowered; being gay or trans makes you stronger, makes you speak out. [*Pauses.*] You know what I mean?

Majdi and Wajdi are two fictional gay characters in the Lebanese sketch comedy *Ma Fi Metlo* (Nothing like it), which airs on the Lebanese MTV. Majdi and Wajdi are overly feminized men represented as always wearing tight-fitting clothes, short colorful T-shirts that expose their torsos, and gaudy sunglasses. They sashay and skip down the streets of Beirut holding hands, though they are meant to be only friends. Their comedy scenes present them as obsessed with the phallus. For example, they are depicted using hookah tubes as replacements for penises and sometimes mistaking microphones for penises. Randa humorously says that while some Lebanese men act like that, it does not represent the whole spectrum of gender performances.

Representations such as Majdi and Wajdi are less about Lebanese culture and more about producing abject subjects and further policing everyday-life gender performances. Portraying gay men as masculine contradicts Lebanese popular knowledge that gay men are and can be gender normative, if not masculine. Randa's point on the potential empowering effects of the visibility of gender-nonnormative representations illustrates how potentially harmful images can be taken up by those they claim to represent. These images, however, are not meant for gay audiences but are directed to the wider public. Such representations allow gender-nonnormative gay men, who are unintentionally visible, to benefit from having outspoken, overly feminine gay characters on Lebanese TV. This "paradoxical visibility," as sociologist Joshua Gamson (2014, 231) calls it, presents an image that is not necessarily only about the experiences of suffering that gay men encounter in their lives. An unintended consequence of such depictions is that they redraw the lines between what they consider to be normal and abnormal gender and sexual practices. Randa insists that presenting gender-nonnormative gay men on television allows people to get more used to the idea:

> I don't think it is bad; you are exposing people to homosexuality and the fact that there are homosexuals in this community. These examples are entering homes that watch TV; the fact that almost every TV station is having that character and that every TV has its own sectarian audience, then they are all exposed. [*Pauses.*] It is mostly good because they have this gay character on every TV station and every home and the kids are exposed to it; however, it is bad because it shows that all the gays act like Majdi and Wajdi, and they only care about the penis.

Randa pauses and laughingly says, "Now, they're not really lying about this, but still [*pauses*] you have the thinkers, the people who want to change, the people who are harassed, made fun of, the prisoners; there are many factors that they don't include." Randa sees some merit in the exposure these representations provide, but they exclude many people. Randa is upset that these shows do not represent various masculinities or any lesbian or queer women. She asserts that this phenomenon, which she referred to as "the eternal lesbian invisibility," is a global one.

In addition to soap operas and comedy sketch shows presenting the increasing visibility of gay characters, talk shows tackling the topic of homosexuality in Lebanon and the Arab world are the other major venue for representation of homosexuality on Lebanese television. These shows invite guests who present their personal testimonies and life stories, as well as experts from the Arab world (usually psychologists and/or religious authorities) who provide commentary on the narratives and the issue at hand. Even though some aspects of these representations have shifted, particularly by adopting more neutral language in discussions of homosexuality, these TV shows almost always conflate gender nonnormativity with sexual nonnormativity and conflate homosexuality with trans issues. In addition, the invited guests, or "informants," are often made anonymous by blurring their faces and distorting their voices, though more guests have been appearing without distortion more recently. The questions asked of guests usually revolve around gender identity, stigma, sexual desire, and societal reactions.

For example, a quintessential episode of the Lebanese talk show *Ahmar Bil Khat Al Areed* (Red in bold font), which aired on January 28, 2009, by the Lebanese Broadcasting Corporation (LBC), tackled the topic of "homosexuality in the Arab world." In a spectacle-like interrogation, Malek Maktabi, the host, questions one of his guests, Alfred, a Lebanese man in his late thirties who does not identify as either homo- or heterosexual. Alfred wears an earring and is somewhat gender nonnormative:

MAKTABI: Did you decide to come here as a woman or a man?
ALFRED: I come as Alfred, who is different.
M: I am asking you about your sexual identity. Are you a man or a woman?
A: I am a man.
M: Alfred, I have a question: you have an earring on . . .
A: This is an accessory.
M: Does a man wear accessories?
A: If he wants to, why not?
M: Doesn't that negate the concept of manhood?
A: For some people, yes.

M: No, not for some people, for *most* people.

A: Maybe.

M: It's the great majority. With your behavior, aren't you creating more revulsion against another category of people—more specifically, of homosexuals?

A: Maybe. If they care about the way I look.

Maktabi explicitly interrogates Alfred's sexual identity by asking if he identifies as a man or woman. He focuses on Alfred's gender identification and presentation to speak to and make his homosexuality intelligible to the audiences.

Maktabi, like many other Lebanese TV hosts, enacts a trial-like spectacle, questioning and interrupting invited guests while inviting medical and religious expertise to support poorly researched arguments and moral judgments. He clearly does not listen to his invited guests but interrupts and asks questions, which contradicts any democratic attempt at letting people freely express their ideas or conceptions on the topic. In addition, the topic of homosexuality is treated with no consideration of the fact that individuals have multiple positions and standpoints that complicate their experiences. Lebanese talk shows like Maktabi's reinforce values of respectability by distinguishing between normative and nonnormative desires, practices, and sexualities. Similar to Alfred's case, Lebanese talk shows take the form of interrogations. The shows always end by focusing on how law, mental health, and religion delineate what counts as acceptable and normal gender and sexual behavior and identifications. While these representations provide a type of visibility for gender and sexual nonnormative individuals, the stories conflate gender and sexuality and police the line between what is or is not considered moral and acceptable. This policing is not only limited to TV representations but is also quite dominant among gay men, who in their everyday lives distance themselves from what they consider to be feminine-acting men.

Visibility and Masculinities

In 2007 and 2008, I conducted interviews with nonheterosexual Lebanese men about masculinities. All the men were aware of popular culture's conflation of gender with sexual nonnormativity. While they considered this conflation to be inaccurate, they still felt most vulnerable and lost power when they were seen and considered as gender nonnormative. Thus, gender normativity confers social privileges on gay men, whereas overtly feminine men are the targets of routine harassment and exclusion. However, gender nonnormativity is highly classed and raced; the men who do not have classed benefits are the most harassed. For example, crackdowns and police arrests usually target working-class individuals, migrant workers, and refugees (Makarem 2011). A number of my interlocutors mentioned that establishments are less likely to target or refuse service to gender-nonnormative men from the Arab Gulf states, since they are wealthy tourists. Class and race are very central in understanding exclusions targeting gender-nonnormative men in Beirut.

Even though almost all the men I interviewed reject notions of hegemonic straight masculinity, they also reject what they perceive as feminine men. Being regarded as a *rijjal* (real man) is a central concern. My interlocutors speak of a relational conception of masculinity that distances them from straight masculinities, on the one hand, and nonnormative enactments of masculinities, on the other hand. They point out that both are harmful to the image of men, since they rely on stereotypical and exaggerated gendered performances. Many assert that their gender-normative enactments are not a performance, since they are naturally masculine and do it without consciously trying. Even though they have slightly differing conceptions of Lebanese masculinity, almost all of them characterize it by the image of the *rijjal*: a man who is physically strong, well groomed, loud, and proud of his sexual prowess. While they disagree with the general public and media's conflation of gender nonnormativity and sexual nonnormativity, they still distance themselves from gender-nonnormative men.

Whereas women and genderqueer individuals express the importance of context and the multiple ways they can play with gender, men had a more rigid conception of gender. When I asked men whether they consider themselves masculine, those who said no also insisted that they are not feminine either, even though I did not ask. Most define their masculinity in terms of not being typically masculine, but also not being feminine. They reject both the extreme ideal of heterosexual masculinity and the stigmatized status of feminine men. Thus, almost all of my male interlocutors consider themselves broadly masculine and express a decidedly negative view of feminine men. Even though they distance themselves from heterosexual masculinity, they define themselves in opposition to the abject position of nonnormative and feminine men.[4]

Unlike Randa's claim that men might benefit from the representations of gay characters such as Majdi and Wajdi, the men I interviewed found such depictions to be harmful. By distancing themselves from the abject positions of feminine gay men, gay men *become* men. Thus, masculinity is highly relational (Connell 1995; Pascoe 2007; Pascoe and Bridges 2016). Though many of my male interlocutors fear that people conflate gender nonnormativity and sexuality, they still use the same method when talking about themselves. For instance, when I asked Mazen, a gay medical student in his mid-twenties, whether he considers himself to be masculine, he wondered whether I could tell he was gay. Thus, he understands his gender performances and visibility to be indicative of his sexuality. Though he believes that people should not conflate gender and sexuality, he still assumes that his gender performance indicates something about his sexuality. On more than one occasion, many of my interlocutors ridiculed feminine gay men in Beirut. "It is funny how gay men make fun of other gays in the community," Mazen said. "Everyone is a *tante*." Mazen was quite uncomfortable with feminine-acting men and argues that gay men should not act feminine. "If you want to be a woman," he said, "then be one." According to him, a man's mannerisms are quite important, and he considers it quite central for a man, whether gay or straight, to maintain gender normativity. He adds that he does not have any feminine-acting gay friends and that all of his gay friends are "straight acting." "I wouldn't be comfortable with a guy who is very feminine, especially in ordinary places" (places that are not gay friendly). Like Tarek, Mazen expresses discomfort in being seen with feminine-acting men in routine social situations.

Salim, a twenty-four-year-old gay graphic designer, also ridiculed feminine gay men on more than one occasion during our interview. Salim claims that feminine gay men, whom he refers to as "queens," harm the gay community in Lebanon. He draws parallels between the way "feminine gay men" project a negative image of the gay community and the way "hypermasculine" men project a bad image of straight men. The harm is linked to the fact that they present a stereotypical image of a gay man as lacking valued masculine traits. "They are not doing well for the community and for its public image as a whole," he says.

Joe, a gay man in his mid-twenties from a working-class background, expresses outrage at those he considers to be "closeted" gay men and extremely flamboyant men. Yet he is aware that he displays some feminine attributes, most apparent in the way he walks and gestures with his hands. He relates that men, even after having sex with him, tend to distance themselves from him in public:

> I will be walking with a man on the streets after having been with him for the night, and he will constantly tell me how to act and how not to act. For example, he would give me comments on the way I move and walk by telling me to stop moving my hands or stop walking the way I do. So what if I moved a little bit feminine? Some men

also walk in front of me or behind me and refuse to walk next to me on the streets.

Joe adds that even his sister used to get upset at him because of his gender-nonconforming mannerisms when, for example, they would go out dancing. At the same time, even though Joe does not consider himself to be masculine, he does not see himself as feminine either. In fact, he rejects feminine men: "Even though I am gay, I get pissed off and angry when I see a feminine guy. I don't know why. I just don't want to be with a feminine guy." When I inquire more into his perception of feminine men, Joe says that these are men who wear makeup and refer to each other by feminine pronouns. He believes that some people view him as gay not because he is feminine but because he has what he calls a "soft" (na'im) demeanor. That is, he is soft-spoken and does not display rugged masculinity.

Almost all the men I interviewed agree that there is discrimination against gender-nonnormative men in Beirut, and Karim says that the same discrimination also exists even within the gay community. "They are not very welcome," he says, "because if you're seen with someone who is feminine, you are directly associated with or thought of as gay. It makes many people uncomfortable." In fact, Karim asserts that things are getting worse for non-normative men in Beirut because men are obsessed with their body image and with being muscular and fit. "Part of it is reaffirming their masculinity. The image is very important. There's an obsession with being fit and looking good and being viewed as ordinary." Karim acknowledges that he too was once quite uncomfortable with feminine gay men, but this attitude changed: "If I want people to accept me for who I am, then I have to accept the other guys for who they are."

Raed, a twenty-three-year-old graphic designer, and Wael, a college student in his early twenties, also talked about how feminine men are excluded within the gay community. Wael terms this exclusion "sissyphobia," which is even more pronounced in the broader culture. Wael recalls being ridiculed at school for not performing normative masculinity. During his high school years, he was called names, such as *tobje* (fag), even though he had not thought of himself as gay at that time. Tarek knows a few gay-identified feminine men, but his fear has meant that he is not close to them: "I don't mind them, but I don't understand why they have to be so obvious or why they act that way. I am sure they're not doing it on purpose, but I still don't understand why." When I ask him to describe a feminine guy, he says that it is a man who "acts like a woman, uses hand gestures and body language, [and] is interested in makeup and shopping." Khaled was the only who does not mind feminine-acting men: "I completely understand where they're coming from. They are very courageous. They have a lot of guts to do what their instincts tell them to do." Finally, and most strikingly, Tarek summarizes the views of many men I interviewed:

> In Lebanon, if you're gay, you're no longer considered a man. It is the close-minded and illiterate people who think that. You're not considered a man, even if you are very masculine, as long as you are gay. It doesn't matter. There might be some exceptions, but generally this is the rule. If you're straight and feminine, you also have a problem.

Tarek's fear of being viewed as "less of a man," shared by many of my male interlocutors, suggests that being gay implies a loss of one's masculine status. This is reminiscent of Hamadeh's statement, discussed previously, that "men are extinct," in reference to the fact that she believes that all men have become gay. Tarek, like Hamadeh, asserts that being gay emasculates men, especially in the minds of the general public. Tarek also claims that if one is straight and not normatively masculine, he also faces some setbacks. Masculine gender identities and performances are the mechanism by which men retain their privileged status and experiences in Beirut. Instead of using masculine performances strategically in response to certain moments and contexts, as is the case with women and genderqueer individuals, the men I interviewed claimed that they have to "be men" (act masculine) at all times, particularly in public, so as not to be harassed.

Visibility, Disrupted

My interlocutors' experiences of visibility disrupt the dominant Euro-American binary of LGBT visibility and invisibility and render metrics around LGBT visibility to be less relevant in gauging the presence or progress of LGBT life in places. Instead, conditions of visibility and legibility become more central to whom, when, and where and what work that visibility does. My interlocutors disrupt fractal distinctions that rely on notions such as out versus closeted and visibility versus invisibility to assess whether places are gay friendly or not. For example, Rabab and Sirine's experiences of cities (in Lebanon and France) help us unsettle the idea that urban spaces, such as those in Beirut, are assumed to be generally more open and progressive than those in the rest of Lebanon.

While describing how they navigate the city, my interlocutors argue that negotiating and maneuvering various parts of the city and country do not have to do with "concealing" or "publicly asserting" their sexuality but about how they are read in certain contexts. They rely on shifting performances—as forms of "code-switching"—to maneuver various parts of the city differently.[5] Being aware and reflexive of how one is read (whether intentionally wanting to present normatively or unintentionally being read as belonging to a certain category), whether it is in a village, Beirut, European cities, or at checkpoints or bars, is very important. In addition, many recount multiple forms of intentional and unintentional visibilities, disclosures, and strategies that are not about sexuality. For example, many have to hide or conceal certain political viewpoints that were not always considered popular in a particular neighborhood or area. This, of course, changes based on shifting Lebanese groups' political alliances, geopolitics, and wars.

My interlocutors recounted their experiences of visibility on the streets of Beirut, as well as in LGBT circles, in ways that account for the multiplicity of their social locations. While gender plays a central role in people's understandings of gay, lesbian, and trans visibility, visibility in Beirut is negotiated primarily in relation to context and gender, class, ethnicity, immigrant status, political identification, and religious sect.

Gender nonnormativity is policed on the streets and in private establishments in Beirut, as well as Lebanese media; however, it usually targets those who are nonnormative in their gender expression and from low-income backgrounds. For example, Rabab explains how her reception as a working-class Shia man rather than a Shia woman afforded her distinct sets of experiences. While an intersectional analysis is important for illustrating the multiple positions that inform people's visibility and strategies of visibilities, it is not enough to account for or explain the political economies of visibility and unintentional visibilities. Thus, strategies of visibility involve complex tactics of maneuvering through the city rather than decontextualized manifestations of closetedness or outness—tropes used by fractal Orientalist depictions to gauge gay life and progressiveness. The next chapter examines the ways that my interlocutors use queer strategies of retreating from *al-wad'*. While community has failed a number of them, they still create spaces and relationships, what I call "bubbles," that allow them to "recharge." In some cases, these bubbles unwittingly deny *al-wad'* and reproduce exceptionalist narratives about Beirut.

5

The Bubble

"Whether we like it or not, the majority of us live in our own bubble, and even though we believe we are radical, we are not," Souraya tells me as she describes "the bubble," a temporary sheltered "place" where she and her friends retreat to resume their lives in Beirut amid *al-wad'*. Being radical, for Souraya, means having to face the conditions of everyday-life disruptions without denying them or hiding. Souraya goes as far as to say that even activists who think they are radical are not really so since they do not acknowledge their privilege, one of which is inhabiting or living in a bubble:

> Some people can afford to; they can protect themselves and not see the other face of reality, and other people create trenches, like me, who live in them and don't need to deal with things they don't want to deal with because they are simply *tired*. They can, of course, if they can afford to.

Rather than speaking about the power of "resilience," Souraya, a feminist and LGBT activist, openly expresses being exhausted from *al-wad'* and needing a safe place to retreat. Thus, what Souraya and many of my interlocutors call a "bubble" serves as an in-between space where people can retreat alone or among other queer kin and then resume their everyday activities. Souraya describes her experiences of the bubble as a trench, explicitly invoking the image of soldiers' shelter in the battlefields. While a trench is much more about place and groundedness—since people dig out ground to hide in—the bubble is not necessarily a material place; rather, it is an experience or a space of pause and suspension. Souraya acknowledges that it takes a certain amount of privilege to lead a (semi)sheltered life and inhabit a bubble. Not everyone has access to temporary protections or bubbles as a way to retreat from *al-wad'* and feel a sense of bounded security in Beirut. In addition, Souraya is concerned that those who do inhabit bubbles might end up becoming too immersed in them, that they might end up forgetting or denying the larger sociopolitical context in which they live.

This chapter examines *al-wad'* as a problem from which one must retreat. It addresses how my interlocutors employ queer strategies of creating and living in bubbles, which serve as temporary spaces of retreat from both conditions of *al-wad'* and gender and sexual normativity. It builds on my interlocutors' usage of the term "bubble" and illustrates that it refers to a time-bound aspect of one's social world, where one can feel a sense of mental and emotional retreat. The bubble is both temporal and affective; it is not a condition that one is always living in, and when one does, it creates a temporary feeling of safety, disaffection, hope, or possible exuberance. This chapter moves away from the idea that LGBT people in the Global South are either resilient heroes or victims and focuses on the queer strategies of creating and inhabiting bubbles. While discourses of resiliency may be empowering, they tend to focus on individual efforts/strengths rather than structural systems of oppression and, in this case, *al-wad'*. Such narratives abstract structural conditions such as *al-wad'* and individualize resistance and everyday survival.

Though many of my interlocutors, such as Souraya, are aware that bubbles are short-lived and unstable, they see them as an alternative to what is typically thought of as an LGBT community, which many claim has failed them. Rather than talk about LGBT communities per se, my interlocutors speak of their distinct and various experiences of bubbles, which respond to *al-wad'* and the failures of (LGBT) communities. A bubble, unlike a community, does not assume longevity or a continuity of institutions. Thus, this chapter sheds light on how my interlocutors use queer strategies of seeking and constructing bubbles with the awareness that they are fleeting and, like *al-wad'*, perpetually unstable.[1] Whereas communities have been conceptualized as longer-term spaces and relations that engender a sense of belonging (Woolwine 2010), bubbles are liminal and precarious spaces where people retreat and recharge so they can continue with their everyday life. My interlocutors experience bubbles differently. For some the bubble is a physical space, such as a neighborhood or organizing space; for others it refers to relationships and ties with people, whereas for some it signifies a mental space.

While the metaphor of the bubble has been employed in urban studies of inequalities, governance, and gated communities in reference to closed-off safe spaces (Caldeira 2001; Hentschel 2015) and in social movement litera-ture to represent ideal and sometimes equalizing spaces of deliberation that are protected from outside forces (Mische 2015), my intervention is twofold. First, I argue that bubbles are temporal rather than necessarily spatial. They are an interruption or a form of suspension that provides temporary relief since they can burst at any moment. Since a bubble is suspended, it cannot survive; it is always temporary and will eventually rupture. Focusing on the bubble as temporal, I move away from location or the concept of safe spaces as a privileged site of understanding LGBT life and mobilizations, including gay or queer spaces.[2] Second, I show that bubbles are not idealistic spaces of retreat; rather, they can be positive or ambivalent or even contribute to a denial of *al-wad'* and reproduce already-existing hierarchies within the larger society and community.[3] To think of bubbles as ideal spaces is to abstract the material conditions through which they are produced.

Bubbles as counterpublics allow us to better appreciate everyday-life strat-egies in the midst of precarity. Queer theorist Michael Warner reminds us that counterpublics, like publics, have "contradictions and perversities in-herent in the organization of all publics" (2002, 81).[4] Thus, I touch on how privilege operates within queer spaces, bubbles, and publics that reproduce already-existing inequalities. While the bubble can represent a physical space for some, instead of asking what the bubble *is*, this chapter is concerned with what the bubble *does*: It suspends, interrupts, and does various things for dif-ferent people, which community fails to provide.

The bubble occupies what queer studies scholar Sharon Holland calls the "interstices" between Lebanese society and LGBT communities (2012, 6). Bubbles require at least moderate privilege, especially in regard to class, gender, and access to networks. To a certain extent, bubbles may allow individuals with certain privileges to experience Beirut and Lebanon as exceptional and to ignore those who are excluded and the larger geo- and sociopolitical context. Some people who inhabit multiple bubbles of privilege are able to experience Beirut as exceptional and modern, while others cannot, primarily because they do not have privileges and/or access to networks that form these bubbles. In some cases, these bubbles allow one to possibly ignore and deny "the situation" and, hence, reproduce fractal narratives of Beiruti exceptionalism. Keeping these concerns in mind, I ask: Who has access to bubbles, and who can afford to create bubbles? What do bubbles do, and what are their relations to *al-wad*? First, I define how I conceive of the bubble and distinguish it from other conceptions. Then I present narratives of the LGBT community in Lebanon by looking at its history as recounted by two interlocutors. Finally, I rethink community by showing how the bubble as a queer tactic better captures the experiences of my interlocutors.

Constructing the Bubble

My conceptualization of the bubble benefits from Michael Warner's (2002) concept of counterpublics and Ann Mische's (2015, 45) theory of publics as performative and relational places of "suppression" rather than necessarily open identification with one's multiple positionalities and identities.[5] While Mische invokes bubbles in the case of contentious politics and various political groups' mobilizations in Brazil, I use it to think about how LGBT Beirutis create spaces (not necessarily physical) for retreat and respite. Mische argues that different Brazilian political groups and factions mobilize and negotiate publics by highlighting and/or downplaying or suppressing certain aspects of their identities. Following Mische, I use the notion of suppression to think about how people inhabiting bubbles suppress not identities but time and space amid *al-wad'*. While Mische's theorization is useful for thinking about how identities are suppressed in forming collectivities, it does not attend to affective elements of the bubble. If one of the primary shared experiences of *al-wad'* is affective (shared feelings of anxiety and suspension), similarly, affect is what draws people to forming bubbles and keeping them intact for a bounded period of time. One might ask what the end goal of bubbles is. However, instead of thinking about an end goal, I show that bubbles are primarily affective spaces of temporary shelter.

Disruptions are chaotic; however, there are patterns to the violence and unrest that they engender. Although individuals in Beirut live amid constant disruption, *al-wad'* does not necessarily produce complete chaos or unpredictability. The queer tactic of creating bubbles happens because people are aware of some patterns that exist or they can predict what needs their bubbles must serve. These bubbles, or comfort zones, are made up of people, spaces, and ideas that act as temporary support systems and spaces of retreat, and the definition of a bubble can change from person to person. The bubbles can do only so much to try to maintain a bounded period of respite or sense of stability, which is a moment of suspension from the larger situation. Bubbles bring people together and provide short-lived experiences of exuberance, comfort, pain, hope, sadness, and possible disaffection. Shared feelings of unease that *al-wad'* produces connect people, as queer theorist Sara Ahmed puts it, "like a thickness in the air" (2013, 10). Shared feelings, as Ahmed argues, do "not only heighten tension, but they are also in tension" (10). For example, while bubbles provide temporary feelings of respite at the microlevel, at a macrolevel, these bubbles, oftentimes coupled with everyday practices of denial of *al-wad'*, serve to unwittingly maintain narratives of modernity and progress and of Beirut's exceptionalism. I conceive of the bubble as a shared sense of a public that is best understood as a contradictory formation, both an expression of privilege and protection, critique and investment. It becomes both a strategy for the negotiation of life in Beirut and a part of the larger ideology of exceptionalism and progress. This is not only a feature of bubbles, and the following discussion distinguishes between bubbles and communities.

Defining Community

While there is no consensus of what an LGBT community in Beirut looks like, for many interlocutors, LGBT activism seemed to be at the center of what a community does. Thus, a number of them recounted the history of what they consider to be the LGBT community in Beirut, either through personal experiences or through stories that have been passed down. Turning to the history of LGBT organizing in Beirut, I contrast the stories presented by two individuals: Randa is in her early thirties and has been involved with the community for more than ten years; and Samira, at age twenty-one, although newer to the activist community in Lebanon, is very active. Randa asserts that community can mean several things:

> I believe people make a city, people make a country, and people make a community. So it all depends on how you want your community to be. I am using the word "community" here, but I mean environment, your surroundings. You know, like "occupy Wall Street," occupy space; if you want a space to be yours, you have to occupy it the way that you are.

Randa has an expansive definition of community to mean one's environment and surroundings. At the same time, she focuses on the importance of material spaces for a community's survival. She argues that one needs to occupy or take space to survive in Beirut. While Randa says that Beirut gives people the space that they want, she explains that people experience harassment very differently and that trans women have limited spaces:

> [Beirut] allows you the space you want; let's be fair. [*Pauses.*] Okay, if we go the extreme, who are the most people who get harassed in Lebanon? They are the transsexuals. The[ir] status is even worse than women['s], especially male to female. If someone hasn't done any op-

eration and for people she looks like a sissy boy . . . these people . . . will be harassed by the rest. However, there are a few places they can be relatively safer in, but these places are very few. The more special or queer you are, your circle is more likely to get smaller and more limited. We also have to talk about safety; maybe a trans person can go out during the day but is not able to go to most places.

In recounting the history of the lesbian and gay activist organizing in Beirut, Randa starts by telling me about how she first went about searching for other gay people in the city on the internet. In the year 2000, she first found about "the community" online, when she joined the "gayLebanon" mailing list. After subscribing to the online mailing list, she started receiving emails from people who called for meetings in various coffee shops every now and then. Individuals on the Listserv had to ask for the group's permission to bring one of their friends to different meetings, who later would become part of the group. This, Randa describes, is how the community started forming. In addition, for anyone new to the group, it would send out an email introducing the new person, followed by a meeting with the organizers. The other major gay outlet for meeting other lesbians and gay men was a channel on the chat network mIRC (Internet Relay Chat), called #gaylebanon. Randa had started chatting with a woman there:

> I met her online; we both liked Melissa Etheridge and Alanis Morisette. No one knew them in Lebanon at the time. I met her the next time. It was the first lesbian I officially met. She took me to Jounieh, she introduced me to another woman, and then she took me back home. This was my first outing when I met someone from the community.

Randa met a man from the mailing list who later took her to her first meeting in 2000. Randa describes the meeting:

> There was a table full of people [*pauses*] like twenty-four, and he introduced me by my screen name, and everyone started cheering to welcome me. We had rented the coffee shop for our meeting. It was private. I met many people; you put a face to a screen name. I met someone with me in university. Most of the people I met back then are still my friends today.

The first meetings took place in private coffee shops that the group rented. These served as meeting spaces since there were not any other available spaces.

Randa reflects on that moment as a time when "there really was a community." What made it such for Randa was the fact that "people liked each other; they used to help each other and offer support. If someone was kicked out of the house, they would offer a place for them to stay." However, with time, the community grew, and some member of this group of people started an underground support group called Club Free, which was later critiqued by other activists as being predominantly upper-middle-class individuals focused only on sexual identities (Naber and Zaatari 2014). Randa recounted stories about several places where gay men and lesbians would hang out and meet, including Sheikh Mankoush (Merabet 2014). She explained that some places became "occupied" by the community at the time; however, many of the original places have closed down: "This is how you occupy spaces, but then you get kicked out. Yes, at the end you get kicked out. I didn't use to go, but yes, then [the management] of Sheikh Mankoush got nasty. [*Pauses.*] They became rude." At that time, women had created a separate mIRC chat channel for themselves, and members of the community started forming separate groups. She recounted that the community got bigger and developed from Club Free to the more visible Helem.

Samira is much newer to LGBT organizing in Beirut, as she had recently moved to Beirut from the Arab Gulf, where she grew up. Talking about the "older generations" and the community in the past, Samira says:

> From what I hear from the old generations, it was all organized but underground in a scary way. They were scared for their own well-being and safety. They still needed their parents [for financial support]. Now, one has a fight with one's parents, packs her bags, and leaves. She has her friends; she finds a job. Back then, they were terrified. The sense of independence didn't exist. Now it does; now there are more connections.

For Samira, the earlier LGBT community's lack of visibility (underground organizing) and the financial dependence on parents conjures up a fear she feels is no longer as salient. She claims that people now are not as scared as they once were, particularly since they have built connections and support networks more akin to bubbles. Building an LGBT support network gave people the courage to be more visible:

> Back then, people didn't mix as much; you couldn't have found lots of Christians and Druze, Muslims and Christians, the connections you found and the networks you built. If you can't find something

in your domain, you now can rely on people outside the family. You know what I mean? I do have a choice.

Samira asserts that now people have a choice about whether to be visible, as a by-product of having a strong support network. Interestingly, Samira mapped on religious and sectarian relations and networks to further explain how things have gotten much better. She continues, describing the fear that people felt earlier in organizing:

> Yes, people were scared; now they are not. We have something here in Lebanon; everyone is scared to lead because they don't want to be left out on their own because they will be screwed. We are brought up on the concept of family; without family you are nothing. We are seen as a collective, not as an individual. The individual has no identity; one is seen as a group. So any individual couldn't or wouldn't risk being individualized and criminalized alone because they would be left with nothing. They have to stick with the collective until they find someone else like them [in this case another collective, but queer]. When they found it, they tried to lead underground. With time, the media, sense of freedom, and the economy started to flourish; people started to slowly open new holes, new passageways, until they surfaced in society where you could organize in a much more efficient way. And this couldn't have been done until [the] internet was properly used and grasped and people found each other.

In recounting the history of organizing, Samira uses the terms "underground," "holes," and "passageways" to describe the process by which organizing forms changed from being hidden to more open. People were particularly scared to lead a group or movement, as they feared potential backlash from their families. Samira describes Lebanese society as "collectivist," whereby she claims that "without family you are nothing." She mentions the importance of finding and relying on queer circles as networks, which represent another type of collective. Things have changed, however, particularly since people can rely on queer networks, which according to Samira, afford individuals more choices and freedom. Many individuals echo Samira's claims about the importance of queer circles and safety, yet they refer to multiple circles that quickly change and take different forms with time.

Both Samira and Randa suggest that networks and the internet are central to LGBT organizing. While Randa believes that there was more sense of a community in the early 2000s, Samira claims that there is a stronger sense of an LGBT community today. Even though they both define the community similarly—networks and connections—for Samira the underground nature and lack of visibility of a community are not very appealing. Samira expresses on more than one occasion the need for visibility and the need for individuals in the community to know that there are multiple other queers. This is something that Randa agrees with, though she does reminisce about the past, when, as she claims, a "community used to exist." Samira paints the older community as "very fearful," which is not the case anymore. In such a statement, she is not taking into account the diverse gendered and classed experiences and the different contexts in which people live. Even though they both talk about the history and the present experiences of the gay and lesbian community, they do not mention the experiences of transgender individuals in the community. While Randa talks more about trans exclusion and invisibility, Samira focuses on the feeling that it seems to be safer for gays and lesbians now.

Samira never got the chance to go to any of the older gay spaces and nightclubs, such as Acid, which she hears people refer to nostalgically as "those times." "There aren't as many gay clubs [now] as there [once were]," Samira says. In the past few years, the number of gay and lesbian bars has indeed decreased. However, since Samira is relatively new to Beirut, her experience of Beirut is always in relation to her experiences in the Gulf, where she grew up and lived. Randa, however, had been part of gay organizing in Beirut for a longer time and had a longing for the earlier times when she claims "it felt more like a community." She says it no longer feels like a community but more like friendship networks and circles.

Some of my interlocutors more strongly contest the meanings of gay and LGBT communities in Beirut, including those who believe that an LGBT community does not exist. The presence of LGBT communities in Beirut has been problematized by academics, who are skeptical of the very notion of a gay community in Beirut. Indeed, anthropologist Sofian Merabet argues:

> One might contend that there is no such thing as a "gay community" in Lebanon at all, providing, of course, one defines a community as a coherent and encompassing group of people sharing similar, even if competing, positions, and aspirations and where the sexual preference becomes a cardinal point of identity construction. (2004, 4)

While it is not clear what Merabet means by "coherent," some of my interlocutors are also skeptical of the presence of LGBT communities, though they conceive of communities differently. Merabet's Euro-American usage of "gay community," without naming its Eurocentrism, puts identity at the center of the definition. My interlocutors, however, define community by how they conceive of projects of politicization and depoliticization. Those who are or were active in queer and/or LGBT organizations *queer* communities by refusing a narrow focus on shared sexual identities. Many claim that focusing only on sexual identities is a form of depoliticization that does not attend to larger structural issues. Thus, to be political is to seek to build communities beyond a shared notion of LGBT identities.

Reflecting on her experiences in feminist and queer organizing in Beirut, Mays, who was involved in LGBT and feminist organizing in Lebanon, states that a Beiruti "gay community" does not exist per se; rather, people organize together according to common political goals:

> If people might just meet at a common denominator, does that mean we suddenly have a community? When things don't fit, we call it "diversity"; we decorate it. A community doesn't exist. [*Pauses.*] It can be a political project at best. [*Pauses.*] People can have a common political project; however, there is nothing called gay community. It's simply pockets of people who have found each other.

Mays asserts that while people might have a common political project, when disagreements do arise, individuals use the term "diversity" to showcase the distinct viewpoints. While events like gay pride in Beirut attempt to demonstrate the presence of a diverse community, she believes it gives the false impression of having one LGBT community in Lebanon. Pride events tend to remain exclusive by highlighting middle-class, cisgender gay men and exclude nonnormative persons who might not identify as LGBT.

Rabab recognizes that class and gender privilege are formative of unequal access to LGBT spaces and, similar to Mays, contests the presence of one LGBT community:

> I believe there are little communities inside big communities. [*Pauses.*] What sucks is that people assume that I belong to some community, just by looking at me, such as the LGBT community, whether I like it or not. Yes, I sleep with women and I identify as bigender, and then I am grouped whether I like it or not with other LGBT people. I get random smiles from butch women [on the street]. However, there are multiple communities. [*Pauses.*] Here in Lebanon we also have the LGBTQ and LBTQ, lesbians and gays, and then you have Helem and Meem. There are also other communities that reject both of them. [*Pauses.*] They are the hardest people to find.

For Rabab, the concept of an LGBT community is limiting, since there are various queer communities in Beirut. She is frustrated when others assume or identify her as part of an LGBT community simply based on her gender nonbinary identification and sexual attraction. She is more comfortable identifying as part of groups that take into account her multiple positions. She references people who reject being part of activist networks such as Meem or Helem because they do not want to be defined by the categories that these groups provide or possibly impose. Like Rabab, Sirine feels limited by how communities construct and are formed around one central identification:

> Depending on the person I am with, I would express myself in different ways, so I can't limit myself to one identity or whatever. I used to say, "I am this," but it takes so much away from the experience. It becomes so calculated in a sense, and it makes you feel restricted because you are blocking things you want to express, whether it is with your body or your language and words.

Sirine realizes that she needs multiple groups and spaces so she is not constantly suppressing multiple aspects of herself, such as her gender identity or Armenian heritage. Rabab, Mays, and Sirine use the English-language term "community" to refer to a group of people who have a common primary identification and a political project. At the same time, they express ways that the LGBT community has failed them. Instead, they turn to the term "bubbles," which better captures their experiences of living in Beirut. For example, bubbles provide Sirine with the space to express aspects of herself that she chooses to express, that are intelligible in certain contexts and in relation to others.

Rabab mentions that there are multiple exclusions within LGBT groups in Beirut that take on different forms. For example, LGBT organizers do not take into account people's differential mobilities within the city. Rabab, who used to live in the southern suburbs of Beirut, had a harder time accessing events taking place in central Beirut because there was no dependable public transportation. Others also had a tough time accessing private gay-friendly spaces where LGBT meetings were held since they could not afford them.

The Bubble as Privilege

"There's no use in claiming we are not the products of the shit around us," Mays tells me, in reference to many of her friends and acquaintances deny-

ing or not fully expressing how *al-wad'*, the traumas of wars and imminent threats of violence, and inequalities in Lebanon shape them and their
experiences. While bubbles might seem like equalizing spaces or states of
short-lived tranquility, they are still reflective of raced, gendered, and classed
exclusions. As anthropologist and queer studies scholar Martin Manalansan
rightfully reminds us in his discussion of queer of color critique: "Queers
and queers of color are not distant figures looking from afar or from above,
rather they are entrenched in the morass that structural inequalities cause"
(2018, 1288). Without acknowledging that we are the "products of the shit
around us," as Mays says, bubbles potentially seem like idealistic spaces separate from the larger sociopolitical realities and environment, including structural inequalities. Thus, bubbles can unwittingly maintain a sense of Beiruti
exceptionalism by providing individuals the possibility of not being attuned
to or aware of what is happening around them and by ignoring the exclusive
nature of these bubbles.

For Souraya, the bubble represents living in a reality that she acknowledges is not shared by the majority of people around her. She understands
that living in a bubble is a form of privilege that most people cannot afford:

> It is people who don't need to live the "other" [real] life, the other real-
> ity; these are the people who believe [in life in the bubble]. They don't
> need to see this other reality: how the government works, the people
> who belong to a class that protects them or they have privileges that
> protect them, those who have another passport, or those who come
> from a certain class or a certain area. They are protected. They don't
> need to see the other reality of Lebanon. Or those people who are able
> to create their own bubble and live in safety.

Souraya frames the bubble as a longer-term experience that privileged people
inhabit and move in safely, separated from the daily lived experiences of
people with less socioeconomic means. While this might contradict previous claims of the temporary nature of the bubble, Souraya's experience of
the bubble as a space of privilege is important to unpack. For her, the bubble
grants people the possibility of going on in their lives while temporarily sus-
pending the realities of *al-wad'* or the realities of those around them who do
not have access to bubbles. She references multiple bubbles, focusing on the
idea that the experience of the bubble shelters people from reality. The privilege of inhabiting a bubble allows the reality of *al-wad'* to be glossed over or
to become invisible, which is precisely why to her it is a bubble rather than
reality. Souraya conceives of the bubble as a temporary experience of shelter

and also as a way for some to make possible a state of ongoing denial of the situation. This is most clear when she says that "it is people who don't need to live the 'other' life" or "don't need to see this other reality," since they can afford to live in their own bubbles. For example, Lebanese individuals who reproduce fractal Orientalist accounts of Beirut's exceptionalism in the Arab Middle East are not paying attention to the uneven effects of everyday experiences of violence and disruptions. Therefore, the bubble can make it possible to deny *al-wad'* and reproduce exceptional narratives of cosmopolitan Beirut. However, that is not the case for everyone.

Some people, as Mays and Souraya suggest, forget that they inhabit bubbles but might be reminded of their existence when disruptions take place. While Souraya is critical of those who do not want to acknowledge what she refers to as "the reality," bubbles may force individuals to face *al-wad'* since these bubble formations are quite temporary and can easily collapse. For example, Souraya points to the privileges and protections that Lebanese dual citizens have, primarily those with North American or European passports. A disruption, such as war, forces people to acknowledge violence and *al-wad'*, yet they continue to inhabit a bubble because they can leave the situation. Those with transnational mobility are afforded a means of escaping when the situation gets too intense or wars break out, such as occurred in 2006. During that war, dual citizens were among the groups who were evacuated by their respective governments, while holders of only Lebanese passports, undocumented persons, Palestinians, and South Asian and East and North African nationals were left behind. This creates a hierarchy and valuations of life—those who deserve to survive and those who do not. Those with transnational mobility can live their everyday lives with the knowledge that they have an escape route if an escalation or a war were to break out; it is a privilege that most Lebanese people do not have, despite other class, neighborhood, or economic privileges.

Others, such as Samira, acknowledge that for some, living in certain parts of Beirut also functions as a type of bubble: "I am in Hamra, which is a bubble. You wake up to realize that you are in a bubble and not everyone lives like that and Lebanon is not that pretty. It's sad, but you wake up to it eventually, and you get slapped on the face." Here, Samira realizes that Hamra, as a wealthier neighborhood, is a bubble that represents a different reality than the rest of Beirut and Lebanon, particularly since it is a diverse neighborhood where both American universities are situated and is usually distanced from other parts of Beirut, including the southern suburbs. People who cannot afford to live in wealthier (and safer) neighborhoods more often construct their bubbles around relationships rather than physical spaces such as residences or clubs.

The Bubble as a Network and Support System

If community, as described by many of my interlocutors, does not capture their experiences of LGBT life in Beirut, what do people rely on for support? My interlocutors employ queer strategies of creating and inhabiting bubbles as an alternative to community. Through the lens of *al-wad'*, I see the bubble as a temporal formation—as opposed to only material—that better captures and reflects the experiences of living amid precarity, where disruptions are the conditions of everyday life. In recounting their lives in Beirut, many of my interlocutors use the term "bubble" to describe their social circles and/or coping mechanisms on which they rely to survive. While they are aware that bubbles are liminal and precarious, some, such as Souraya, also made it clear that creating a bubble requires some form of privilege.

"These comfort zones are so temporary. There is no stability. [*Pauses.*] It's like you're driving your car in a storm and you can't see beyond quarter of a mile," Mays says. While Mays asserts that individuals have the possibility of creating their own comfort zones in Beirut, she reminds me that these spaces are temporary and very unstable. When I inquire into what a comfort zone is, Mays tells me:

> It is made up of people, spaces, and ideas. You try to create a support system, but you always feel it might crumble. People leave. Very few people live here. Everyone I know has a plan B to leave. There is no sense of emotional stability, especially if you build your support system around people. Everyone is on their way out. It can [easily] crumble.

While some might refer to these comfort zones or bubbles as communities, Mays's insistence that these people, spaces, and ideas can provide only temporary comfort (and safety) and are always at risk (or on the verge) of crumbling raises the question of whether we can think of bubbles as communities. Capturing her experiences of living amid the perpetual precarity of *al-wad'*, Mays draws attention to the temporary nature of feeling respite, comfort, and stability in Beirut. Though Mays does not use the term *al-wad* in this quotation, her invocation of driving one's car in a storm with no immediate or long-term visibility ahead illustrates what living amid constant disruptions feels like to her. She says that you attempt to take ownership, to know that you are moving—"driving your car"—yet you do not know what lies down the road or even immediately ahead. Despite that, Mays asserts:

> You have the possibility of creating your own comfort zone, which means you don't have to deal with normative aspects of the city *as much*. As you grow up, they become less dominant in your life. But at the same time, you feel that those comfort zones are temporary. You can't envision a future that is nonnormative. If you don't want to do what everyone else is doing, what other options do you have?

Mays says that many anti- and nonnormative individuals seek and create individual and shared comfort zones, which give them the space of not having to consistently deal with various normative aspects of the city, including heteronormative spaces. Normativity, as Ahmed reminds us, is "comfortable for those who can inhabit it" (2013, 147). Though *al-wad'* and disruptions constitute and are constitutive of everyday life in Beirut—contesting Euro-American conceptions of normative lives—Mays is particularly talking about heteronormative spaces in the city. However, Mays also found that queer spaces and networks in Beirut reproduce similar hierarchies of class and gender.

Bubbles, unlike communities, are precarious queer strategies of disrupting borders, exclusions, and identities. "I came to queer issues by questioning borders, physical borders, like nations, not by questioning sexuality," Sirine says; "this is what community was for me." She continues: "Then I realized that I still have awesome friends. [*Pauses.*] There is no community left for me; I am out. In Lebanon, there are many communities." Sirine explains that though she was involved in queer activism and felt that she was part of a community at some point, she does not feel she belongs to an LGBT community, as she continuously questions how borders are created and maintained: from the borders that communities assume to national borders. Drawing on her experiences as genderqueer and Lebanese-Armenian, she felt policed and constricted, given that the LGBT community did not allow her a space to embody or express multiple aspects of her identity, such as her Armenianness. For Sirine, to queer an LGBT community is to question its borders, formation, and exclusions.

Sirine experienced a sense of conflict or friction with the LGBT community's sole focus on sexuality. While frictions can imply closeness and proximity, they are also about rupture. Thus, Sirine's response to the failures of LGBT communities in Beirut is to create a rupture and find bubbles as spaces of retreat, which allow her to express her multiple experiences and thus feel less bounded.

Bubbles change with time and take on different forms based on different needs and contexts. Though Sirine experiences everything around her as temporary (invoking everyday-life disruptions and imminent violence), she still thinks of her relationships with people as a sort of "home": "It is not about borders; everything is so temporary. However, it is with the *whom* that is the permanent thing." Sirine defines her bubble as her relationships with people and thus distinguishes it from communities, which she finds to be more precarious. Relationships feel less precarious than communities because she has more personal control over them than over communities. Having some form of personal control is central to the formation of bubbles and for maintaining a feeling of relative safety amid *al-wad'*.

Mays, who was also active in feminist, LGBT, and queer organizing, considers herself to be someone who has "dropped out" of the LGBT and queer movements in Lebanon:

> This comes from a lot of disappointment—and the moment you have this type of consciousness that I am not outside my society or the shit that I have been trying to fight. The moment you realize that, what then? If I am not here or there, where am I? Does that mean the change I was advocating for or the oppressions I was talking about and fighting for [didn't matter], since you see others reproducing it?

Mays is disappointed with the outcomes of some of the activist work she and others have done, especially since she feels that they have reproduced types of violence and exclusions similar to the ones they were fighting to change. Though Mays and others formed bubbles as a retreat or as a rupture from LGBT communities and other realities, they find that they are far from being idealistic spaces.

Mays, like Sirine, queers LGBT spaces by creating bubbles, which she recognizes take on different manifestations:

> The bubble changes with time. You create different bubbles based on your wants and needs. We create our queer bubbles as a reaction to the oppression and the vulnerability we feel. It is a reaction. Thus, we create a rift or a rupture between us and society. [*Pauses.*] I am trying to understanding this rupture, and I do believe, as organizers, we have a lot work that needs to be done in order to understand this rupture. What kind of alternative spaces are we seeking?

Mays was involved in queer organizing in Lebanon as an alternative to LGBT organizing, which relied heavily on identity politics and rights. She regards bubbles, such as her previous organizing bubble, as a form of rupture from mainstream LGBT organizing and everyday-life disruptions, oppressions, and vulnerabilities. This queer strategy of creating a separation from *al-wad'* and LGBT organizing is a response to a collective need and desire for alternative spaces or counterpublics. Mays recounts her experiences of building and maintaining the queer bubble, which later disappointed her:

> At the beginning, the bubble was made up of a support system that you built and slowly understand; it depends on the kind of life you ultimately envision for yourself. It might include like-minded friends, a physical space as well. My first support system was linked to Meem and Nassawiya. I got a lot of strength from these places and the ideas circulating in these spaces. [*Pauses.*] It is spaces like these that make you believe in the power of a collective. The first couple of years are euphoric. There is a process: First, you live in a heteronormative world. You build these spaces, and it is euphoric, and everything is amazing, and we are all feminists. But then you realize everyone around me perpetuates a similar kind of violence that we had initially built for protection.

Mays's bubbles initially included the feminist and queer activist circles she was part of, which gave her strength and possibilities to imagine a different world. Mays recounts the need to form bubbles to create a queer present and a future that one envisions. The bubble becomes a support system and network of like-minded people and friends. In addition, it is also a physical space, such as the feminist organizing spaces that Meem and Nassawiya provided. However, in this example, Mays recounts how the bubble became a queer organizing community that ultimately failed her and others, since they ended up reproducing a similar kind of violence to that of society at large. While in the beginning these feminist spaces and circles produced a sense of euphoria, it turned into disappointment. Like a bubble, both Meem and Nassawiya burst and no longer exist as entities.

The bubble produces feelings of kinship, networks, and possible support systems, especially amid *al-wad'*. Yara and Souraya also focus on the importance of support networks that they seek through bubbles. "This is what I hate about Beirut the most; it chews you very badly. It's a rough; it's a very rough city, especially if you are trying to be independent and trying to make your own money and stuff," Yara tells me. Given the harsh conditions of living independently in Beirut, Yara has focused on building support networks and systems with other like-minded individuals. Similarly, Souraya points to the central role that networks occupy in maintaining the bubble, even if it is only temporary. Souraya tells me about the importance of inhabiting bubbles with people who share similar values. While explaining her own life and experiences of the bubble, Souraya recounts that she inhabits multiple bubbles: her family bubble, activist circles, and her university bubble. According to her, bubbles change and take on different forms based on their context and the networks included in the particular bubble, or with whom it is shared. Bubbles, however, are not immune to the reproduction of hierarchies and/or denial of the situation. They are part and parcel of *al-wad'*.

Chaos and Denial

Many of my interlocutors recounted the unsettling nature and anxieties that *al-wad'* produces on a daily basis and the need to find mental or physical spaces of retreat. Ziad, a medical doctor in his late twenties, focuses on the chaos of the streets in Beirut:

> The negative chaos in the way that people drive is a reflection of our own society. People have no respect for pedestrians, rules, regulations, or anything. People act like there are no boundaries; it's like [they feel] they can do whatever they want without accountability. The way they drive reflects the way they live; you can do whatever you want because there is a lack of accountability. People have no boundaries. The other day a fight broke out in Hamra because someone was putting a flag of this other political party. This is all reflected in how we drive.

Ziad recounts the lack of boundaries and respect that people have for each other in mundane actions as a reflection of Lebanese society. He continues, "This chaos gets to me inside; I feel it inside. I want to change things; the chaos makes me angry and hopeless that this will not change. [*Pauses.*] My screams are futile. People disregard each other." Ziad expresses the rage and hopelessness he feels. A bubble for him becomes a mental space of respite, where he can set some form of boundary. He says that anyone who does not follow "the norm" needs a bubble: "You can live in your own bubble; everyone can be in their own bubble as long as others don't enter." Ziad invokes the need for bubbles as a space of retreat so individuals can go on "fighting" for their right to live peacefully, alone.

The chaos of everyday life that Ziad describes is institutionalized in Lebanon. Souraya echoes Ziad's concerns about the lack of accountability in the everyday: "Our country is a very confrontational, violent, and aggressive [one]. [*Pauses.*] You see it in the laws; I don't think such things are symbols of openness and being progressive and being civilized, as people understand openness and progressiveness." Souraya contests narratives of Beiruti exceptionalism and progress by pointing to institutionalized violence. She asserts that it is not only in everyday life that one encounters aggression; one also experiences it through the violence of the legal system toward women, refugees, migrants, and gender and sexual-nonnormative people. However, people's lack of awareness of the systemic violence embedded in the law makes it possible for individuals to deny the existence of such practices.

After moving to Beirut from the Arab Gulf, Samira was surprised at how many people she met were in denial of the situation:

> What I hated was the social problems that people were in denial about that now they are becoming aware of. I hated the racism, and I hated the entire concept of sectarianism. You come here, and you're like, what is Shia and Sunni, and why do you people hate each other?

Samira cites the repeated denial of the situation as a major issue that gets enacted on a daily basis. Bubbles contribute to such denials when they become particularly exclusive and secluded from realities around them. Yara echoes Samira's concern, citing her experiences of living in the predominantly Christian city of Jounieh:

> In Jounieh, people are closed off on themselves; if they see a veiled woman, they would freak out. Now the fear of Syrians is on the rise. It really is a Christian ghetto. Being part of this community, you know it's a ghetto, and there is no way to open it up. I don't know what would make Jounieh open up to the world, but there are people if you tell them you are going to Hamra, they would be so scared and tell you, "Are you going to West Beirut?" This still happens—what I am telling you is recent—or they say, "Beirut, it's too far away," when in fact, it's only forty-five minutes *in traffic.*

Yara describes how civil war terminology of partition—West and East Beirut—is still employed among residents of Jounieh, even though the civil war ended in 1990. She shows that residents of Jounieh imagine Beirut to be quite distant and, particularly West Beirut (predominantly Muslim), to be dangerous and unsafe for Christians. In another manifestation of fractal Orientalism, East Beirut (predominantly Christian) becomes considered safer and more progressive than West Beirut.

The bubble does not transcend some of the sedimented divisions that exist in Lebanese society. For example, Yara describes her queer bubble as a feminist one, whose members shared more in common than just being queer. Her queer bubble prioritizes and mobilizes around feminist issues and the rights of migrants and refugees in addition to queer issues. Yara, however, refuses to organize with queer individuals who are partisan and belong to political parties that do not share her views on immigration and refugee issues.

In some instances, the bubble becomes explicitly linked to everyday practices of denial, where people resume their own lives by ignoring parts of the city and/or country that are experiencing violence, armed clashes, or bombings. During the war in the summer of 2006, which primarily targeted Shia residential areas, private establishments, including nightclubs and bars, relocated from downtown Beirut to the safer mountain areas where others who were not directly targeted resumed their nightlife and continued to party. As Naber and Zaatari show, there was a rift between LGBT activists during this time, during which those who were active in relief work "distanced themselves from mainstream LGBTQ activists who had the privilege of isolating themselves from the invasion, and continued to focus only on keeping gay nightclubs alive during the invasion" (2014, 104). I am not suggesting that individuals should not find spaces to resume their lives amid conflict; rather, I am pointing to the ways that these strategies can sometimes coexist with practices of denial and contribute to narratives of Beirut's exceptionalism.

Bubbles as Strategy

Why is it important to examine how community fails people and how it takes on different manifestations such as bubbles? What are the links between bubbles, *al-wad'*, and narratives of progress? To navigate *al-wad'*, many individuals find respite in sheltered bubbles that give them some breathing space from precarity and the disruptions of the everyday and provide normalcy. Many describe the bubble as a place where they feel a certain distance from reality. Respite is equated with taking a break from what constitutes realities of everyday life in Beirut. Since these bubbles provide only temporary emotional stability, I suggest that we think of them as temporally bound experiences of shelter from ongoing violence and as responses to the failure of the promise of LGBT communities.

Bubbles are a queer strategy of creating an experience of safety where individuals can resume their lives and maneuver the city with a certain sense of caution with friends and networks. Bubbles are in-between spaces that require the need for shared emotions that can bring people together. In a state where community fails people and where shared definitions and meanings of the past, such as the civil war, and the present do not hold, bubbles may provide a sense of shared understanding and a feeling of safety. Bubbles produce a distance, a place to breathe, and a place to be contained. Thus, they *orient* and also *displace*—like air bubbles displacing water.

At a microlevel, these bubbles are privileged spaces not accessible to everyone. Thus, bubbles are not immune to reproducing the inequalities and hierarchies of Lebanese society at large. The privileged nature of the bubble also reminds us that not everyone can afford shelter. One of the ways that some of my interlocutors resume their lives in Beirut is by denying the larger sociopolitical context in which they live. They deny it so they can live with it. Even though many people are anxious and share a deep sense of despair about the present and future, they try to maintain a sense of normalcy and an ability to adjust to a constantly changing "new normal."

Many turn to bubbles when communities fail them. For example, Mays's reference to the violence that communities perpetuate illustrates one way in which these bubbles become a mechanism for creating new spaces and connections that, like *al-wad'*, are constantly shifting. While bubbles are not idealistic spaces and are not immune to disruption, they help us understand the possibility of exuberance amid pain and violence and the way that even spaces of retreat have the potential of circulating narratives of progress and exceptionalism.

Conclusion

Feeling Exceptional and Queer (Dis)Locations

For me, the [civil] war hasn't ended; I am living a second war.
Because the war is not over, within me. Within me, the war is still
ongoing, and I don't know how to end it.

—HANA, in *Phantom Beirut*

On November 12, 2015, two ISIL suicide bombers carried out a double suicide attack in a busy working-class market in the southern suburbs of Beirut, killing 89 people and injuring more than 200 others. This came a day before the Paris ISIL attacks, which resulted in the death of 130 people. While people on Facebook around the world changed their profile pictures in solidarity with Paris and Facebook enabled a safety marker for people in Paris, Beirut did not receive nearly as much coverage. However, this was not *any* part of Beirut—it was an overpopulated working-class Shia suburb.

I was in New Jersey finishing my dissertation at the time. I woke up and read the news, realizing that my aunt and cousin were at the site of the attack. I called my family to check on them and was told that while both suffered serious injuries, my cousin was in a critical condition—pieces of shrapnel had penetrated her head. Recently divorced, my thirty-two-year-old cousin had gone out that day to buy new pajamas for her two children, whom her ex-husband had taken, and he was not allowing her to have contact with them. She had wanted to buy them pajamas in an attempt to win back their love. She was in a coma for twenty days. Fortunately, she and my aunt survived. My cousin's story is only one of the narratives of the people who had gone out that day to shop in the busy working-class neighborhood of Burj al-Barajneh.

The global coverage was meager compared to the scale of the casualties, not simply because it happened in Beirut (and not Paris) but because it did not happen in central Beirut, at a cultural event, or at a high-end shopping mall. It was, after all, in a working-class Shia area of Beirut, next to a large Palestinian refugee camp. I had to continue working on my dissertation and prepare for an invited talk the following week. However, as stated in the Introduction, these disruptions and violence of *al-wad'* do not leave me. In retrospect, perhaps it was a queer tactic for me to go on. Or perhaps it could have been a bubble I have created for myself, which might have resulted in my denial or suspension of *al-wad'*, at least temporarily.

In *Disruptive Situations*, I try to show that erasures, such as downplaying the double suicide attack in the southern suburbs of Beirut, is one example of how fractal Orientalism works. This attack did not take place in downtown Beirut or in a wealthy area where tourists might have been. Fractal Orientalism presents some lives as worthier, or as Judith Butler (2010) says, more "grievable" than others. Thus, the lack of coverage of the event presumes that the lives lost are not *as* worthy. In light of this story, I ask: Why is there more coverage of gay life (or the possibilities of gay life) in Beirut than of such violent incidents, especially when they take place outside central Beirut? What does it mean to think of Beirut as an exceptional cosmopolitan city? What happens to the concept of justice in the context of *al-wad'*? These are questions that came up in discussions with many of my interlocutors and stayed with me as I wrote this book. As this book illustrates, modernity and progress are inadequate frameworks to assess the queer or cosmopolitan potential of cities, since modernity itself depends on the exclusion of certain people—Muslim, working-class, gender-nonnormative and trans individuals, as well as refugees and migrant workers—who are defined as outside modernity.

On (Not) Reconciling Paradoxes

What does it mean to conduct research on sexuality in times of war or possibilities of war? How does using a lens of perpetual everyday-life disruptions challenge our understandings of queerness? How does one define war? Am I overtheorizing in times when more pressing issues are present? These are questions that have lingered and I have wrestled with while conducting research and writing the book. While I cannot answer all of the questions that arise, my hope is that I have answered these two major theoretical questions: How do people make sense of difference and normativity in a city that is anything but normative? How do we make sense of or understand the contours of normativity, which as many have pointed out, are shifting, unstable, and highly contextual, just as *al-wad'* is?

Instead of a formal summary of the questions in the book, I wish to recognize the ongoing nature of *al-wad'* and thus to recognize the inability of reconciling the different manifestations of *al-wad'*. While this concluding chapter offers theoretical, methodological, and empirical insights from my research, *Disruptive Situations* does not attempt to provide a coherent narrative, as that would betray my experiences of research and the experiences of my interlocutors. Rather, I ask the reader to consider how paradoxes and unanswered questions can be productive. While Rabab's story, like those of many of my interlocutors, can be simplified, I present it in the complex form in which it is embodied and experienced. For example, what do Rabab's experiences of being regarded as "not queer" and undesirable in certain establishments but also as a "cool *muhajjaba*" tell us? Rabab, who identified as bigender when interviewed, told me on multiple occasions, "It took me time to understand people who viewed it as oppressive, when I was attacked for wearing a veil. I was treated differently in queer circles and establishments for wearing a veil." Here, Rabab is referencing that she did not feel welcome in most gay establishments, as they considered her to be not legitimately or appropriately "queer," given her hijab. Instead of reconciling her hijab with her sexual and gender nonconformity, Rabab used the queer strategy of embracing what others considered to be a contradiction, which helped her better negotiate her multiple positionalities. "I either got the meanest looks from women," she says, "or a look that suggested that I am a cool *muhajjaba*." I am not suggesting that Rabab or any of my interlocutors are heroes or victims. As queer studies scholar Gayatri Gopinath reminds us:

> Queerness here is not so much a brave or heroic refusal of the normative, as it appears in some narratives of queer subjectivity, as much as it names the impossibility of normativity for racialized subjects who are marked by histories of violent dispossession; for such subjects, a recourse to the comforting fictions of belonging is always out of reach. (2010, 167)

As a nonnormative working-class Shia, Rabab is not attempting to fit into any narrative that made sense or provided comfort for others. She also did not find or feel comfort in queerness; rather, she used her everyday-life queer tactics to navigate the disruptions and discomfort. As Sara Ahmed rightfully points out, "Discomfort is itself a sign that queer spaces may extend some bodies more than others. . . . We can feel uncomfortable in the categories we inhabit, even categories that are shaped by their refusal of public comfort" (2013, 151).

In this book, everyday-life disruptions and violence better capture the experiences of my interlocutors and research than using the traditional lenses of sexuality, culture, and religion. Sexuality alone cannot be used to understand the lives of LGBT people; instead I highlight how queer experiences cannot be separated from political ones (Naber and Zaatari 2014). Thus, this book is not only not about sexual subjectivities but about queer tactics or strategies that tell us about survival amid constant disruptions. While I focus on one city, the narratives I share throughout this book refuse fixity of both people and place. Paying attention to queer tactics of everyday life illustrates that my interlocutors do not think of themselves as another minority. Hence, they disrupt such positionings and discourses through their everyday-life practices of negotiating disruptions. Drawing on the case of queer subjectivities and tactics in contemporary Beirut, I examine the links between gender, sexuality, and discourses of modernity and progress. I argue against the tendency in scholarship and representations of gender and sexuality in Lebanon (and the Arab Middle East) to focus almost exclusively on culture and rights. Using the lens of culture and rights for understanding gender and sexual nonnormativity obscures complexities and lived experiences and assumes that individuals are impacted in similar ways, regardless of gender, class, religious sect, and migrant and refugee status. One such is example is that of negotiating visibility.

Strategies of concealment, passing, and disclosure(s) are not structured along a necessary binary; nor are these performances oppositional. Therefore, if one wants to pass as a woman in a certain context and pass as a man or as androgynous in other contexts, it does not imply oppositional thinking but rather strategies, what Ann Swidler calls "toolkits" of maneuvering situations (1986, 273). Edward Said's memoir *Out of Place* (2000) includes a good example, particularly his discussion of the various ways he presented himself in the United States (e.g., stressing his first name) and in the Arab world (e.g., stressing his last name). Said writes about his strategic focus:

> For years, and depending on the exact circumstances, I would rush past "Edward" and emphasize "Said"; at other times I would do the reverse, or connect these two to each other so quickly that neither would be clear. The one thing I could not tolerate, but very often would have to endure, was the disbelieving, and hence undermining, reaction: Edward? Said? (2000, 3–4)

Similar to Said's claim that people react to his full name as impossible, contradictory, or in need of some necessary reconciliation, my life and those of my interlocutors are assumed by many to be similarly "impossible and unimaginable" (Gopinath 2005, 16). Thus, my experiences and those of my interlocutors collapse the binary of visibility and invisibility. We have had to conceal, fashion, and refashion multiple performances and positionalities, particularly as we cross everyday boundaries in Beirut.

For example, my status as a Lebanese man does not grant me access to all areas of Beirut equally. Given the historical and growing suspicion of the other in Beirut, this sense gets heightened when individuals are present in a part of the city where they are "not from." Borders and checkpoints become spaces where individuals must present themselves as nonthreatening and knowledgeable about the area that they are entering. One way to do is to code-switch, or to leverage social networks or families in the area. Having to cross multiple neighborhoods of Beirut, I have to situate myself in multiple and shifting ways to ensure my safety and also make me pass as an "insider" or "from the neighborhood" (*ibn il mantiqa*). As the Introduction shows, *al-wad'* complicates the politics of insider versus outsider, which are constantly shifting based on the historical moment or period and which populations get marked as potentially threatening.

Fractals as Disruptive Situations

Using *al-wad'* as a critical analytical lens helps capture the nuances and complexities of contradictory experiences and fractal representations of queer life amid everyday-life disruptions. I suggest moving away from Foucauldian analyses, which assume a normative status that needs to be shaken or upset, to account for situations and places where the normative is already and always disruptive. My analysis is informed by queer of color critique and intersectionality, though they do not always account for the transnational. Incorporating fractals, however, provides us with a better understanding of the changing landscape of queer "regionalism," or how some global regions get understood and represented as more gay or queer friendly than others (Gopinath 2007, 341). A central feature of fractal Orientalism is that disruptions become only a background or descriptor and Beirut is highlighted at the expense of other cities, villages, and areas of Lebanon. While Beirut becomes exceptional in the Arab world, it also becomes exceptional in Lebanon, where the rest of the country becomes presumably uncharted territory. While Beirut has an international spotlight, like other major global cities, other parts of the country are forgotten or downplayed. Discourses on Beirut's exceptionalism hide and conceal inequalities within Beirut and Lebanon.

The political economy of such erasures affects the everyday lives of individuals in other areas of Lebanon, including the outskirts of Beirut. Beirut, the economic hub of the country, receives the most attention and governmental services, including basic supplies, such as electricity. Beirut also has more attention from the local and international press than do other parts of the country, including its southern suburbs. Souraya echoes this:

> Don't forget the security policies that give more importance to Beirut. If something happened in Beirut, people pay attention; but if people are killing each other in Tripoli, no one cares. It only gets a small news segment about it. This economic center also produces a cultural center, whereby the city becomes the center of emotions and art; most of the poems and songs are about Beirut. Are there any songs about Sidon or Tripoli? The only songs about the south [of Lebanon] are songs about resistance [to the Israeli occupation].

Beirut becomes the center of intellectual, economic, and cultural life, causing other areas to appear to lack such attributes. This phenomenon cannot be simply explained in terms of metronormativity, since other major cities in Lebanon do not get the same attention. Whereas Beirut has a culture and a history, other cities are invisible or are assumed to be behind in relation to Beirut. Thus, discourses of Beirut's exceptionalism happen simultaneously at the regional, national, and global levels.

Many of my interlocutors were concerned with the paradoxical depictions and erasures of parts of Beirut and contested representations of Beirut as an open and modern city: "Just because I can walk on the streets of Beirut in shorts and a gay man may freely sashay and not get beaten up doesn't mean that this is openness," Souraya says. "For me, openness is about justice, material justice." Souraya believes that a greater freedom in dress and nonnormative presentation for gay men is a shallow understanding of openness: "It's very stupid for someone to say that Lebanon is an open country. The law to protect women from family violence has not been passed for twenty years. [*Pauses.*] It has been at the parliament for ten years, and then our parliament extended its own term."[1] For a place to be open or forward-thinking, according to Souraya, it needs to prioritize and be invested in social justice issues by ensuring legal fairness and the priority of justice, and Lebanon is not one of those places. As a case in point she tells me, "Two days ago a woman was murdered by her husband in Akkar [a northern city in Lebanon], and I haven't heard the government say anything about it." She points to the paradoxes inherent in the claims that Beirut and Lebanon are "open," when the legal protection of women from family violence is not even available. "Beirut is a cruel and harsh city," she says. Contrary to the representations of Beirut as a cosmopolitan city, Souraya argues that the definitions of openness and modernity need to be changed.

While Souraya is responding to representations of Beirut as a cosmopolitan, open, and fun city, others, such as Ziad, find that Beirut is often (mis)represented as backward. He tells me that his encounters with people in the United States and his observations of how Beirut is depicted in Euro-American media make him feel that life in Beirut is misunderstood: "Beirut is a city that is *happening*. Your stereotypes don't fit here; it's not a desert, [there are no] tents, and [it's not] a war zone. I try to clarify that it is not." Souraya and Ziad's engagements with the discourses of Beirut's openness (or lack thereof) are only two examples of the various ways that queer Beirutis engage with the fractal Orientalist representations of Beirut as both "the Provincetown of the Middle East" and yet not quite modern enough. While Beirut might be represented as a cosmopolitan space, it is *still* in the Middle East. Hence, it is cosmopolitan and exceptional only in relation to other cities in Lebanon and the Arab Middle East. These two Orientalist depictions, though seemingly paradoxical, complement each other. Fractal Orientalism, as the book shows throughout, is what allows Beirut to occupy the imagination as both a "gay mecca" and as a war-torn terrorist hub, as in the 2018 Hollywood movie *Beirut*.

Temporalities of "the Modern"

The 1998 novel *Koolaids* by the Lebanese American author Rabih Alameddine, about the Lebanese civil war and the 1980s AIDS epidemic in the United States, best captures how geopolitics, war, and sexuality are entangled. Toward the end of the novel, one of the narrators, a gay Lebanese American man dying of AIDS, recounts his experiences of watching the 1986 American movie *Delta Force*: "When the hijacked plane lands in Beirut, one of the passengers said this used to be a wonderful city. You could do whatever you want. I couldn't believe what he said next: 'Beirut used to be the Las Vegas of the Middle East.' . . . Now that's fucking insulting" (Alameddine 1998, 244).

While "Paris of the Middle East" presents a more colonial depiction of Beirut, "Las Vegas of the Middle East" likens it to an artificial and hedonistic U.S. playground. *Disruptive Situations* starts with the 2009 depictions of Beirut as the "Provincetown of the Middle East," another U.S. reference; however, many also wish for Beirut to regain its title as a Paris and seek to distance it from places such as Kandahar. When Beirut is compared to other Euro-American cities, it is positioned as exceptional in its pre–civil war period (prior to 1975). Chapter 1 shows that such discourses produce a Beirut that *was* exceptional: it *was* the Paris or the Switzerland of the Middle East. The flip side of this discourse is the claim that Beirut is bound to regain its title as Paris or Switzerland of the Middle East. While these discourses seem oppositional, they are held up and made possible by fractal Orientalism. More often than not, the focus is on the past or the future of Beirut, not on the present, except as a possible gay touristic destination. Temporally speaking, Beirut is always either in the past or in the future, although the constancy of *al-wad'* might seem static and challenge conceptions of any change. However, this Orientalist positioning of Beirut begs the question, What becomes of Beirut today? What does a discourse that always orients us to the past and/or future, but never the present, reveal?

Beirut's exceptionalism is based on a remembered past and a promised future. Focusing on the present, this book disrupts these discourses. *Al-wad'*, with its constant disruptions, is what connects the past and the future—or fills the void of the present. The Beirut of the present and *al-wad'* disrupt and make a contemporary narrative of exceptionalism impossible. For example, Beirut can be cosmopolitan and exceptional only if one disregards or denies the myriad sets of violent and exclusionary practices: from state practices against refugees and other vulnerable populations, to the inability of most LGBT Lebanese people to experience Beirut as gay friendly.

Interestingly, and perhaps counterintuitively, I argue that Beirut has to go back to the past to reach its potential future—that is, the promise of its future is located in its past. While narratives of modernity and progress are presented as linear and teleological, they obscure the circular and fractal ways in which they actually operate. In her work on the colonial history of Puerto Rico and the United States, critical theory scholar Sandra Ruiz provides us with a concept of temporal looping in lieu of linear narratives of time. Ruiz argues that the colonial relationship between Puerto Rico and the United States is best understood as "temporal looping whereby actions to redress the past lead us into the future and back again to something prior; this is the affective consequence of colonialism—an active state in the here and now, looping forward and back into itself as if time never started or stopped ticking" (2019, 3). In a similar way, I use *al-wad'* to argue for a circular conception of time that attends to disruptions and trauma. A circular narrative—one with no clear beginning and end—dislocates linear narratives of modernity, queer exceptionalism, and progress. This dislocation happens in two ways. First, it challenges conceptions of linear time, not by focusing on a "queer future" (Muñoz 2009) but rather by showing how the future, past, and present are co-constituted and blurred (and need to be) so that these fractal narratives can exist on global, regional, and local scales. Second, trauma and perpetual everyday-life disruptions of *al-wad'* also challenge a linear conception of time and temporality by the copresence of the present and the past. When one is not able to tell a linear story of disruptions or *al-wad'*, one unwittingly challenges linear time and a clear unfolding of events.

Queer Tactics as Method: Fractal Orientalism and *Al-Wad'* Today

Disruptive Situations makes a methodological contribution to studying queer lives amid everyday-life disruptions. The book focuses on LGBT Beirutis' queer tactics in navigating disruptive situations and touches on the precarity of the research process, especially amid violence and war. While queer tactics shed light on how LGBT Beirutis navigate everyday-life precarity, I suggest that we think of *al-wad'* as a methodological lens or tool. Conducting research and writing a book about disruptions and queerness, both messy situations, I had to let go of predefined ways of approaching research fields and narratives. Since queer tactics help us understand how individuals maneuver, feel, and create their worlds amid perpetual disruption, I had to constantly shift and change research methodologies based on *al-wad'*, funding, and personal feelings of safety, among others. As I reflect on the research and writing process, I find that I was enacting some queer tactics learned from my interlocutors: embracing contradictions, code-switching, accepting disruptions, and not forcing coherent narratives.

Following anthropologist Aseel Sawalha, who discusses "flexible methodologies and techniques to accommodate the emerging needs" during her fieldwork in Beirut (2010, 14), I argue for the need of queer flexible methodologies. While Sawalha does not expand on her conception of flexible methodologies, I suggest queer flexible methodologies as an orientation that asks us to consider the constant changing nature of the field, disruptions, and nature of access—in its local and transnational manifestations. My research methods reflect the disruptive situations I live in and write about. A queer flexible methodology accepts that our methods are co-constituted by the field and are part and parcel of fieldwork. It requires a certain form of letting go and of being humble.

Letting go is not abandoning the field or making ourselves heroes for staying. Here, I respond to and extend the urgent call made by queer theorists David Eng, Jack Hallberstam, and Jose Esteban Muñoz for queer theory to move toward an "ethics of humility" (2005, 15). Queer flexible methodologies require humility and an acceptance of uncertainty. Thus, they beg rethinking the artificial separation between researcher and interlocutors and understanding that the field as one co-constituted by disruptions both in the field and in the lives of researchers and interlocutors.

While our experiences are not uniform, we are living in a more precarious time when there is growing concern for researchers conducting work amid unexpected and unsettling disruptions. Queer flexible methodologies give us an orientation rather than an answer. Much like the queer tactics employed by my interlocutors, such a methodology orients us and sheds light on the context and situation in which we are conducting research. Thus, rather than downplay or force context, situations we find ourselves in become a central part of how we learn and stay more accountable to our field. Many of my theoretical and methodological questions are born out of *al-wad'*. For example: What kind of sense or senses of security do we need (or develop) during the research and writing process? How does one determine what are priorities in the field and the research? How important is context in abstracting or decontextualizing the interview process?

In May 2019, I returned to Beirut on a research trip. On my flight, I overheard two British men asking another British woman—a frequent visitor to Beirut—what Beirut is like. The woman, presumably in her forties, recounted that she visits Lebanon often to see her sister who lives there. "Oh, Beirut is great," she said. "People ask me all the time, 'What, you're going to Beirut? Why?' They don't know what it's like. [*Pauses.*] Sure, the area next to the airport [the southern suburbs of the city] looks like World War III just happened, but go to downtown Beirut, and it looks like Abu Dhabi." To make Beirut seem glamorous and fun—and like a legitimate place to visit— the British traveler situated it as *like* Abu Dhabi and *different from* Beirut's southern suburbs. In a fractal Orientalist fashion, she uses the wealth and presumed cosmopolitanism associated with Abu Dhabi to make Beirut intelligible on regional and local levels. As the book shows throughout, to make Beirut exceptional is to compare it to other cities in the Arab world rather than only Euro-American cities. The southern suburbs for her, however, represent a war-torn poor area of the city, which she uses only as a contrast to downtown Beirut—or Beirut proper.

A few days later, as I was walking through downtown Beirut and snapping pictures of new buildings, a soldier stopped me and laughingly said, "Enjoy it while it lasts; a war is coming." The soldier was referencing a possible U.S.-Iran war, since tensions have been on the rise. I was not surprised to hear that; rather, it made what Martin Manalansan describes as "the shock of the familiar" more familiar (2003, 136). Those who live amid *al-wad'* (whether in Beirut or not) experience its disruptions through its anticipatory, continuous, and circular nature. Perhaps what is exceptional about Beirut (and queerness) is the *feeling* that there is always something disruptive on the horizon. There, but as José Esteban Muñoz says, "not yet here" (2009, 1).

Appendix

Methodology and Beirut Neighborhoods

METHODOLOGY

This book draws on three types of data: ethnographic observations, life-history interviews, and textual and discourse analysis.

For Chapter 1, I analyzed seven gay travelogues from the years 2005–2016, including more than twenty tourism pieces on Beirut. Five of the articles, since they are published in gay magazines such as *Out Traveler* and *Winq Magazine*, are targeted primarily to gay audiences. The two others, such as the article in the *New York Times*, address a general public. Two articles appeared in German and Dutch publications, whereas the others appeared in U.S. publications. See Table A.1.

I conducted ethnographic fieldwork among LGBTQ individuals in Lebanon for a total of fifteen months in 2008–2009, 2013, and 2014, in addition to a number of research visits to Beirut during 2010, 2011, and 2012. Even though I rely primarily on life-history interviews conducted in 2007–2008 and 2013–2014, my analysis is drawn from all my time spent there, talking to and interacting with people, attending LGBT events (such as IDAHOT, a queer public reading by Meem in 2009, and book discussions at Meem), and socializing. My interviews were conducted face-to-face, with the exception of two conducted through Skype with individuals who were not currently in Beirut, and lasted between one and a half to two and a half hours. All face-to-face interviews took place in public in Beirut, primarily gay-friendly coffee shops. All my interlocutors (ages eighteen to thirty-one), though not necessarily born in Beirut, had lived there for most of their adult lives. I conducted interviews primarily in Arabic, with some in English or French, and translated them into English. My interlocutors include cisgender men, cisgender women, and genderqueer and bigender individuals. The interviewees include college students, NGO workers, graphic designers, health-care professionals, and medical doctors. Some were involved in Lebanese LGBT organizing at some point in their lives. Their religious backgrounds include Maronite Christian, Sunni Muslim, Shiite

TABLE A.1 ARTICLES ANALYZED FOR CHAPTER 1

Article title	Date	Publisher
"Beirut: Hotbed of Vice of the Middle East"	June 2005	*FlyerTalk* (U.S.)
"Beirut Unexpected"	January/February 2006	*Out Traveler* (U.S.)
"Beirut, the Provincetown of the Middle East"	July 2009	*New York Times* (U.S.)
"Beirut's Flourishing (Albeit Illegal) Gay Scene"	September 2010 (accessed)	*Daily Clarity* (U.S.)
"Gay Life in Lebanon: Bounce Back Beirut"	Winter 2010	*Winq Magazine* (Netherlands)
"Lebanon Write Up"	February 2010	International Gay and Lesbian Travel Association
"Destination: Gay Beirut and Beyond"	April 2010	*San Diego Gay and Lesbian News*

Muslim, Christian Orthodox, and Druze. All names and identifying information have been changed to protect the interviewees and ensure their anonymity.

To analyze my interviews, I use grounded theory or a "grounds-up approach" in which data are "the foundation of our theory and our analysis of these data generates the concepts" (Charmaz 2006, 2). I transcribed the interviews shortly after conducting them and was thus able to reflect on, code, and note themes that emerged beginning with the initial interviews. I organized my data based on emergent and recurrent themes from the interviews, such as visibility, safety, access to space, and cosmopolitanism. I did not explicitly ask about "safety" or "access to space"; rather, these themes, which are a focus of this book, emerged from my interviews. Analyzing my data, I found that people's experiences of gay-friendly Beirut were largely based on co-constitution of gender (and gender normativity) and class. In addition, many of my interlocutors engaging differently with the dominant narrative of Beiruti cosmopolitanism and exceptionalism pushed me to reflect on and probe this further.

Given the sensitive nature of the topic, I relied on snowball sampling to recruit individuals for all my interviews conducted in both 2007–2008 and 2012–2014. In 2012–2014, I made my first contact through feminist networks by email when in the United States. In early 2013, I was directed to Rabab as a key person involved in queer organizing in Beirut, and after exchanging a number of emails, we met in May 2013 in Beirut. During our initial meeting, I described my research as focusing on the relationship between gender, sexuality, and ideas of progress and modernity in Beirut. I explained that I was looking for individuals who identify as LGBT or nonheteronormative and who have lived or currently live in Beirut. Understandably, Rabab wanted to screen me and told me that she had to get to know me before introducing me to people in the queer and trans community. Since we shared a somewhat similar background and grew up in a similar part of the city, it was a little easier for us to develop rapport. Rabab recounted that many feminist and queer activists are wary about speaking to researchers, particularly Euro-American white men and women who study LGBT people and life in Lebanon. It was apparent that there were fine lines being drawn between activists and researchers, as some activists believe that researchers come into a field, conduct their research, and leave, often misrepresenting activists' lived realities. Rabab's unease with academics is also a reflection of her experiences as an activist, her working-class background, and her discomfort with what she rightfully associates with positions of privilege. Thus, during our first few encounters, Rabab told me half-jokingly that she and her friends will be "watching" and paying attention to me, as I was yet another queer academic conducting research on Beirut. Rabab and my other interlocutors set boundaries from the start, explaining that not every interaction or "hanging out" we have, especially at people's homes, is meant to be part of my research. Thankfully, this helped our interactions and getting to know each other better and gave my interlocutors an important say and decision in shaping our relationship. Therefore, while I do rely on informal interactions and ethnographic observations to inform my analysis, the major part of my data is based on the formal interviews I conducted. In addition, I conducted two separate interviews with one Helem and one Meem representative and visited both of their centers. I also visited and spent some time at Marsa Sexual Health Center in Beirut.

Conducting research on gender and sexualities in a highly unstable region provided several challenges. First, at times, it was physically unsafe to be there. Second, given "the situation," people were less likely to respond and/or to engage with such topics, given the more pressing issues. Therefore, I assume and understand that discussing such issues for many individuals was not always a priority. Third, my research was disrupted on multiple occasions. For example, bombings made it impossible to follow through with some scheduled interviews and thus led to the cancellation of multiple events and meetings. It also made it challenging to schedule meetings in general. Particularly after bombings, people understandably were less likely to go out and want to talk about gender and sexuality and their experiences of the city. Given these limitations, I supplement my formal in-depth interviews with informal discussions and interviews that I conducted. In addition, I incorporate the larger sociopolitical environment and attempt to capture and represent how the situation affected my everyday life, the everyday lives of my interlocutors, and life in Beirut in general.

The ways that my interlocutors set boundaries between me as a researcher and my research project and their everyday lives is productive in thinking about feminist and queer methodologies that do not simply treat the field or interlocutors as sources of data. The researcher/ethnographer is not viewed as a "hero" entering the field to represent or give voice to marginalized populations in the Global South, and at the same time, interlocutors are not regarded through the binary of victims and heroes themselves (Vidal-Ortiz 2010; Rios 2011). Such interactions, while still mediated by uneven power relations in the field, moved me more toward humanizing the experience of the field and sharpened my accountability to the field.[1]

DESCRIPTIONS OF SELECT NEIGHBORHOODS IN BEIRUT

Most if not all of my interlocutors talked about navigating common parts of the city, mainly the neighborhoods of Hamra, Gemmayzeh, Achrafieh, Mar Mikhael, and occasionally the southern suburbs, where the individuals live and circulate.

Achrafieh is a major Christian district in East Beirut.

Beirut's Central District, known as "downtown," separates Hamra and Achrafieh. Post–civil war, Beirut's Central District was reconstructed by the company Solidere, owned by former prime minister Rafic Hariri.

Gemmayzeh is an old residential neighborhood in East Beirut, predominantly a Christian area. It experienced a lot of reconstruction and has been a hub of nightlife in Beirut since the mid-2000s.

Hamra is a bustling commercial and residential neighborhood in West Beirut. It is a religiously diverse neighborhood known for its shopping, coffee shops, and nightlife. It is also an intellectual and artistic hub that includes a number of theaters and the two major American universities: American University of Beirut and the Lebanese American University in the neighborhood of Ras Beirut. Many Beirutis consider Harma to be the cosmopolitan hub of Beirut.

Mar Mikhael is more recently an up-and-coming neighborhood; it is a lower-middle-class Christian community on the border of the predominantly Armenian neighborhood of Bourj Hamoud. Mar Mikhael has become gentrified and is now open to many shops, bookstores, and coffee shops, Airbnbs, and bars. Rue Armenia, the major street that leads to Bourj Hammoud, is lined with many small two- to three-story buildings. Through gentrification, Mar Mikhael has attracted young people as a place to live, especially for its rents, which are more affordable than those in Hamra and other parts of Beirut.

Notes

INTRODUCTION

1. My understanding of religious sect refers more to the positionalities that individuals occupy in Lebanese society with regard to their sect and the history of sect than to religiosity and social sect. Sociologist Rima Majed's theorization of sects and sectarianism as political categories and processes is particularly instructive for my analysis. Sect, according to Majed (forthcoming), is "a practice of categorization (as self-identification or identification by others) that is based on the politicization of religious identity (regardless of religiosity). It can serve as a tool for identification through state institutions, as well as a vehicle for political mobilization and economic competition." For more on the conceptualization of sect, see Mikdashi 2014.

2. *Almaany Dictionary*, s.v. "al-wad'," available at https://www.almaany.com/en/dict/ar-en (accessed February 20, 2020).

3. For a more generalized understanding of fractals, see Rose 2012.

4. For example, such accounts of nonnormative gender and sexualities in the Arab Middle East and the Muslim world are circulated by gay travelogues and tour guides.

5. Feminist geographers have also considered precarity, gender, and sexuality, particularly in accounting for experiences of natural disasters (see Johnston 2018).

6. This understanding of precarity is best captured by cultural anthropologist Anne Allison. In her work on precarity in Japan, she states, "I try to maintain, rather than weed out, these senses of my precarious subjects. I am more interested in entering the pain—messy, murky, and meandering as it may be—and touching the circumstances, the conditions, and the everyday effects and effects of how precarity gets lived" (2013, 17).

7. In *Queer Beirut* anthropologist Sofian Merabet (2014) examines gay life and the production of gay spaces in Beirut. While Merabet conceives of "gay" through the

prism of same-sex desires and identifications, I look at queer strategies of everyday life that shed light on negotiating everyday-life disruptions in Beirut.

8. For a critique of the artificial divide between queer theory and area studies, see Mikdashi and Puar 2016.

9. Queer of color critique sheds light on multiple genealogies of queer theorizing, particularly women of color feminisms and black feminist thought, which I find crucial to my understanding of how race, class, gender, and sexuality are always co-constitutive categories of experience (Hames-Garcia 2011).

10. However, as historian Ussama Makdisi writes, as early as the nineteenth century, "European travelers, missionaries, and consuls saw Mount Lebanon as a non-Muslim enclave from which the movement to civilize and reform the 'fanatical' and 'Mohemmedan' Ottoman Empire could be launched" (1996, 24).

11. Solidere, the Lebanese Company for the Development and Reconstruction of Beirut's Central District, is owned by the ex-prime minister Rafic Hariri (Masri 2010).

12. Other examples include TV shows such as a program on Orange TV (OTV) in Arabic translated as *Here in Lebanon*, on which the host Randa Sarkis shows apartment complexes, new restaurants, resorts, clothing stores, and the like and attempts to sell the country to Lebanese in the diaspora and to people in Saudi and Gulf states. The show, which has been running since 2011, is a prime example of the neoliberal logics behind selling the country.

13. Totten's article is emblematic of the Euro-American articles circulated about Beirut, as Chapter 1 describes.

14. The al-Dahiyeh, though represented as a homogeneous Hezbollah stronghold, is actually a diverse and dense area with working- to middle-class people and families from a number of religious sects, including Maronite Christians and Shias (Deeb 2006). To many Lebanese, "the suburb," as urban planner Mona Harb documents, is meant to be "shunned for its chaos, filth, poverty and backwardness; [it] is a place to avoid, as it is shameful, fearful and hateful" (2007, 16). These discourses are not limited to journalistic or media accounts but are circulated by some academics, such as Lebanese sociologist Samir Khalaf (2012), who in his book *Lebanon Adrift* contrasts the cosmopolitan Beirutis to the "backward" and fanatic Shias of the southern suburbs.

15. For more on the productivity of mess in ethnographic research, see Manalansan 2014.

16. For more on LGBT rights and modernity, see Reddy 2011.

17. Similar to antisodomy laws, these practices are French colonial inventions and regimes of control. These tests were first introduced by French forensic doctor Auguste Ambroise Tardieu in his 1857 book *The Forensic Study of Assaults against Decency* as a way of "detecting" homosexuality and proving which men engage in homosexual sex-acts (Long 2004, 137).

18. Helem is an acronym for Lebanese Protection for Lesbians, Gays, Bisexuals and Transgenders (see the organization's website, at http://www.helem.net). The name Meem was derived from the Arabic letter "m," which stands for Majmouaat mou'azara lil-mar'a al-mithliya, a support group for queer women. Meem no longer exists as Meem. There are newer LGBT groups, such as Arab Foundation for Freedoms and Equality (see http://afemena.org) and Proud Lebanon (see https://www.proudlebanon .org).

19. For a review of studies on precarious gender and sexuality in geography, see Johnston 2018, and in sociology, see Millar 2017.

20. Judith Butler, as feminist geographer Lynda Johnston (2018) writes, distinguishes between precarity and precariousness and their links to vulnerability. "Precarity" refers to "the specific ways socio-economic and political institutions create unequal life conditions for all, and precariousness relates to the idea that vulnerability is an avoidable aspect of life" (Johnston 2018, 930). Precarity becomes a "rubric that brings together 'women, queers, transgender people, the poor, and the stateless'" (930–931, quoting Butler).

21. Sociologist Kathleen Millar reminds us that precarity is a "concept, a condition, and an experience across place and space" (2017, 1).

22. See the Appendix for a detailed discussion.

23. Though one develops friendships during fieldwork, I do not call my interlocutors' friends so that I do not obscure the power dynamics inherent in writing about their experiences.

24. Berry and colleagues employ fugitive anthropology because "activist research that does not pursue epistemological decolonization will, we argue, inevitably reproduce the very hierarchies of power that it seeks to help dismantle" (2017, 538).

25. The Appendix explores this in more detail.

26. For studies on the bubble in urban settings, see Calderia 2001 and Hentschel 2015.

CHAPTER 1

1. Two of the seven articles appeared in German and Dutch publications, and the others appeared in U.S. publications. See the Appendix for more detailed information.

2. I found seven gay travelogues about Beirut written in or translated into English since 2005. Since I am concerned only with the cultural production and content of these texts, I do not consider the reception of the articles in the Lebanese context. Instead, I focus on the recorded descriptions of the travelers' experiences of gay Beirut and on analysis of written texts rather than accompanying images.

3. Even though the Lebanese gay tour agency Lebtour promotes gay tours to the region, this chapter focuses on the narratives of progress and essentialized masculinities circulated in the Euro-American travelogues. Lebtour is discussed only when it appears in the travelogues being analyzed. For an ethnographic study on Lebtour's gay tours and marketing strategies, see McCormick 2011.

4. Although implied in the articles, this becomes more evident in articles by Teulings (2010) and Totten (2013).

5. I benefit from Gayatri Gopinath's concept of queer "regionalism" as a method that deconstructs the binary of local-global (2007, 341).

6. The origin of the term "fractal," which comes from a French word meaning "broken" or "fractured," sheds light on the segmented nature of fractals. *Oxford English Dictionary*, s.v. "fractal," available at https://www-oed-com.proxy2.library.illinois.edu/view/Entry/74094?redirectedFrom=fractal (accessed January 13, 2020).

7. The late Anthony Bourdain's Beirut episode of the CNN show *No Reservations* in 2006 (season 2, episode 12) is a good example. It illustrates that despite the exciting

instability of Beirut, once the 2006 Israeli war started and the airport was bombed, Bourdain and his crew were stuck in the country until they were evacuated by the United States. While Bourdain assumed that he was simply experiencing manifestations of *al-wad'*, disruptions escalated quickly into a state of emergency and the thirty-four day-Israeli war against Lebanon.

8. Such journalistic depictions are not exclusive to men in the Global South. For example, Benoit Denizet-Lewis's 2003 piece on the down-low, the double sexual lives that presumably heterosexual black and Latino men lead, uses similar tropes of racialized underdeveloped gay identities (see Vidal Ortiz, Robinson, and Khan 2018).

9. Jared McCormick (2011) thoroughly explores the focus on the image of the bear, its complexities, and how it is appropriated and negotiated in a Lebanese and Syrian context, both by self-identifying bears and as a marketing tool by Lebtour.

10. A cub refers to a younger bear in the gay community.

11. Here, I am referring to his representations in the 1962 Hollywood movie *Lawrence of Arabia*, starring Peter O'Toole.

12. This notion is circulated in a number of other articles and books on gay life in the Middle East, most notably in Whitaker 2006 and El-Feki 2013.

CHAPTER 2

1. For more on how same-sex sexualities have become a litmus test of national and cultural advancement, see Manalansan 1995, 2003; Massad 2007; Puar 2007; Nair 2010; Reddy 2011; Haritaworn 2015; and Perez 2015.

2. For more about Proud Lebanon, see its website, at http://www.proudlebanon.org.

3. Unless otherwise noted, all quotations come from interviews I conducted in Beirut in 2008–2017.

4. This is not particular to the Lebanese case; for example, Jyoti Puri's (2016) concept of sexual states sheds light on how a state's governance of sexuality, particularly in times of instability or change, serves to reassert the state's power.

5. For a discussion on public spaces, see Merabet 2014.

6. Shifting the focus away from the global business and leisure class, scholars have redefined cosmopolitanism by conceiving it in terms of everyday practices and competences. Examples of nonelite forms of cosmopolitanism include working-class cosmopolitans (Werbner 1999) and cosmopolitanism "from below," exemplified by migrants, such as "practical" (Pecoud 2004, 15) and "strategic" (Kothari 2008, 500) cosmopolitanisms.

CHAPTER 3

1. Rabab distinguishes between gender identity, experience, and how one is perceived/read.

2. While Rabab now identifies as trans masculine rather than bigender, I use only the pronoun "she" in the book, since it captured his experiences at that time. In addition, he wanted me to use "she," since my fieldwork was conducted and reflects this part of his life and experiences.

3. As Monroe notes, in the period 2004–2006, "motor scooter drivers were more suspect by security forces because it was thought that this type of vehicle, loaded with explosives, was connected to the spate of bombings" (2011, 95).

4. *Oxford English Dictionary*, s.v. "reconciliation," available at https://oed.com (accessed January 14, 2020).

5. Such narratives, similar to those circulated by the Euro-American travelogues and studies discussed in Chapter 1, rely on essentialist and flattened understandings of culture and identity that posit parts of the Arab Middle East and some populations as inherently more homophobic than others.

6. For example, see Collins 2005; Acosta 2013; and Moore 2011.

7. Scholars, including Carrillo (2017), Cantú (2009), Decena (2011), and Manalansan (2003), have focused on disruptions of coming-out strategies produced by and through one's migration status. In this case, it is not about a transit period; rather, the queer strategies employed disrupt and navigate everyday-life uncertainty and disruptions.

8. I define and understand meaning making not strictly as cognitive practices but rather as part of processes of embodiment.

9. Many of my interlocutors who were involved in LGBT organizing more readily used the term "queer" than "LGBT." While these terms were sometimes used interchangeably, others who were more involved in queer organizing made a distinction between queer and LGBT. For some, "queer" was an umbrella term to mean LGBTQ.

10. This practice is also documented in anthropologist Sofian Merabet's (2014) *Queer Beirut* in his discussion of gay men's relationship to their families.

11. Sofian Merabet touches on similar experiences of his interlocutors in Beirut; for example, he notes that the parents of one interlocutor know, but they do not talk about it (2014, 2).

12. In many other cases they refused to talk about harassment against women, as is evident in the harassment issues in Helem. See "Helem and Sexual Harassment" 2012.

CHAPTER 4

1. This chapter focuses on another facet of "queer strategies," but I do not intend to frame my interlocutors as simply rational-choice actors.

2. This strategy was not employed by other groups during the 2006 war, presumably given the response to crisis situations and the need for resources and relief work.

3. Bobby Benedicto illustrates the sociohistorical specificity of femme phobia in Manila: "While the denigration of femininity has long been a feature of gay male spaces in the West, so-called femme phobia was complicated in Manila by the historical dominance of kabaklaan in Filipino public culture and the associated, class fear that one's homosexuality might be interpreted as female identification" (2014, 85).

4. This is similar to sociologist C. J. Pascoe's discussion of the "constitutive outsider" in her examination of the uses of the fag discourses among high school boys (2007, 14).

5. The term "code-switching" refers to strategies and performances that help individuals negotiate visibility and safely navigate certain parts of Beirut. In this instance,

it is not used linguistically. For more on code-switching, see Minning 2004 and Decena 2011.

CHAPTER 5

1. A bubble, according to the *Oxford English Dictionary*, is "a protected or fortunate situation which is isolated from reality or unlikely to last." *Oxford English Dictionary*, s.v. "bubble," available at https://www.oed.com/view/Entry/24071#eid12770039 (accessed November 20, 2019).

2. For more discussion on gay spaces in Beirut and the complicated nature of private/public spaces, see Merabet 2014.

3. For more information on racism in LGBT spaces and communities, see Hanhardt 2013; Han 2015; Blair 2016; Orne 2017; and Greene 2019.

4. Warner defines a counterpublic as "a scene in which a dominated group aspires to re-create itself as a public and, in doing so, finds itself in conflict not only with the dominant social group, but also with the norms that constitute the dominant culture as public" (2002, 80).

5. Mische defines publics in her discussion of partisan publics in Brazil as performative and relational. She argues that they are "complex and multivalent, with many more identities and projects *potentially* in play than could be expressed in any given encounter" (2015, 45). Mische revises our understanding of publics to be "not as spaces of free expression, but rather of performative and relational *suppression* that enables and inhibits certain modes of political communication" (45).

CONCLUSION

1. This law was passed on July 22, 2014, a week after this interview. The Lebanese parliament, elected in 2009 for a four-year term, extended its own term instead of holding elections because of what it claimed to be "security reasons," citing the fear of possible ISIL attacks and suicide bombings at poll stations and among large congregations of people.

APPENDIX

1. I am indebted to conversations with Salvador Vidal-Ortiz for making this dynamic visible to me and for encouraging me to write about it.

References

Abbott, Andrew. 2001. *Chaos of Disciplines.* Chicago: University of Chicago Press.

Acosta, Katie L. 2013. *Amigas y Amantes: Sexually Nonconforming Latinas Negotiate Family.* New Brunswick, NJ: Rutgers University Press.

Ahmed, Sara. 2013. *The Cultural Politics of Emotion.* New York: Routledge.

Alameddine, Rabih. 1998. *Koolaids: The Art of War.* New York: Picador.

Alexander, Jacqui. 1998. "Imperial Desire/Sexual Utopias: White Gay Capital and Transnational Tourism." In *Talking Visions*, edited by Ella Shohat, 281–286. Cambridge, MA: MIT Press.

———. 2005. *Pedagogies of Crossing: Meditations on Feminism, Sexual Politics, Memory, and the Sacred.* Durham, NC: Duke University Press.

Allen, Jafari S. 2011. *¡Venceremos? The Erotics of Black Self-Making in Cuba.* Durham, NC: Duke University Press.

Allison, Anne. 2013. *Precarious Japan.* Durham, NC: Duke University Press.

Altman, Dennis. 1996. "Rupture or Continuity? The Internalization of Gay Identities." *Social Text* 48 (Autumn): 77–94.

Anzaldúa, Gloria E. 2002. "Preface: (Un)Natural Bridges, (Un)Safe Spaces." In *This Bridge We Call Home: Radical Visions for Transformation*, edited by Gloria E. Anzaldúa and AnaLouise Keating, 1–5. New York: Routledge.

Barrington, Lisa. 2018. "Beirut Pride Canceled after Organizer Held Overnight by Authorities." *Reuters*, May 16. Available at https://www.reuters.com/article/us-lebanon-lgbt/beirut-pride-canceled-after-organizer-held-overnight-by-authorities-idUSKCN1IH0XT.

Bayat, Asef. 2015. "Neo-Orientalism." *ISA: The Futures We Want*, September 19. Previously available at http://futureswewant.net/asef-bayat-neo-orientalism.

"Beirut's Flourishing (Albeit Illegal) Gay Scene." n.d. *Daily Clarity.* Previously available at http://mydailyclarity.com (accessed September 2, 2010).

Benedicto, Bobby. 2008. "The Haunting of Gay Manila: Global Space-Time and the Specter of *Kabaklaan*." *GLQ: Gay and Lesbian Quarterly* 14 (2–3): 317–338.

———. 2014. *Under Bright Lights: Gay Manila and the Global Scene*. Minneapolis: University of Minnesota Press.

Berry, Maya J., Claudia Chávez Argüelles, Shanya Cordis, Sarah Ihmoud, and Elizabeth Velásquez Estrada. 2017. "Toward a Fugitive Anthropology: Gender, Race, and Violence in the Field." *Cultural Anthropology* 32 (4): 537–565.

Bhabha, Homi. 1994. *The Location of Culture*. London: Routledge.

Binnie, Jon. 2014. "Relational Comparison, Queer Urbanism and Worlding Cities." *Geography Compass* 8 (8): 590–599.

Blair, Zachary. 2016. "Boystown: Gay Neighborhoods, Social Media, and the (Re) Production of Racism." In *No Tea, No Shade: New Writings in Black Queer Studies*, edited by E. Patrick Johnson, 287–303. Durham, NC: Duke University Press.

Boone, Joseph. 1995. "Vacation Cruises; or, The Homoerotics of Orientalism." *PMLA* 110 (1): 89–107.

Bourdieu, Pierre. 1986. "The Forms of Capital." In *Handbook of Theory and Research for the Sociology of Education*, edited by John Richardson, 241–258. New York: Greenwood.

———. 1998. *Acts of Resistance: Against the Tyranny of the Market*. New York: New Press.

Bracke, Sarah. 2012. "From 'Saving Women' to 'Saving Gays': Rescue Narratives and Their Dis/continuities." *European Journal of Women's Studies* 19 (2): 237–252.

Brown, Wendy. 2006. *Regulating Aversion: Tolerance in the Age of Identity and Empire*. Princeton, NJ: Princeton University Press.

Butler, Judith. 2006. *Precarious Life: The Powers of Mourning and Violence*. London: Verso.

———. 2010. *Frames of War: When Is Life Grievable?* London: Verso.

Calderia, Teresa P. R. 2001. *City of Walls: Crime, Segregation, and Citizenship in São Paulo*. Berkeley: University of California Press.

Cantú, Lionel. 2002. "De Ambiente: Queer Tourism and the Shifting Boundaries of Mexican Male Sexualities." *GLQ: Journal of Lesbian and Gay Studies* 8 (1–2): 139–166.

———. 2009. *The Sexuality of Migration: Border Crossings and Mexican Immigrant Men*. New York: New York University Press.

Carrillo, Héctor. 2017. *Pathways of Desire: The Sexual Migration of Mexican Gay Men*. Chicago: University of Chicago Press.

Caton, Steven. 1999. *A Film's Anthropology*. Berkley: University California Press.

Cervulle, Maxime, and Nick Rees-Roberts. 2008. "Queering the Orientalist Porn Package: Arab Men in French Gay Pornography." *New Cinemas: Journal of Contemporary Film* 6 (3): 197–208.

Charmaz, Kathy. 2006. *Constructing Grounded Theory: A Practical Guide through Qualitative Analysis*. London: Sage.

Cohen, Cathy. 1997. "Punks, Bulldaggers, and Welfare Queens: The Radical Potential of Queer Politics?" *GLQ: A Journal of Lesbian and Gay Studies* 3 (4): 437–446.

Collins, Patricia H. 2005. *Black Sexual Politics: African Americans, Gender, and the New Racism*. New York: Routledge.

Connell, R. W. 1995. *Masculinities*. London: Allen and Unwin.

————. 2001. *The Men and the Boys.* Berkeley: University of California Press.

Cruz-Malavé, Arnaldo, and Martin Manalansan, eds. 2002. *Queer Globalizations: Citizenship and the Afterlife of Colonialism.* New York: New York University Press.

Dann, Graham. 1992. "Travelogs and the Management of Unfamiliarity." *Journal of Travel Research* 30 (4): 59–63.

Dawson, Graham. 1991. "The Blond Bedouin." In *Manful Assertions: Masculinities in Britain since 1800*, edited by Michael Roper and John Tosh, 113–144. London: Routledge.

Decena, Carlos. 2008. "Tacit Subjects." *GLQ: Gay and Lesbian Quarterly* 14 (2–3): 339–359.

————. 2011. *Tacit Subjects: Belonging and Same-Sex Desire among Dominican Men.* Durham, NC: Duke University Press.

Deeb, Lara. 2006. *An Enchanted Modern: Gender and Public Piety in Shi'i Lebanon.* Princeton, NJ: Princeton University Press.

"Destination: Gay Beirut and Beyond." 2010. *San Diego Gay and Lesbian News*, April 10. Available at https://sdgln.com/entertainment/2010/04/07/destination-gay-beirut-and-beyond.

El-Feki, Shereen. 2013. *Sex and the Citadel.* London: Chatto and Windus.

El-Tayeb, Fatima. 2011. *European Others: Queering Ethnicity in Postnational Europe.* Minneapolis: University of Minnesota Press.

Eng, David L., Judith Halberstam, and José Esteban Muñoz. 2005. "Introduction: What's Queer about Queer Studies Now?" *Social Text* 23 (3–4): 1–17.

Fadda-Conrey, Carol. 2010. "Writing Memories of the Present: Alternative Narratives about the 2006 Israeli War on Lebanon." *College Literature* 37 (1): 159–173.

Ferguson, Roderick. 2004. *Aberrations in Black: Toward a Queer of Color Critique.* Minneapolis: University of Minnesota Press.

Gamson, Joshua. 2014. "'It's Been a While since I've Seen, Like, Straight People': Queer Visibility in the Age of Postnetwork Reality Television." In *A Companion to Reality Television*, edited Laurie Ouellette, 227–246. Malden, MA: John Wiley.

Geertz, Clifford. 1998. "Deep Hanging Out." *New York Review of Books* 45 (16): 69.

Giorgi, Gabriel. 2002. "Madrid en tránsito: Travelers, Visibility, and Gay Identity." *GLQ: Journal of Lesbian and Gay Studies* 8 (1–2): 57–80.

Gopinath, Gayatri. 2005. *Impossible Desires: Queer Diasporas and South Asian Public Cultures.* Durham, NC: Duke University Press.

————. 2007. "Queer Region: Locating Lesbians in Sancharram." In *A Companion to Lesbian, Gay, Bisexual, Transgender, and Queer Studies*, edited by George E. Haggerty and Molly McGarry, 341–354. Malden, MA: Blackwell.

————. 2010. "Archive, Affect, and the Everyday: Queer Diasporic Re-visions." In *Political Emotions: New Agendas in Communication*, edited by Janet Staiger, Ann Cvetkovich, and Ann Reynolds, 165–192. New York: Routledge.

Greene, Theodore. 2019. "Queer Cultural Archipelagos Are New to Us." *City and Community*, March 5. Available at https://doi.org/10.1111/cico.12382.

Guzman, Manolo. 2005. *Gay Hegemony/Latino Homosexualities.* New York: Routledge.

Hajj, Lama. 2018. "Major Milestone for Gay Rights: Lebanese Court of Appeals Rules Homosexuality Is Not a Crime." *Beirut*, July 13. Available at https://www.beirut.com/l/55881.

Halberstam, Jack. 2005. *In a Queer Time and Place: Transgender Bodies, Subcultural Lives.* New York: New York University Press.

Hames-Garcia, Michael. 2011. "Queer Theory Revisited." In *Gay Latino Studies: A Critical Reader,* edited by Michael Hames-Garcia and Ernesto Javier Martinez, 19–45. Durham, NC: Duke University Press.

Han, C. Winter. 2015. *Geisha of a Different Kind: Race and Sexuality in Gaysian America.* New York: New York University Press.

Hanhardt, Christina. 2013. *Safe Space: Gay Neighborhood History and the Politics of Violence.* Durham, NC: Duke University Press.

Harb, Mona. 2007. "Deconstructing Hizballah and Its Suburb." *Middle East Report* 242 (Spring): 12–17.

Haritaworn, Jin. 2015. *Queer Lovers and Hateful Others: Regenerating Violent Times and Places.* Chicago: Pluto Press.

Healy, Patrick. 2009. "Beirut, the Provincetown of the Middle East." *New York Times,* July 29. Available at http://travel.nytimes.com/2009/08/02/travel/02gaybeirut.html.

"Helem and Sexual Harassment." 2012. *NFASharte,* September 14. Available at https://nfasharte.wordpress.com/2012/09/14/helem-and-sexual-harassment.

Hentschel, Christine. 2015. *Security in the Bubble: Navigating Crime in Urban South Africa.* Minneapolis: University of Minnesota Press.

Hoad, Neville. 2000. "Arrested Development or the Queerness of Savages: Resisting Evolutionary Narratives." *Postcolonial Studies* 3 (2): 133–158.

Holland, Sharon. 2012. *The Erotic Life of Racism.* Durham, NC: Duke University Press.

Hubbard, Phil. 2012. *Cities and Sexualities.* Abingdon, UK: Routledge.

Human Rights Watch. 2018. "Lebanon: Police Shutter Pride Events." May 18. Available at https://www.hrw.org/news/2018/05/18/lebanon-police-shutter-pride-events.

Jameson, Fredric. 1990. *Postmodernism; or, The Cultural Logic of Late Capitalism.* Durham, NC: Duke University Press.

Jimmy67. 2005. "Beirut: Hotbed of Vice of the Middle East." *FlyerTalk,* June 8. Available at http://www.flyertalk.com/forum/glbt-travelers/441302-beirut-unspoiled-gay-paradise.html.

Johnston, Lynda. 2018. "Gender and Sexuality III: Precarious Places." *Progress in Human Geography* 42 (6): 928–936.

Khalaf, Samir. 2012. *Lebanon Adrift: From Battleground to Playground.* London: Saqi Books.

Kothari, Uma. 2008. "Global Peddlers and Local Networks: Migrant Cosmopolitans." *Environment and Planning D: Society and Space* 26 (3): 500–516.

"Lebanese Authorities Arrest Two Men for 'Sodomy.'" 2012. *Al-Akhbar,* August 17. Previously available at http://english.al-akhbar.com/content/lebanese-authorities-arrest-two-men-sodomy.

Lebanon Ministry of Tourism. n.d. "About Lebanon." Available at http://mot.gov.lb/AboutLebanon (accessed November 19, 2019).

Long, Scott. 2004. "When Doctors Torture: The Anus and the State in Egypt and Beyond." *Health and Human Rights* 7 (2): 114–140.

Luongo, Michael. 2007. *Gay Travels in the Muslim World.* New York: Routledge.

———. 2010. "Lebanon Write Up." IGLTA Symposium, February. Previously available at http://www.beirut2010.com.

Lyotard, Jean-François. 1984. *The Postmodern Condition: A Report on Knowledge*. Minneapolis: University of Minnesota Press.

M., Nadine. n.d. "Arab Queer Women and Transgenders Confronting Diverse Religious Fundamentalisms: The Case of Meem in Lebanon." Available at https://www.awid.org/sites/default/files/atoms/files/feminists_on_the_frontline_-_arab_queer_women_trans.pdf (accessed February 17, 2020).

Majed, Rima. 2016. "The Shifting Salience of Sectarianism in Lebanon, 2000–2010." Ph.D. diss., University of Oxford.

———. Forthcoming. "The Theoretical and Methodological Traps in Studying Sectarianism in the Middle East." In *Routledge Handbook on the Politics of the Middle East*, edited by Larbi Sadiki. London, UK: Routledge.

Makarem, Ghassan. 2011. "The Story of Helem." *Journal of Middle East Women's Studies* 7 (3): 98–112.

Makdisi, Ussama. 1996. "Reconstructing the Nation-State: The Modernity of Sectarianism in Lebanon." *Middle East Report* 200:23–26.

Manalansan, Martin. 1995. "In the Shadows of Stonewall: Examining Gay Transnational Politics and the Diasporic Dilemma." *GLQ: A Journal of Lesbian and Gay Studies* 2 (4): 425–438.

———. 2003. *Global Divas: Filipino Men in the Diaspora*. Durham, NC: Duke University Press.

———. 2013. "Queer Worldings: The Messy Art of Being Global in Manila and New York." *Antipode* 47 (3): 566–579.

———. 2014. "The 'Stuff' of Archives: Mess, Migration, and Queer Lives." *Radical History Review* 120:94–107.

———. 2018. "Messing Up Sex: The Promises and Possibilities of Queer of Color Critique." *Sexualities* 21 (8): 1287–1290.

Marama-Cavino, Hayley. 2018. "Decolonizing Rape and an Indigenous Response to #Metoo." Paper presented at Race Sex Power 2018 Conference, April, Chicago, IL.

Marquardt, Alexander. 2014. "Topless Images of Olympic Skier Jackie Chamoun a Scandal in Lebanon." *ABC News*, February 11. Available at https://abcnews.go.com/blogs/headlines/2014/02/topless-images-of-olympic-skier-a-scandal-in-lebanon.

Marwan, Yumna. 2013. "Lebanese Mayor Cracks Down on Homosexuality in His Town." *Al-Akhbar*, April 24. Available at http://actup.org/news/lebanon-dekwaneh-mayor-cracks-down-on-homosexuality-in-his-town.

Masri, Ghada. 2009. "Tourism, Sex, and Beirut." *Global-E* 3 (5). Available at https://www.21global.ucsb.edu/global-e/june-2009/tourism-sex-and%C2%A0beirut.

———. 2010. "Resurrecting Phoenicia: Tourist Landscapes and National Identity in the Heart of the Lebanese Capital." In *City Tourism: National Capital Perspectives*, edited by Robert Maitland and Brent W. Ritchie, 225–238. Wallingford, UK: CAB International.

Massad, Joseph. 2002. "Re-orienting Desire: The Gay International and the Arab World." *Public Culture* 14 (2): 361–385.

———. 2007. *Desiring Arabs*. Chicago: University of Chicago Press.

McCormick, Jared. 2011. "Hairy Chest, Will Travel." *Journal of Middle East Women's Studies* 7 (3): 71–97.

Meijer, Roel. 1999. *Cosmopolitanism, Identity, and Authenticity in the Middle East.* London: Routledge.

Melamed, Jodi. 2006. "The Spirit of Neoliberalism: From Racial Liberalism to Neoliberal Multiculturalism." *Social Text* 24 (2): 1–24.

Merabet, Sofian. 2004. "Disavowed Homosexualities in Beirut." *Middle East Report* 23 (Spring): 30–33.

———. 2014. *Queer Beirut.* Austin: University of Texas Press.

Mignolo, Walter. 2000. "Introduction from Cross-genealogies and Subaltern Knowledges to Nepantla." *Nepantla: Views from South* 1 (1): 1–8.

Mikdashi, Maya. 2014. "Sex and Sectarianism: The Legal Architecture of Lebanese Citizenship." *Comparative Studies of South Asia, Africa and the Middle East* 34 (2): 279–293.

Mikdashi, Maya, and Jasbir Puar. 2016. "Queer Theory and Permanent War." *Gay and Lesbian Quarterly* 22 (2): 215–222.

Millar, Kathleen M. 2017. "Toward a Critical Politics of Precarity." *Sociology Compass* 11 (6): 1–11.

Minning, Heidi. 2004. "Qwir-English Code-Mixing in Germany: Constructing a Rainbow of Identities." In *Speaking in Queer Tongues: Globalization and Queer Language,* edited by William Leap and Tom Boellstorff, 46–71. Urbana: University of Illinois Press.

Mische, Ann. 2015. "Partisan Performance: The Relational Construction of Brazilian Youth Activist Publics." In *Social Movement Dynamics: New Perspectives on Theory and Research from Latin America,* edited by Federico M. Rossi and Marisa von Bulow, 43–71. Burlington, VT: Ashgate.

Monroe, Kristin V. 2011. "Being Mobile in Beirut." *City and Society* 23 (1): 94–111.

———. 2016. *The Insecure City: Space, Power, and Mobility in Beirut.* New Brunswick, NJ: Rutgers University Press.

Moore, Mignon. 2011. *Invisible Families: Gay Identities, Relationships and Motherhood among Black Women.* Berkeley: University of California Press.

Moussawi, Ghassan. 2013. "Queering Beirut, the Paris of the Middle East: Fractal Orientalism and Essentialized Masculinities in Gay Travelogues." *Gender, Place and Culture: A Journal of Feminist Geography* 20 (7): 858–875.

———. 2015. "(Un)Critically Queer Organizing: Towards a More Complex Analysis of LGBTQ Organizing in Lebanon." *Sexualities* 5 (6): 593–617.

Muñoz, Jose E. 1999. *Disidentifications: Queers of Color and the Performance of Politics.* Minneapolis: University of Minnesota Press.

———. 2009. *Cruising Utopia: The Then and There of Queer Futurity.* New York: New York University Press.

Naber, Nadine, and Zeina Zaatari. 2014. "Reframing the War on Terror: Feminist and Lesbian, Gay, Bisexual, Transgender, and Queer (LGBTQ) Activism in the Context of the 2006 Israeli Invasion of Lebanon." *Cultural Dynamics* 26 (1): 91–111.

Nair, Yasmin. 2010. "What's Left of Queer? Immigration, Sexuality, and Affect in a Neoliberal World." *Yasmin Nair* (blog), May 12. Available at https://www.yasminnair.net/yasminnairwhatisleftofimmigration.

Orne, Jason. 2017. *Boystown: Sex and Community in Chicago*. Chicago: University of Chicago Press.

Oswin, Natalie. 2015. "World, City, Queer." *Antipode* 47:557–565.

Pascoe, C. J. 2007. *Dude, You're a Fag: Masculinity and Sexuality in High School*. Berkeley: University of California Press.

Pascoe, C. J., and Tristan Bridges. 2016. *Exploring Masculinities: Identity, Inequality, Continuity and Change*. New York: Oxford University Press.

Patil, Vrushali. 2018. "The Heterosexual Matrix as Imperial Effect." *Sociological Theory* 36 (1): 1–26.

Pecoud, Antoine. 2004. "Entrepreneurship and Identity: Cosmopolitanism and Cultural Competencies among German-Turkish Business People in Berlin." *Journal of Ethnic and Migration Studies* 30 (1): 3–20.

Peitgen, Heinz-Otto, and Peter Richter. 1986. *The Beauty of Fractals: Images of Complex Dynamical Systems*. Heidelberg, Germany: Springer-Verlag.

Perez, Hiram. 2015. *A Taste for Brown Bodies: Gay Modernity and Cosmopolitan Desire*. New York: New York University Press.

Phantom Beirut. 1998. Directed by Ghassan Salhab. GH Films.

Plummer, Ken. 2015. *Cosmopolitan Sexualities*. Cambridge, UK: Polity Press.

Puar, Jasbir K. 2002. "Circuits of Queer Mobility: Tourism, Travel, and Globalization." *GLQ: Journal of Lesbian and Gay Studies* 8 (1–2): 101–138.

———. 2004. "Abu Ghraib: Arguing against Exceptionalism." *Feminist Studies* 30 (2): 522–534.

———. 2007. *Terrorist Assemblages: Homonationalism in Queer Times*. Durham, NC: Duke University Press.

Puri, Jyoti. 2016. *Sexual States: Governance and the Struggle over Antisodomy Law in India*. Durham, NC: Duke University Press.

Reddy, Chandan. 2011. *Freedom with Violence: Race, Sexuality and the US State*. Durham, NC: Duke University Press.

Rios, Victor. 2011. *Punished: Policing the Lives of Black and Latino Boys*. New York: New York University Press.

Ritchie, Jason. 2010. "How Do You Say 'Come out of the Closet' in Arabic? Queer Activism and the Politics of Visibility in Israel-Palestine." *GLQ: Journal of Lesbian and Gay Studies* 16 (4): 558–575.

Rose, Michael. 2012. "Explainer: What Are Fractals?" *The Conversation*, December 11. Available at https://theconversation.com/explainer-what-are-fractals-10865.

Ruiz, Sandra. 2019. *Ricanness: Enduring Time in Anticolonial Performance*. New York: New York University Press.

Said, Edward. 1978. *Orientalism*. New York: Vintage.

———. 2000. *Out of Place*. New York: Vintage.

Sawalha, Aseel. 2010. *Reconstructing Beirut*. Austin: University of Texas Press.

Schwedler, Jillian. 2010. "Amman Cosmopolitan: Spaces and Practices of Aspiration and Consumption." *Comparative Studies in South Asia, Africa, and the Middle East* 30 (3): 547–562.

Sedgwick, Eve. 1990. *Epistemology of the Closet*. Berkeley: University of California Press.

Seidman, Steven. 2002. *Beyond the Closet: The Transformation of Gay and Lesbian Life*. New York: Routledge.

————. 2012. "The Politics of Cosmopolitan Beirut: From the Stranger to the Other." *Theory, Culture, and Society* 29 (2): 3–36.

Sherwood, Seth, and Gisella Williams. 2009. "Where to Go: 2009." *New York Times*, January 11. Available at https://archive.nytimes.com/query.nytimes.com/gst/fullpage-9A0DE7D7173AF932A25752C0A96F9C8B63.html.

Skeggs, Beverley. 1997. *Formations of Class and Gender: Becoming Respectable*. London: Sage.

Slevin, Kathleen, and Thomas Linneman. 2010. "Old Gay Men's Bodies and Masculinities." *Men and Masculinities* 12 (4): 483–507.

Smith, Lee. 2006. "Beirut Unexpected." *Out Traveler*, January–February. Available at https://www.outtraveler.com/features/2005/12/09/januaryfebruary-2006-beirut-unexpected.

Smith, Linda Tuhiwai. 1999. *Decolonizing Methodologies: Research and Indigenous Peoples*. London: Zed Books.

Smith Galer, Sophia. 2018. "Lebanon Is Drowning in Its Own Waste." *BBC Future*, March 28. Available at http://www.bbc.com/future/story/20180328-lebanon-is-drowning-in-its-own-waste.

Somerville, Siobhan. 2000. *Queering the Colorline*. Durham, NC: Duke University Press.

————. 2014. "Queer." In *Keywords for American Cultural Studies*, edited by Glenn Hendler and Bruce Burgett, 203–207. New York: New York University Press.

Spartacus International Gay Guide. 2009. 38th ed. Edited by Briand Bedford. Berlin: Bruno Gmunder.

Spartacus International Gay Guide. 2011–2012. 40th ed. Edited by Briand Bedford. Berlin: Bruno Gmunder.

Spartacus International Gay Guide. 2016. 45th ed. Edited by Briand Bedford. Berlin: Bruno Gmunder.

Standing, Guy. 2011. *The Precariat: The New Dangerous Class*. London: Bloomsbury Academic.

Swidler, Ann. 1986. "Culture in Action: Symbols and Strategies." *American Sociological Review* 51 (2): 273–286.

Teulings, Jurriaan. 2010. "Bounce Back Beirut." *Winq Magazine*, Winter. Available at https://www.globalgayz.com/gay-lebanon/297/.

Totten, Michael J. 2013. "Can Beirut Be Paris Again?" *City Journal*, Summer. Available at https://www.city-journal.org/html/can-beirut-be-paris-again-13586.html.

Traboulsi, Fawwaz. 2007. *A History of Modern Lebanon*. London: Pluto Press.

Tucker, Andrew. 2009. *Queer Visibilities: Space, Identity and Interaction in Cape Town*. Chichester, UK: Wiley Blackwell.

Tyler, Imogen. 2013. *Revolting Subjects: Social Abjection and Resistance in Neoliberal Britain*. Chicago: University of Chicago Press.

Vidal-Ortiz, Salvador. 2010. "Blurring the Boundaries of Being, the Field, and Nation: Santeria in the Bronx, Puerto Rico." In *Fieldwork Identities in the Caribbean*, edited by Erin B. Taylor, 197–220. Coconut Creek, FL: Caribbean Studies Press.

————. 2014. "Introduction: Brown Writing Queer; A Composite of Latina/o LGBT Activism." In *Queer Brown Voices*, edited by Uriel Quesada, Letitia Gomez, and Salvador Vidal-Ortiz, 1–27. Austin: University of Texas Press.

————. 2019. "Borders Are Both Real and Imagined: Rejoicing on Lionel Cantú's '*De Ambiente*: Queer Tourism and the Shifting Boundaries of Mexican Male Sexualities.'" *GLQ: Gay and Lesbian Studies* 25 (1): 73–77.

Vidal-Ortiz, Salvador, Brandon Andrew Robinson, and Cristina Khan. 2018. *Race and Sexuality*. Cambridge, UK: Polity Press.

Waitt, Gordon, and Kevin Markwell. 2006. *Gay Tourism: Culture and Context*. New York: Haworth.

Warner, Michael. 2002. "Publics and Counterpublics." *Public Culture Journal* 14 (1): 49–90.

Werbner, Pnina. 1999. "Global Pathways: Working Class Cosmopolitans and the Creation of Transnational Ethnic Worlds." *Social Anthropology* 7 (1): 17–36.

Weston, Kath. 1998. *Long Slow Burn: Sexuality and Social Science*. New York: Routledge.

Whitaker, Brian. 2006. *Unspeakable Love: Gay and Lesbian Life in the Middle East*. London: Saqi Books.

Woolwine, David. 2010. "Community in Gay Male Experience and Moral Discourse." *Journal of Homosexuality* 38 (4): 5–37.

Yazbeck, Natacha. 2009. "Sleepless in Beirut, Sin City of the Middle East." *Mail and Guardian*, August 16. Available at https://mg.co.za/article/2009-08-16-sleepless-in-beirut-sin-city-of-the-middle-east.

Zoepf, Katherine. 2007. "What Happened to Gay Beirut?" *Observer*, August 17. Available at https://observer.com/2007/08/what-happened-to-gay-beirut.

Index

Ghassan Moussawi is an Assistant Professor of Gender and Women's Studies and Sociology at the University of Illinois at Urbana–Champaign.